HOW THE RIGHT
LOST ITS MIND

T0275170

HOW
THE
RIGHT
LOST ITS
MIND

Charles J. Sykes

 ST. MARTIN'S GRIFFIN 🐾 NEW YORK

**For my father, Jay G. Sykes,
curmudgeon, contrarian, and mentor**

www.stmartins.com

The Library of Congress has cataloged the hardcover edition as follows:

Names: Sykes, Charles J., 1954– author.
Title: How the right lost its mind / Charles J. Sykes.
Description: New York : St. Martin's Press, [2017] | Includes bibliographical
    references and index.
Identifiers: LCCN 2017018870 | ISBN 9781250147172 (hardcover) | ISBN
    9781250147219 (ebook)
Subjects: LCSH: Conservatism—United States. | Right and left (Political
    science)—United States. | Political culture—United States. | United
    States—Politics and government.
Classification: LCC JC573.2.U6 S95 2017 | DDC 320.520973—dc23
LC record available at https://lccn.loc.gov/2017018870

ISBN 978-1-250-19953-9 (trade paperback)

Our books may be purchased in bulk for promotional, educational, or business
use. Please contact your local bookseller or the Macmillan Corporate and
Premium Sales Department at 1-800-221-7945, extension 5442, or by email at
MacmillanSpecialMarkets@macmillan.com.

First St. Martin's Griffin Edition: October 2018

D   10   9   8

CONTENTS

[Back] of all political institutions there are moral and philosophical concepts, implicit or defined. Our political economy and our high-energy industry run on large, general principles, on ideas—not by day-to-day guess work, expedients and improvisations. Ideas have to go into exchange to become or remain operative; and the medium of such exchange is the printed word.

—"PUBLISHER'S STATEMENT," IN THE FIRST ISSUE
OF *NATIONAL REVIEW* (NOVEMBER 1955)

Conservatism must, however, be wiped clean of the parasitic cant that defaces it, and repels so many of those who approach it inquiringly. Up against the faith of a conservative, the great surrealistic ideologies reduce to dust.

—WILLIAM F. BUCKLEY, *UP FROM LIBERALISM* (1959)

I'm going to be honest with you, I'm not a reader. I don't like to read long books. I like to read news. So I couldn't tell you that there was a book that I read that changed my life. More so, I love to read news and I love to read commentary and I love to watch TV. I love to watch news. I'm a watcher and I'm a writer. A reader in the sense that I like to read news but I have a very short attention span, so sitting down with a book is very difficult for me.

—TOMI LAHREN (2016)

I told them, you know, it's really funny to me to see the splodey heads keep 'sploding over this movement.

—SARAH PALIN (2016)

PREFACE TO THE
PAPERBACK EDITION

LATE IN THE AFTERNOON of October 7, 2016, I texted an old friend, fellow Wisconsinite Reince Priebus.

The Access Hollywood videotape had just been released, showing the GOP presidential nominee describing his approach to seducing and perhaps assaulting women. "You know I'm automatically attracted to beautiful—I just start kissing them," Donald Trump says on the tape. "It's like a magnet. Just kiss. I don't even wait. And when you're a star, they let you do it. You can do anything. Grab 'em by the pussy. You can do anything."

Over the course of his campaign, Trump had insulted POWs, women, disabled reporters, members of minority groups, and his opponents without derailing his candidacy. But this felt like it might be different, and events were moving quickly.

Trump was due to visit Wisconsin the next day, for a rally with Speaker Paul Ryan, their first joint appearance of the campaign. Relations between Trump and Ryan had been fraught, with the speaker accusing his party's nominee of "textbook racism," while Trump derided the speaker as "our very weak and ineffective leader." The Wisconsin event was the culmination of Priebus's peacemaking efforts. Like other members of the GOP mainstream, Priebus had been a Trump skeptic, but as chairman of the Republican National Committee, he had embraced Trump's candidacy with apparent enthusiasm. As one of Ryan's best friends, Priebus helped organize the joint event as a symbol of his efforts to normalize Trump's candidacy and rally the disparate wings of the GOP behind the erratic billionaire.

But now all of Priebus's friends and colleagues from Wisconsin would have to stand onstage with their pussy-grabbing nominee. It would be the photo-op from hell, a month before the general election.

Despite our deepening political differences over Trump, Reince and I had kept in touch throughout the campaign. At one point, despite my opposition, he had arranged a one-on-one meeting with vice presidential nominee Mike Pence at Milwaukee's airport. (Pence assured me that he was a "big Paul Ryan guy.")

At lunch in Milwaukee in September, Reince and I talked about our lives after the election. He wanted to stay on as RNC chair to pick up the pieces before returning to law or perhaps a cable television deal. I told him that I was writing this book; he said we should stay in touch because, unlike Trump's campaign staffers, he had never signed a nondisclosure agreement.

So that afternoon after the tape was released, I texted Priebus. He wasn't going to allow Trump to drop a bomb on Wisconsin Republicans, was he?

Priebus responded quickly: "I am the guy trying to fix this!" he texted me. "I am in tears over this."

Within a few hours, Ryan withdrew the invitation to Trump. For a moment, it seemed like a turning point. But it wasn't, or at least not in the way that I thought would be.

As we later learned, Priebus actually told Trump he should drop out of the race (for which Trump never forgave him). Across the country, Republicans rescinded their endorsements. Ryan announced he would no longer defend Trump.

But one by one, they drifted back. After Trump's improbable win, Priebus became White House chief of staff. Ryan, who had so often expressed his disgust with Trump's comments, became his most important ally in Congress. A year after Trump's election, Ryan declared: "We're with Trump. That's a choice we made at the beginning of the year. That's a choice we made during the campaign, which is we merged our agendas."

Over the last several years, there were many other potential turning points for conservatives and red lines that were never drawn. But in retrospect, the Access Hollywood video foreshadowed the degree to which the Right was willing to surrender its remaining principles and enable many of Trump's worst impulses.

So it should not have come as a surprise when the GOP stuck with Trump as he became embroiled in a growing series of scandals, fired the FBI director, and tried to undermine the special counsel's investigation into his conduct. Nor should it have come as a surprise when evangelical Christian leaders gave the president a pass on reports he had an affair with a porn star and paid her hush money. They were merely reprising the moral compromises they had made during the campaign.

The Right's rolling acquiescence to Trump's hostile takeover also foreshadowed the metamorphosis of the conservative movement on issues ranging from personal character and public ethics to fiscal conservativism, crony capitalism, free trade, immigration, global leadership, human rights, and the rule of law.

In April 2018, Ryan, who had once been the party's rising conservative star, announced that he was stepping down as speaker. "Ryan's departure is not some kind of inflection point," wrote Stephen Hayes, editor of the *Weekly Standard*, "it is an exclamation point."[1]

It is Trump's party now, marked not only by the GOP Congress's rituals of sycophantic abasement (especially after the passage of tax cuts), but also by poll numbers suggesting the degree to which the conservative base has made itself over in Trump's image. In February 2018, in the wake of the passage of tax reform, 90 percent of Republican voters told Gallup pollsters they approved of Trump's performance.[2] Approval of GOP voters also seemed to extend beyond his policies to his personal qualities as well. In January 2018, the Quinnipiac poll found that the overwhelming majority of Americans—71 percent of independent voters, 67 percent of male voters, and 68 percent of female voters—had come to the conclusion that Trump was not setting a good example for children. The one glaring exception? Seventy-two percent of Republican voters said they thought that Trump "is a good role model for children." Even after a year of juvenile taunts on Twitter and his repeated assaults on truth, 82 percent of Republicans said that Trump shared their values, and four out of five think he "provides the United States with moral leadership."[3] The percentage of Republican voters who thought sexual misconduct by a president was an important issue dropped from 70 percent during Bill Clinton's presidency to just 25 percent under Trump's.[4]

Since Trump's election, we keep hearing the same question again and again: What will it take? What has to happen for Republicans to break with their mad king? The honest answer is: Who knows? Whatever people have said has to happen *has, in fact, already happened, over and over again, and the GOP has swallowed it anyway.* At least so far.

NORMALIZING TRUMP

In early 2016, *National Review,* the magazine founded by William F. Buckley Jr., devoted an issue to essays gathered under the headline: "Against Trump." By February 2018, the same magazine's cover featured a smiling President Trump and the headline: "A Year of Achievement: The Case for the Trump Presidency."

Indeed, many Republicans insist that they support the Trump agenda and policies, rather than the man. Tax cuts, they reasoned, were worth ignoring a few tweets, even the ugly ones. They convinced themselves that their cynicism was savvy realism. There was uneasiness about his chaotic style, his management by humiliation, and his penchant for surrounding himself with a remarkable menagerie of misfit toys. But many conservatives rallied around Trump in reaction to what they saw as media bias and the hostility of his critics and opponents. Anti-anti-Trumpism has proven a powerful glue among conservatives seeking a reason to stick with the president; the more he is besieged, the tighter his supporters cling to him and the deeper they dig in.

Other Republicans told themselves that if you squint hard enough, Trump can look like a somewhat normal Republican president who has delivered a series of conservative wins. Under Trump, they point out, the GOP has been able to pass sweeping tax reform, eliminate the individual mandate for health insurance, roll back the regulatory state, toughen immigration enforcement, fund the military, and install conservative judges throughout the federal judiciary, including, most notably, the Supreme Court, where his two appointments (so far) could ensure a conservative majority for decades. The stock market went up, unemployment down. In any case, the choice remains binary; whatever his flaws might be, Trump is still preferable to the ghastly alternative of Hillary Clinton or the progressive Left.

In this telling, Trump's lack of any fixed principles and invincible ignorance on policy means that he is an empty vessel that the establishment GOP could use to accomplish many of its dearest objectives. "Trump has governed so far as more of a Republican and conservative than I expected," *National Review* editor Rich Lowry wrote in 2017.[5]

But claims that Trumpism had delivered major conservative wins were undermined by the GOP's dramatic abandonment of even the pretense of fiscal conservatism, adding trillions of dollars to the national debt. Rather than draining the swamp, they fully funded it.*

In a series of votes on tax cuts and spending, Trump and the GOP Congress blew through spending caps imposed during the Obama years. After Trump signed a massive $1.3 trillion omnibus spending bill in

---

*Even without those tax cuts, the Congressional Budget Office estimated an aging population will push the deficit from 3.6 percent to 5.7 percent of the country's economic output by 2027. Spending for mandatory programs will increase from $2.5 trillion in 2017 to $4.3 trillion in 2027, and interest payments on the national debt alone will double as a share of the GDP.

March, economists estimated that it would add $2 trillion to the national debt over the next decade. Within a decade, debt payments alone could top $1 trillion a year.* The GOP's abandonment of fiscal prudence was followed by its retreat from free trade. Trump threatened to derail the booming economy and set off a trade war by imposing tens of billions of dollars of tariffs (taxes) on imports. Free-market conservatives denounced Trump's protectionism, but again the GOP failed to push back in any meaningful way. This, however, has been only part of the story.

WAS IT WORSE?

So, has the Trump era turned out better or worse than I expected? Back in May 2016 (on what I'm pretty sure was my last appearance ever on Fox News) I said:

> Donald Trump is a serial liar, a con man who mocks the disabled and women. He's a narcissist and a bully, a man with no fixed principles who has the vocabulary of an emotionally insecure nine-year-old. So no, I don't want to give him control of the IRS, the FBI, and the nuclear codes. That's just me.

Nothing that has happened since then has changed my opinion one bit.[†]

Even so, it has been worse than I thought, but not because of Trump. Nothing he has done as president should come as a surprise to anyone

---

*Despite its earlier praise for Trump's presidency, *National Review* joined other conservatives in denouncing the deal. "The omnibus spending bill was crafted in secret and will be passed under pressure; raises discretionary spending as the national debt grows; and fails to deliver on any major GOP priorities except increased defense spending," the editors wrote. ("The Omnibus Disgrace," *National Review*, March 22, 2018.)

†I later signed on as an analyst with NBC/MSNBC. When this book appeared, I also made appearances on CNN, PBS, ABC, NBC, and CSPAN, but was not invited to discuss it on Fox News.

who paid any attention to his career or his campaign in 2015 and 2016. He is who we expected him to be; there was never going to be a pivot. Conservatives have, unfortunately, been a different story. The original edition of this book focused on the mind-set of a movement that had enabled and capitulated to Trump, but it was still shocking to see the *extent* of the moral, intellectual, and political surrender by conservative leaders once he was in power. The 2016 election dramatically highlighted the role of tribalism in American politics, but since the election we have seen the degree to which conservative politics has become not merely tribal, but also transactional.

In this book, I describe the network of cranks, careerists, grifters, eccentric billionaire funders, and think tanks who had reshaped the conservative movement. Since the election, one after another they made their peace with Trump's chaotic incoherence, as they jostled and shoved for a place at the table. At the same time, many conservatives have drifted even deeper into the Alt Reality silos I describe later in this book.

During his hostile takeover of the GOP, Trump secured the nomination with only a minority of the primary votes. During the general election, many conservatives voted for him reluctantly because they saw the election as a "binary choice" (see chapter 14). But the GOP submission since Trump's election has a different feel: Now that it is in power, the Trumpian Right often feels more like a cult than a political movement. It is one thing to support tax cuts (a staple of GOP politics for decades), quite another to cheer on his attacks on the special prosecutor, the Department of Justice, and the FBI. The House Intelligence Committee under Congressman Devin Nunes became a virtual extension of the Trump White House, issuing reports that sought to discredit findings of the intelligence community about Russian interference in the election. The Republican National Committee took the lead in attempts to discredit former FBI director James Comey even before the publication of his memoir, setting up a website with the Trumpian title Lyin' Comey. Of course, this had nothing to do with conservative principles or even making America great again, but it has become the new normal for the GOP; Republicans have grown accustomed to the politics of rationalization and a daily diet of codswallop.

xvi   PREFACE TO THE PAPERBACK EDITION

The president's many rationalizers often insist that objections to Trump are merely matters of taste or style or the president's "personality." But that is an obvious dodge because Trump's presidency is a reflection of his character and his judgment, and the consequences are substantive. Trump did not adjust to the responsibilities of the presidency, so conservatives adjusted to him.

When Trump retweeted racist videos from a British fascist group, Republican leaders ignored it. As Trump's lies became more flagrant, they shrugged. His conflicts of interest generated little attention, his juvenile taunts and ignorance and indifference to policy hardly a blink.

SHERIFF JOE ARPAIO was a caricature of law enforcement—living up to every stereotype of a lawless, brutal, racist cop, who ignored fundamental rights and reveled in calculated cruelty. When Trump used his presidential authority to pardon him, most Republicans shuffled their feet and changed the subject. Trumpists doubled down. In an appearance in Arizona, in May 2018, Vice President Pence gave a shout out to Arpaio, who was now running for the U.S. Senate, calling him "a great friend of this president and tireless champion of strong borders and the rule of law."[6]

At the same time, Trump bullied critics, including a Gold Star family, attacked and threatened the media, and used his office to enrich himself and his family. Ushering in a new era of crony capitalism, he rewarded his political allies, while using his bully pulpit to vindictively attack successful businesses, like Amazon, in part because its owner also owns the *Washington Post,* which has been critical of his presidency.

As the #MeToo movement gathered momentum, critics noted that he had been credibly accused of harassing or assaulting numerous women. His response has been to call them liars and threaten to sue them. Throughout his first year in office, he stoked racial animosity by picking fights with prominent African Americans, including NFL players, and suggested that neo-Nazi protesters in Charlottesville included many "fine people."

His foreign policy, including his nuclear saber rattling, often seemed driven more by impulse than grand design. His refusal to sign the G7 summit's final communique, his repeated questioning of the value of NATO, his attacks on the European Union, and his disdain for many of our traditional allies risk isolating the United States while undermining the international order built up on a bipartisan basis over more than seven decades. Trump's bitter attacks on allies like Canada's Justin Trudeau contrasted sharply with his fawning praise of global thugs like North Korea's Kim Jong-un and Russia's Putin.

Perhaps inspired by their example, he has repeatedly suggested prosecuting or jailing his political opponents. In the weeks leading up to Trump's first State of the Union speech, the man who had begun his campaign by lashing out at "Mexican rapists" derailed negotiations over immigration reform by objecting to refugees from "shithole countries."

Heart-wrenching scenes of migrant children being separated from their parents at the border and held in cages drew international condemnation, but seemed a logical culmination of the Trumpian embrace of a policy of calculated cruelty.

There were dissenting voices, including former president George W. Bush, and Senators John McCain, Bob Corker, and Jeff Flake, but they found themselves isolated and routinely derided by the loudest voices in the conservative media. Flake took to the floor of the Senate to challenge his colleagues. "We must never regard as 'normal' the regular and casual undermining of our democratic norms and ideals," Flake said.

> We must never meekly accept the daily sundering of our country—the personal attacks, the threats against principles, freedoms, and institutions, the flagrant disregard for truth or decency, the reckless provocations, most often for the pettiest and most personal reasons.

But the reality is that the GOP is, in fact, fine with all this. Even though other Republicans shared Flake's views, few were willing to speak out, and Flake's decision not to seek reelection highlighted his isolation.

By any measure, the makeover was remarkable. Until Trump, Republicans were members of a party that insisted that "character matters." But, goaded into a tribalism that treats ideas, facts, truth, and basic decency as expendable, the GOP seems a party blanched of any fixed principles. "It's more than strong; it's tribal in nature," Senator Corker explained to the *Washington Examiner.* "People who tell me, who are out on the trail, say, 'Look, people don't ask about issues anymore. They don't care about issues. They want to know if you're with Trump or not.'"[7] Republicans had shifted so far on the issue that loyalty to Trump in the days after the release of the Access Hollywood tape became a litmus test in GOP primary elections in 2018.*[8]

Because the GOP has cast its lot so thoroughly with Trump, he has succeeded in a remarkably short period of time in moving the window of acceptability in our politics, especially on the Right. As a result, the rules of the game have changed in ways that are still hard to grasp, as conservatives accept behaviors and ideological shifts that would have been unacceptable a few years ago. The cause and effect of politics has been broken, adding a layer of unpredictability to an already volatile landscape. Although optimists continue to insist that our system of checks and balances has held up well, Americans have also discovered that we are not immune to history. Many of those norms turn out to be based on an honor system rather than hard-and-fast rules. And when we no longer have honorable people in power, those norms turn out to be more fragile that we had imagined.

Conservatives ought to have been alarmed by all of this demagogic indifference to democratic norms and bedrock conservative principles—and to be sure, some were. But if anything, pressure to get on board the Trump train has grown over time. While some commentators (some with contracts with Fox News) have tried to maintain their independence—mixing criticism with praise—the tightrope has

---

* "Fealty to Trump has become more of a litmus test than ever for Republicans. Emboldened by private polling and focus groups that show the president is incredibly popular with the base, GOP candidates are stepping up attacks on their rivals over any daylight they've shown with Trump, even if it stemmed from his personal conduct toward women or apostasy on traditional conservative orthodoxy. It's another illustration of the degree to which Trumpism has come to define the Republican Party. This is no longer the party of Abraham Lincoln, Ronald Reagan or George W. Bush. It's the party of Donald J. Trump." —James Hohmann, "The Daily 202: Loyalty to Trump emerges as a top issue in Republican primary campaign commercials," *Washington Post,* March 29, 2018.

been treacherous. In conservative circles, the failure to go full #MAGA risked irrelevance and exile. Shortly before this book was published, I was fired by a conservative Wisconsin think tank for whom I had edited a magazine for twenty-seven years. The group's president, a long-time friend, had also been a Trump critic, but told me that I was no longer consistent with their "brand." Others paid a much stiffer price. Friendships have ended and careers foundered.

The consequences of the Right's capitulation are likely to be far-reaching and of long duration. Tainted by association with Trump, Republicans are shedding support among young voters, who disapprove of the president by a margin of more than 40 points in one poll.[9] For many of those voters, the face of conservatism will continue to be ignorant, bigoted, and cruel, and polls suggest that the Right could face a generational political tsunami as a result. At the same time, Republicans are embracing hard-line immigration policies (travel bans, deportations, and a wall) and nativist rhetoric that alienate moderates and drive minority voters away from the party, perhaps for a generation or more.

We do not yet know whether Trump's presidency will be farce or tragedy, but it is hard to imagine that it will end well. So this might be a good time to remember that in a Faustian bargain you can indeed get your heart's desire, only to find out that the price is far higher than you imagined.

And yet, many on the Right are still willing to pay it.

WHAT CHANGED

Indeed, pretty much everything described in these pages has gotten worse, even though some things have changed.

Paul Nehlen, the Breitbart-backed congressional candidate described in chapter 12 ("The Bigots Among Us") veered off into the darkest corners of the Alt Right, adopting white supremacist slogans and tweeting anti-Semitic insults and memes. Although Nehlen had been praised by Trump, and backed by right-wing celebrities like Sarah Palin, Ann Coulter, and Michelle Malkin, his overt racism was too much even for Breitbart, which announced that it was severing all ties with him.[10]

After Trump's failure to make progress on the Mexican border wall, Coulter seemed to sour on him, admitting that "I knew he was a shallow, lazy ignoramus, and I didn't care," as long as she got a crackdown on illegal immigration. But Coulter, who had written a book called *In Trump We Trust*, has been forced to admit that he has reneged on many of the promises he made to the base.* [11] (If only she had been warned.) But Coulter's disillusionment was an outlier.

The annual CPAC convention, a gathering of movement conservatives, turned itself into a ranting Trumpathon that included an appearance by Marion Maréchal-Le Pen, a far-right, ethno-nationalist French politician. One of the few conservative dissenters at the conference, Mona Charen, was loudly booed for daring to call out the GOP's hypocrisy on sexual morality. [12]

Evangelical Christian leaders (whose embrace of Trump is described in chapter 15) also made clear that their willingness to compromise their morals for Trump was not a one-off decision. In late 2017, many of the evangelical leaders supported the senate candidacy of accused child molester Roy Moore, an unreconstructed "birther," who believed that Barack Obama was an illegitimate president and had been twice removed from the Alabama bench for failing to respect the rule of law. In a remarkable spectacle of projection, Franklin Graham tweeted: "The hypocrisy of Washington has no bounds. So many denouncing Roy Moore when they are guilty of doing much worse than what he has been accused of supposedly doing. Shame on the hypocrites." [13] Trump also backed Moore, along with the Republican National Committee, in a campaign in which the GOP lost a senate race in a state Trump himself had won by nearly 50 points.

As the Christian Right became more overtly transactional, leaders also expressed few qualms about reports that Trump had paid hush

---

*In an interview with Frank Bruni of the *New York Times,* Coulter said: "It was very easy to brush aside Jeb Exclamation Point. Charlie Sykes. Bill Kristol. The Former Trumpers are the ones who would die for Trump, who would defend him from anything, who did defend him and blew off the 'Access Hollywood' tape— blew off everything. We kept coming back. He could sell Ivanka Trump merchandise from the Oval Office if he would just build the wall." (Frank Bruni, "Ann Coulter to Donald Trump: Beware the Former Trumpers," *New York Times,* April 2, 2018.)

money to a porn star shortly after his third wife, Melania, gave birth to their son. The Family Research Council's Tony Perkins famously said Trump deserved a "mulligan" for his behavior, as long he continued to give them what they wanted on policy.[14]

Some on the Right seemed to recognize that Trump's victory was never really about conservative principles at all. Representative Thomas Massie, a Republican for Kentucky, tried to diagnose the mind-set of conservative voters when he told the *Washington Examiner,* "I thought they were voting for libertarian Republicans." Massie said, "But after some soul-searching, I realized when they voted for Rand and Ron [Paul] and me in these primaries, they weren't voting for libertarian ideas. They were voting for the craziest son of a bitch in the race. And Donald Trump won best in class."[15]

But other critics fell silent, or became active cheerleaders for the new president. During the 2016 campaign, Ted Cruz had ripped Trump as a "pathological liar," and a "sniveling coward," after Trump mocked his wife's looks and suggested that his father may have been involved in the assassination of JFK. But in 2018, Cruz penned a glowing panegyric for the president in *Time* magazine. "President Trump is doing what he was elected to do: disrupt the status quo," wrote a chastened Cruz. "That scares the heck out of those who have controlled Washington for decades, but for millions of Americans, their confusion is great fun to watch."[16]

Steve Bannon also fell from grace, losing both his position in the White House and his job running Breitbart. In his romantic self-regard, Bannon may have thought of himself as the Robespierre of this Trumpian Revolution, who was ultimately destroyed by the forces he helped release. Bannon was among those who imagined that he could control, shape, and use Donald Trump as an empty vessel to fill with his poisonous worldview (he even at one point described him as an "imperfect vessel" for the political upheaval he had long been envisioning). Like so many others on the Right, Steve Bannon thought he could ride the tiger. Instead, he and his allies became roadkill in Trump's shambolic presidency.

In retrospect, it's extraordinary how tone-deaf Bannon was. He helped create a pro-Trump media ecosystem that demanded loyalty, not ideological consistency. But in the process he also helped create something else: a cult of personality that could be immune to the attacks he might now hope to launch. Despite Trump's well-documented indifference to the truth, GOP voters have shown a remarkable willingness take their cues from him, even when it means reversing attitudes toward Russia or American law enforcement. When, for instance, Trump began accusing the FBI of political bias, Republican support for the agency dropped by 22 points.[17]

Even when Trump breaks his promises or betrays his base, they stick with him. The unified field theory among Trumpists appears to be that Trump himself cannot fail; he can only be betrayed by RINOs, weak-kneed congressional leaders, "secret societies," or the deep state.

So, not surprisingly, the defenestration of Bannon did not mark a turn toward normalcy for Trump's presidency, nor did it mark the rejection of nativist, national white identity politics. The fall of Bannon also did not signal a turn toward sobriety or responsibility in the Right's media ecosystem. If anything, the Right media actually became even more obsequious and extreme, ramping up their rhetoric as Trump's administration began to stumble. Much of the conservative media has continued to morph into a gigantic fog machine: ignoring or deflecting damaging stories or engaging in whataboutism (Hillary's emails remain a favorite target). A large segment of the conservative base reacts to disturbing reports about Trump by simply refusing to believe them. This also has long-term consequences for the conservative mind as the Trump base cuts itself off from mainstream sources of information.

We are still only beginning to grasp the scope of fake news, hoaxes, and propaganda that flooded social media during the 2016 campaign or the role that Russian bots may have played in deranging the conservative mind. But what is equally notable here is the lack of moral panic or even mild concern among conservative political leaders for the implications of that attack, or what it says about the intellectual integrity of the Right. Instead of any serious introspection about the susceptibility of the conservative base to fake information, the Trumpian

Right has doubled down on its (largely successful) efforts to delegitimize fact-based journalism.

Back in 2017, one of Bannon's acolytes, Breitbart Washington editor
Matt Boyle, declared that "journalistic integrity is dead . . . So everything is about the weaponization of information." The goal? "We
envision a day when CNN is no longer in business. We envision a day
when the *New York Times* closes its doors. I think that day is possible."[18]
Boyle's prophecy has, so far, not panned out. Even as Breitbart has
slipped into irrelevancy, cable ratings and newspaper readership has
soared. Still, the pro-Trump feedback loop seems to be growing, with
the vocal addition of Sinclair Broadcast Group, which owns nearly
two hundred local television stations (and is seeking the approval of
the FCC to add more). In early 2018, Sinclair's management ordered its
news anchors to read an anti-media screed on the air and the company
demanded that stations carry pro-Trump editorials on a "must-run"
basis.[19] The Salem Media Group, which syndicates conservative talkers like Hugh Hewitt, reportedly also pressured its hosts to be more
supportive of Trump and then fired many of the Trump critics who
wrote for the company's RedState website.[20]

At the same time, Fox News hosts like Sean Hannity trafficked in
the kind of bizarre conspiracy theories that had once been isolated
in the far reaches of the fever swamps. For weeks, Hannity peddled a
rumor linking a murdered Democratic National Committee employee
named Seth Rich to DNC emails that had been leaked to WikiLeaks.
(Rich's family has sued Fox News and others in connection with the
story.)[21]

Despite such embarrassments, Fox News has become even more
overtly pro-Trump, self-consciously turning itself in a virtual house
organ of the Trump presidency. At least in the short term, Fox's overt
Trumpism has paid off with higher ratings and the loyal viewership of
the president himself, who often tweets about things that he has seen
on shows like *Fox & Friends* and who seems to use cable appearances
as auditions for spots in his administration.

Fox's fawning and reflexive support for the regime drew a stinging
rebuke from one longtime contributor, former Army colonel Ralph

Peters, who resigned from the network in early 2018. "In my view," he wrote in his resignation letter, "Fox has degenerated from providing a legitimate and much-needed outlet for conservative voices to a mere propaganda machine for a destructive and ethically ruinous administration." Peters was appalled by Fox's attacks on law enforcement and its penchant for conspiracy theories. "When prime-time hosts—who have never served our country in any capacity—dismiss facts and empirical reality to launch profoundly dishonest assaults on the FBI, the Justice Department, the courts, the intelligence community (in which I served) and, not least, a model public servant and genuine war hero such as [special counsel Robert S. Mueller III]—all the while scaremongering with lurid warnings of 'deep-state' machinations—I cannot be part of the same organization, even at a remove," he wrote. "To me, Fox News is now wittingly harming our system of government for profit."[22]

OBJECTIONS FROM THE LEFT AND THE RIGHT

Not surprisingly, objections have been raised to my critique of conservatism. Ironically, some critics on both the right and left make what is essentially the same argument—rather than seeing Trumpism as a threat to the conservative tradition, they argue, we should regard it as a logical, consistent, and organic outgrowth of that movement.

That is, of course the view from the (Sean) Hannitized Right, which insists that opposition to Trump among the so-called Never Trumpers is a form of apostasy. But it is also an argument advanced by former Trump critics like *National Review*'s Lowry, who insists that despite his many flaws, Trump is not "a wild outlier in the contemporary GOP." On issues like immigration and trade with China, Lowry wrote, "Trump is closer to the national Republican consensus than his conservative detractors."[23]

On the Left, there is also a chorus making the equivalent case. "Donald Trump Was the Inevitable Result of Republicanism," declared a recent headline in *Esquire*.[24] Some progressive critics denounce even the most consistent Trump critics for being "complicit" in Trump's rise, because conservatism itself created the conditions of his rise. "You built this," is a nagging refrain on social media. "No absolution for the Right."

In the chapters that follow, I try to address that question of whether Trump represents continuity or discontinuity in conservatism, and I don't want to relitigate the question here. I readily concede that the dysfunction on the Right was a preexisting condition and that conservatives need to ask themselves some hard questions. (In retrospect I wish I had devoted more attention to Newt Gingrich's role in toxifying the Right and to Sarah Palin, who can be seen as Patient Zero in the current epidemic of crazy.)*

But a few points need to be made about the attempt to equate Trumpism with traditional conservatism. The first is the most obvious: If Trump was the inevitable and predictable outcome of the conservative movement, why did none of those critics predict his coming?

They also need to explain why Trump is more an "authentic" expression of conservatism than previous GOP nominees, like George H. W. Bush, John McCain, or Mitt Romney. Distinctions are important here; it is unhealthy and intellectually sloppy to gloss over the fundamental differences between the conservatism of a Milton Friedman and the raw nationalist nativism of a Steve Bannon, just as it is intellectually dishonest to confuse the progressivism of Adlai Stevenson II with Che Guevera. Nuance matters.

Obviously, Trump has deftly exploited many of the grievances and attitudes that have festered for decades on the Right. But that's not the whole story. Trump has more in common with populist demagogues like Father Charles Coughlin, George Wallace, and Pat Buchanan than

---

* For a longer discussion of some of these questions, see "The Republican Roots of Trumpism," *New Yorker*, October 24, 2014. Jonathan Chait and I go back and forth about whether I had glossed over some of the darker aspects of the right, including the role of William F. Buckley Jr.

with conservatives like George Will or Ronald Reagan. Until the last election, conservatives had the good taste, sound judgment, and wisdom to reject and even marginalize those uglier voices on the Right. In that sense, Trump is the exception, rather than the rule. Perhaps the best way to think about Trump's populist nativism is to see it as a recessive gene in conservatism, but one that had been kept in check for generations. That also suggests another tradition exists, even if it is now in eclipse.

While it's easy (and tempting) to define a political movement by its worst aspects, it bears noting that modern conservatism also gave rise to Charles Krauthammer, Ross Douthat, Peter Wehner, Ben Sasse, and Jeff Flake. In other words, it didn't have to be this way, and it doesn't have to continue in the future.

But the real danger in seeing Trump as the logical, organic product of conservatism is that it *normalizes* him. Discounting the peculiarity of his rise ignores the uniqueness of the threat he poses and the urgency of the need to confront the damage being done to the body politic and our political culture. If he is merely another Republican, there is no emergency, no existential crisis, no cause for more than the usual alarm.

The argument that all conservatives are complicit in his rise also seems to preclude the creation of a genuine Coalition of the Decent, members of the center right and center left who recognize their common values and goals and are trying to make common cause. Declaring all conservatives to be anathema rejects important allies in the recovery efforts that lie ahead. (Unfortunately, there also continues to be strong resistance among some progressives to acknowledging their own contributions to the toxification of our political culture.)

I still believe that it will be up to the battered and beleaguered band of rational and responsible conservatives to save the Republic. We will need all the help we can get.

—**Charles Sykes**
July 2018

INTRODUCTION

THIS IS NOT A book about Donald Trump, even though he will play a central role. It is about the culture and mind-set of a Republican party and a conservative movement that enabled him, capitulated to him, and embraced him, probably much to his own surprise. His nomination and election profoundly changed the face of conservativism, but also revealed the tectonic shifts that had already broken conservatism apart.

It is also a painful book for me to write.

It will be painful not just because it will recount the dissolution of the conservative coalition, but also the betrayal of conservative principles by so many of the trusted leaders, spokesmen, and champions of the Right. This includes the implosion of conservative media, many of whose leading voices turned from gatekeepers to cheerleaders and from thought leaders to sycophantic propagandists. Most painful of all has been the recognition that some of the Left's critiques, while often unfair and overdrawn, were also often far more on target than many of us ever wished to admit.

But somehow a movement based on ideas had devolved into a new tribalism that valued neither principle nor truth; a Brave New Age that replaced Edmund Burke and William F. Buckley Jr. with Ann Coulter and Milo Yiannopoulos. Moral reasoning was supplanted by polls; ideas were elbowed aside by charlatans and media clowns; while ratings spikes were proof that one was not "out of touch." The gleeful rejection of established norms of civility, tradition, and basic decency played well in an era of reality television, but was the antithesis of what conservatism had once represented.

Unfortunately, the election results will surely fill the worst elements on the Right with passionate intensity.

I cannot pretend that I was not part of this story, and not merely for my attempts to construct a firewall of sorts against the march of Trumpism. For a quarter of a century I was part of this conservative movement, both as an observer and as a full participant. Like a number of other conservatives, including talk show hosts, I have to step back and ask uncomfortable questions. There's no point in mincing words: for me 2016 was a brutal, disorienting, disillusioning slog. There came a moment when I realized that conservatives had created an alternative reality bubble and that I had perhaps helped shape it. Somewhere along the line much of the echo chamber turned on the very principles that had once animated it, replacing ideas of freedom, limited government, and constitutionalism with a crude populist nativism that fed into the Right's media zeitgeist.

Sometimes movements or organizations can only be understood from the inside, because only an insider can provide a sense of perspective and motivation or translate the language and the nuance, separating dog whistles from core principles.

But there are also times when it takes an outsider to recognize the essential lunacy of a political cause or strategy; the guy in the room who will raise his hand and say, "This is foolish." The power of group-think to coalesce around awful ideas in closed meetings is well understood, but the process is magnified in a political movement that creates its own silos. Participants often simply do not understand how silly they look from the outside. As someone who had a front row seat for years, but now finds himself exiled from what the conservative movement has become, I hope to straddle those perspectives and be able to look at what has happened as both an insider and an outsider.

Inevitably, this book will also ask whether many of the Left's critiques of conservative rhetoric—charges we have rejected for decades—might not have had a grain of truth. Did we—did I—contribute to this prairie fire of bigotry and xenophobia that seemed to grip so many on the Right? How did the elites miss the signs of division that turned to schism that became a veritable civil war? Did we play with fire, only to see it spread out of control? Did we really "make" Donald Trump? Or is he a merely a cartoonish bizzaro version of conservative values?

In other words, did Trump represent continuity or discontinuity? Was he a logical development in conservativism, or a radical, ominous break with that tradition? Or was it a combination of both?

First a confession: When I set out to write this book, I was prepared to argue that Trump's victory was a black swan event, a hostile takeover of the conservative movement. But that position no longer seems tenable; the roots for the populist/nationalist putsch run too deep.

Another obvious question is whether the sweeping successes of Republicans in 2016 essentially refute my argument that the Right has indeed lost its mind or render this book irrelevant. Actually, I would argue that the 2016 victory makes the need for a reassessment even more urgent. After Trump's defeat of Hillary Clinton, the Democrats need to perform an autopsy; Republicans need an exorcism.

Such is our worship of success and power that we assume that an election triumph wipes away a multitude of sins; instead, it magnifies them. Problems that were exposed during the rough-and-tumble of the campaign are unlikely to disappear when the tribe assumes all of the trappings and perks of power. History seems rich with examples: Success does not necessarily imply virtue or even sanity. One can lose one's mind and still achieve the imperial purple. Kings can be both mad and bad, and the courtiers are usually loath to point out the obvious.

The problems of the Right are no longer a crisis of a political faction or a theoretical conundrum to be hashed over by its pundits. They are now a national problem with potentially sweeping consequences.

Of course, the Left also has its moonbats, its cranks, its hermetically sealed bubbles and alternative realities. They can easily be found on university campuses and the newsrooms of elite media organizations, whose lip service to "diversity" seldom extends to diversity of ideas. Buckley once said, "Liberals claim to want to give a hearing to other views, but then are shocked and offended to discover that there are other views." Evidence is abundant that progressives have experienced their own crackup, but I will leave that book for someone else; this book focuses on what just happened to the Right.

It is not a contradiction to say that conservatism urgently needs to adjust to modern realities and also to regard Donald Trump's victory as a catastrophe for the movement. One of the abiding ironies of the campaign was the way that many of the enforcers of ideological purity, who had made such innovation and creative policymaking politically impossible, were the first to embrace Trumpism.

The dilemma now for many conservatives will be painful: By aligning themselves with Trump they will score significant victories, including the appointment of conservative Supreme Court justices, tougher policies on immigration, and the rollback of the administrative state. But they will constantly have to ask themselves, *What is the butcher's bill for this Trumpian bargain? How much will they overlook? How many other principles will they be required to abandon?*

In *A Man for All Seasons*, Thomas More asks Richard Rich, "It profits a man nothing to give his soul for the whole world . . . but for Wales, Richard?" A more modern version might read, "but for tax cuts, Paul?"

Unfortunately, the effects of Trumpism cannot be measured solely in terms of policy, but also in the way it has coarsened the culture as a whole. The election marked not only a rejection of the Reagan legacy, but also the abandonment of respect for gradualism, civility, expertise, intelligence, and prudence—the values that once were taken for granted among conservatives. This isn't to say that conservatism was ever strictly genteel; that is obviously not the case, especially in recent years. But the distinctive element of 2016 was the open ridicule and contempt for notions of civility, or even basic decency, as values that needed to be protected and advanced.

In the 1990s, as Bill Clinton's scandals unfolded, conservatives insisted that character mattered and worried deeply and often loudly about the toxic effects of our politics on the culture. What message, they asked, were we sending our children?

So, what is the message now?

Consider the problems of raising children in an era in which our most famous role model is Donald Trump, a new symbol of power, success, celebrity, and masculinity. As parents, we struggle to teach our children empathy and compassion. We hope to teach them character, humility, impulse control, kindness, and good sportsmanship. We want them to learn how to win and lose graciously, treat others with respect, avoiding name-calling, and tell the truth even if it's inconvenient. But young people only need to flip the channel to see what success looks like in America today. Whatever we tell them, young people have a keen sense of what traits and behaviors are rewarded and celebrated. They have an acute sense of the hypocrisy of a society that touts virtue but lavishes fame, wealth, and power on people who flout them. Especially for young men still searching for a model of what it means to be a man, Trump's behavior will carry significant weight. And why not? He may be a bully, a fabulist, a serial insulter and abuser of women, but our alpha-male president is a billionaire, who has been elevated to the most powerful job in the world.

And the folks who had been the culture's chief defenders of character and virtue seem to be okay with that. Pre-Trump, former education secretary William Bennett had argued eloquently that: "It is our character that supports the promise of our future—far more than particular government programs or policies." Bennett, the author of the *Book of Virtues* and one of the most prominent virtucrats of the Right, emphasized the importance of the president as a role model. "The

President is the symbol of who the people of the United States are. He is the person who stands for us in the eyes of the world and the eyes of our children."[1] But during the recent presidential campaign, Bennett reversed himself, saying that conservatives who objected to Trump "suffer from a terrible case of moral superiority and put their own vanity and taste above the interest of the country."[2] In August 2016, Bennett wrote an essay making the case for overlooking questions of character in choosing a president. "Our country can survive the occasional infelicities and improprieties of Donald Trump," Bennett wrote. "But it cannot survive losing the Supreme Court to liberals and allowing them to wreck our sacred republic. It would reshape the country for decades."[3]

Like Bennett, most conservatives have been willing to make the trade-off: they were willing to inject toxic sludge into the culture in order to win a political victory. Needless to say, this is a dramatic reversal for the Right. Conservatives once recognized that politics was a means, not an end, because they believed that we live in communities sustained by moral capital, recognizing as social psychologist Jonathan Haidt notes, that moral communities are "fragile things, hard to build and easy to destroy."[4] But now, for many conservatives, a willingness to ignore, rationalize, or defend lies has become a test of tribal loyalty. At the same time, Trump's acolytes in politics and social media have modelled their behavior on his, combining the worst traits of the schoolyard bully, the thin-skinned nastiness that mimics confidence; the strut and sneer that substitutes for actual strength. Vindictive smash mouth attacks have replaced civil engagement. For many of us, this has a familiar feel; it is as if we've all been sent back to the sixth-grade playground.

This book is not a comprehensive chronicle of conservatism. There are inevitable gaps, and critics will note that I have glossed over many of the movement's historic foibles and failures. What I have tried to do is capture some of the developments that led to the Trumpian Revolution and their implications for the conservative mind.

To a certain extent the title of this book is also misleading, because not everyone on the Right lost their minds. There have been consistent, principled voices from the conservative old guard, including George Will, Charles Krauthammer, Peter Wehner, Bill Kristol, Jonah Goldberg, John Podhoretz, Noah Rothman, David French, David Frum, Rich Lowry, Bret Stephens, Jennifer Rubin, and Stephen Hayes. Despite heavy pressure, *National Review,* the *Weekly Standard,* and *Commentary* magazines all stayed true to the faith. But despite its electoral successes, the conservative movement is broken and the conservative media deeply compromised. On the surface the rise of Trump seemed to rend the fabric of the movement, but it merely exposed a preexisting condition: a failure of imagination, principle, political courage, and ultimately of ideas.

Finally, I suspect this book will disappoint some readers who hope to read a full-throated rejection of conservative values. But I hope I have made it clear that I am still a conservative—albeit a contrarian one, who believes that the events of the last several years do not invalidate conservative principles, but rather make them political orphans.

PART I

HOW THE
RIGHT
LOST ITS
MIND

CHAPTER 1

DID WE CREATE
THIS MONSTER?

The best lack all conviction, while the worst
Are full of passionate intensity.

—W. B. YEATS

SO HOW DID THIS happen?

How did the right wander off into the fever swamps of the Alt Right? How did it manage to go from Friedrich Hayek to Sean Hannity, from Ronald Reagan to Donald Trump? How did it create an alternative-reality silo that indulged every manner of crackpot, wing-nut conspiracy theory? How did a movement that was defined by its belief in individual liberty, respect for the constitution, free markets, personal responsibility, traditional values, and civility find itself embracing a stew of nativism, populism, and nationalism? How did the thought leaders of the movement find themselves tossed aside as "cuckservatives"?

When exactly did conservatives start to lose their minds?

Was it the day the Drudge Report began linking to the fevered conspiracy rantings of a guy named Alex Jones? Was it when the GOP thought it might be a good idea to put Sarah Palin a heartbeat away from the Oval Office? Was it the rise of the Tea Party or when Rush Limbaugh called a young female law student a "slut," and his career began to implode? Was it when they outsourced their thought leadership to the perpetually outraged? Or when Ann Coulter began her rants about Mexican rapists? Did the Right's intellectual implosion begin when conservatives began to get their information from their Facebook news feeds? When conservatives replaced Bill Buckley with late-night Twitter rants? When they made fiscal promises they couldn't keep?

Was Stephen King right when he wrote: "Conservatives who for 8 years sowed the dragon's teeth of partisan politics are horrified to discover they have grown an actual dragon"?[1] Or did it start long before that?

From the outside, political movements can look monolithic, even coherent—especially when there is a dearth of actual conversation with the people who comprise it. For years, progressives have indulged in hostile generalizations about the Right, a pastime made easier by the fact that they seldom read conservative books or magazines or listened with much attention to what conservatives were saying.

So the Right may have looked formidable, but the reality is that it was a mess—a contentious collection of disparate, often contradictory ideas and querulous and warring factions of libertarians, chamber of commerce types, traditionalists, and social conservatives. For years there have been deep fissures in a movement that calls itself conservative but supports an economic system that was designed to be creatively destructive, that supports traditional values but also a limited government. There are inherent tensions in a party that claims to be the party of "freedom" but also of national security and law and order. Consider that in recent years "conservative" had come to mean "radical change agent," and you see the difficulties. Those were very real tensions, but not necessarily contradictions.

Over decades, conservative thought leaders had sought to knit together those various interpretations of conservativism, carefully balancing culture, individual responsibility, and politics through the concept of *ordered liberty*. This was the essential equilibrium of modern conservatism that was shattered by the rise of Donald Trump.

Trump, we were told, "tapped into something." Yes he did; something disturbing that we had ignored and perhaps nurtured—a shift from an emphasis on freedom to authoritarianism and from American "exceptionalism" to nativism. The movement's slow-motion repudiation of the Reagan legacy has many dimensions, but none more so than the rejection of his optimistic agenda and its replacement by the darker paranoid side of the Right. Where Reagan had famously called on Mr. Gorbachev to "tear down this wall," Donald Trump was proposing to build one—a big, beautiful wall to shut people out from Reagan's "shining city on a hill." Those of us who pointed that out found ourselves increasingly isolated, disoriented, and ultimately disillusioned. It was, indeed, a clarifying moment for conservatism. The extent of the movement's abandonment of Reaganism was on full display at the first major conservative event of 2017, the Conservative Political Action Conference (CPAC), as the ideas that had animated conservativism—such as small government and free trade—were supplanted by the new cult of personality/entertainment politics that has gripped the Right. Trump aide Kellyanne Conway quipped that CPAC was becoming TPAC; with "Trump" replacing the word "Conservative." Indeed, noted one commentator, the conference revealed an "ideology conforming to an individual rather than the other way around. . . . Anyone searching for a brand of conservatism independent of the new president would have walked away sorely disappointed."[2]*

The reality is that a genuinely "conservative" party would never have nominated a Donald Trump; a right-wing nationalist party or one without fixed principles would have no problem doing so. While

---

*Headlines captured the shift: *Washington Post*: "As Trumpism Coopts CPAC, the Reagan Era Ends"; *Los Angeles Times*: "Trump's Popularity at CPAC Gathering, Which He Shunned a Year Ago, Shows How He's Conquered Conservatives"; Yahoo News: "Trumpism Versus Conservatism at CPAC"; *New York Times*: "Big Tent or Circus Tent? A Conservative Identity Crisis in the Trump Era."

Trump's nomination has been described as a "hostile takeover," it was not a complete outlier, as conservatives had long ago replaced rational policy discussions with the politics of lowest-common-denominator angry populism. A movement once driven by ideas found itself dominated by Kardashian-like talking point reciters, intellectually dishonest shills, cynical careerists, and Alt Right bullies. Recent debates among conservatives, one commentator gibed, "show[ed] the nuanced differences between a YouTube comments section and a chain email to your grandfather." Conservative "leaders" did not merely regurgitate "talking points" but became addicted to word salads of conservative clichés— "establishment," "globalist," "elites"—that became substitutes for actual thought. This has paralleled a surge in the anti-intellectualism in American life, perhaps facilitated by compromises among the people whose judgment and ideas I once relied upon and trusted.

In this environment, conformity was demanded—on language, attitudes, and even tactics. Since even the mildest of dissent was punished by withering fire on air and through social media—"RINO!"—it was not surprising that original, fresh thinking was discouraged. What creative public policy innovation occurred took place far from the increasingly populist, ranting heart of the movement. It is not as if we weren't warned. After years of carefully building an impressive intellectual infrastructure, conservatives thought they were poised to move ahead with a coherent philosophy of governing, only to have principled conservative ideas drowned out in a tsunami of misinformation and demagoguery. But even before the rise of Donald Trump, there were signs of deep dysfunction in the conservative ranks, raising questions about its ability to govern.

Critics on both the right and left warned that the GOP often seemed fat, lazy, and intellectually sclerotic—out of ideas and out of touch. With its increasingly shrill rhetoric and rejection of political compromise, the conservative movement was unable to adapt to changing realities and increasingly alienated from its own constituencies. It was not simply that conservatives chronically overpromised, it was that their message was often contradictory and incoherent. Even as the Republican base became more Southern, evangelical, and working class, the party's actual policies tended to focus on the entrepreneurial and business class. "Most traditional conservatives reliably serve large corporate interests, and can be counted on to ignore the basic interests of middle- and working-class voters," author Joel Kotkin writes.[3] That is perhaps an unduly harsh indictment, but the gap between the Right's actual voting base and the world of conservative think tanks and Washington dealmakers, was widening. Indeed, while the rhetoric of conservatives was often libertarian, their agenda often focused on the use of government power to satisfy the needs of the donor and lobbyist class. In recent years, nearly every major spending bill has been a master class in the art of crony capitalism.

The tone and the language of the Right was also shifting, as columnist Peter Wehner noted, with many conservatives confusing "cruelty, vulgarity, and bluster with strength and straight talk."[4] In the years before embracing Trump, the party flirted with the eccentric candidacies of Michele Bachmann, Newt Gingrich, Sarah Palin, and Herman Cain, making each of them temporary presidential front-runners at one point or another.

Such quixotic, self-defeating strategies were often justified on the grounds that they "made liberal heads explode," or as Palin put it so memorably, "it's really funny to me to see the splodey heads keep 'sploding. . . ." The result has been a compulsion to defend anyone attacked by the Left, no matter how reckless, extreme, or bizarre. If liberals hated something, the argument went, then it must be wonderful and worthy of aggressive defense, even if that meant defending the indefensible and losing elections. So conservatives embraced and defended figures like Christine ("I am not a witch") O'Donnell and lost winnable Senate races with candidates who said bizarre things about rape (Todd Akin) or were just too weird for the electorate (Sharron Angle).

DIVIDED AMERICA

All of this has taken place in the context of our radically divided politics. It is only a slight exaggeration to say that America, far from being "indivisible," has become two separate virtual nations, divided both intellectually and spatially. Increasingly, Americans have constructed what the Associated Press called "intellectual ghettoes," where audiences seldom intersect. But this divide is also increasingly geographical as well, reflected in eye-popping charts that divide the country into red and blue. As recently as 1997, 164 of the House of Representatives' 435 seats were considered "swing districts." Today, according to an analysis by the *Cook Political Report*, only about 72 seats are considered competitive. That is less than one in six congressional seats.[5] While some of this can be blamed on gerrymandering, it also reflects the way that Americans are sorting themselves out by class and ideology. As political columnist Mike Allen noted, "We are increasingly moving next to people who share our political views—and then following and sharing like-minded news on social media when our doors are closed. This can't be fixed with better redistricting laws."[6]

This division is also reflected in presidential elections, as Americans sort themselves out by lifestyle and politics. Author Bill Bishop, who documented the trend in his book, *The Big Sort*, illustrates the sorting out process by calculating the number of voters who live in so-called landslide counties, which were carried by 20 percentage points or more. In 1976, when Jimmy Carter narrowly edged Gerald Ford, only about one in four Americans lived in a landslide county. That proportion has grown steadily as the nation's political polarization accelerated. By 2004 that had risen to 48.3 percent; by 2012, a majority of Americans (50.6 percent) lived in a landslide county. In 2016, the portion of Americans living in deeply blue or deeply red counties surged to 60.4 percent. In rural America, more than three fourths of voters lived in counties that voted overwhelmingly red.

The result, says Bishop is that "any common ground between the two sides has nearly disappeared."[7] Inevitably, that has meant that the worst tendencies of both the right and left have been magnified as we interact less and less with those with whom we may disagree. Our politics becomes less about compromise than confrontation and less about persuasion than about tests of tribal loyalty.

"Cross-party friendships are disappearing," writes Jonathan Haidt. "Manicheaism and scorched earth politics are increasing."[8]

The loudest voices on the Right became increasingly strident as they stoked a mood of perpetual outrage. Long before Trump burst upon the scene, Conor Friedersdorf wrote in the *Atlantic*, "Hugely popular intellectual leaders abandoned the most basic norms of decency, as when Mark Levin screamed at a caller that her husband should shoot himself; stoked racial tensions, as when Rush Limbaugh avowed that in President Obama's America folks think white kids deserve to get beat up by black kids on busses; and indulged paranoid conspiracy theories, as when Roger Ailes aired month-after-month of Glenn Beck's chalkboard monologues."[9]

Further cranking up the volume, charlatans and grifters sought to exploit the anger for cash and clicks, pushing the GOP into shutting down the government in a maneuver that was nearly as pointless as it was suicidal. And, of course, there were the crackpots, from the darker corners of the fever swamps. Many of us in conservative media brushed them off, because we felt that somehow we could control the crackpottery. How naïve.

BRING IN THE CLOWNS

In 2016, the various denizens of Crazytown who had made cameo appearances on the national stage were first emboldened, then empowered, gleefully crashing the party, overturning the furniture and settled hierarchies as they raucously dismissed traditional gatekeepers. Those who were slow to join the bacchanal were denounced as sellouts and traitors, or perhaps, even worse, elitists. This was all heady stuff that required extraordinary nimbleness: conservatives who had just five minutes earlier agreed that Russia posed a global threat pivoted to embrace Vladimir Putin as an exemplar of white Christian civilization; Tea Party activists who had railed against deficit spending now accepted calls for massive infrastructure spending; the party of free markets endorsed protectionism and an economic policy that seemed driven by personal fear and favor; constitutionalists watched silently as the rule of law was undermined and norms of public integrity ignored. Activists who had clamored to "burn it all down" suddenly pivoted to demand party loyalty and virtual lockstep support of policies, even when they conflicted with fundamental principles or contradicted what the dear leader had previously said.

WHO WERE WE?

We learned a great deal about "conservatives" in recent years; they were passionate in what (and who) they opposed, but they were evidently far less clear in what they supported or believed in. Birtherism resonated far more than Paul Ryan's patient, wonky analysis of the tax code. Hatred of the media substituted for a coherent governing agenda.

And, as it turned out, Americans were just not that into conservative values. Among conservative voters, principles like constitutionalism, entitlement reform, and even the belief that character mattered turned out to be pie-crust thin, leaving the movement vulnerable to cult of personality politics. Some of the same media figures who gutted GOP leaders for not adopting scorched-earth tactics on budget issues and were willing to read them out of the movement found themselves carrying water for a man who had actually funded many of the Democrats who advanced those policies. Their about-face reflected the degree to which conservativism has come to be dominated by careerists and opportunists for whom the professed beliefs in small government, fiscal restraint, and constitutionalism were merely means to an end (ratings, cash, clicks, power), and thus easily discarded.

"One of the things we learned this year is that the ranks of conservatives as you and I understand them—limited government, the rule of law, working against the new effort to destigmatize dependency on government . . . that sort of conservative is pretty thin on the ground in the United States," George Will told me after the election. "Mr. Trump did not seek and therefore did not get . . . a mandate for dealing with the most predictable crisis in American history: the crisis of the entitlement state that gets worse every day and is clearly unsustainable. . . . That is because there is no constituency of any significant size for doing some of the kinds of things that this kind of conservatives know have to be done.

"So, the first thing we learned from this was that our numbers are smaller than we thought; that a number of people who called themselves conservatives (and they are free to do so) are not conservatives in the sense that we understand that—of genuinely wanting a smaller government, genuinely worrying about the separation of powers, and the grotesquely swollen president we have under both parties.

"In that sense," he told me, "what we have learned is that we are a smaller band of brothers and sisters than we thought."[10]

THE LEFT AT RAMMING SPEED

There is, of course, another side to this story that also needs to be told; no account of what has happened to the Right would be complete without a discussion of what conservatives thought they were reacting against. For years, conservatives have felt that the Left has been at ramming speed, often ignoring the niceties of congressional action, public opinion, or tolerance of religious differences. There was the passage of Obamacare with the barest of partisan majorities, rammed through on Christmas Eve and a massive stimulus package that threatened to explode the national debt. That was followed (in the eyes of conservatives) by assaults on free speech and religious liberty; the IRS targeting of Tea Party groups, John Doe probes into conservative activists in Wisconsin, complete with predawn paramilitary raids; threats to bankrupt the coal industry; and the ongoing vilification of conservative activists and donors.[11]* On university campuses, activists

---

*In the wake of the Supreme Court's *Citizens United* decision, Kimberley Strassel describes how the Left targeted conservative activists, moving "to harass and scare and shame opponents out of speaking. . . . They called out conservative donors by name, making them targets of a vast and threatening federal bureaucracy. . . . Liberal

began enforcing their demands for ideological conformity, complete with lists of microaggressions, trigger warnings, and "safe spaces."

Decades of scarcely concealed contempt, including the almost reflexive dismissal of conservatives as ignorant racists, had sowed seeds of deep antipathy among conservatives, many of whom felt both disrespected and under attack. All of this often was distorted and exaggerated by the Alt Reality media and their allies, but it is important to understand that the reactionary Right had something to react against.

Democrats often seemed to act as if their victories were preordained, not merely by history but by demographics, assuring themselves that as the nation became younger and more ethnically and racially diverse, it would deliver one victory after another to liberals. Indeed, the liberal Left seldom disappoints in its ability to alienate, offend, and alarm conservatives who may be tempted to stray from the fold; something in its ideological DNA compels it to shock the bourgeoisie, annoy taxpayers, and demonstrate a global disdain for those who are not members of protected classes.

Not content with winning historic victories on gay marriage, some progressives indulged their penchant for labeling opponents as bigots and their religious faith as hatred and discrimination. The goal was not tolerance, but what seemed like a determination to drive dissenters out of polite society and expel them from the public square. Many conservative voters, especially evangelical Christians, came to feel that they were not simply losing the culture war, they were being anathematized by a country they no longer recognized.

During the campaign, commentators on the Left expressed (legitimate) concern that Trump was encouraging violence at some of his rallies. At the same time, conservatives were inundated with stories,

---

activists took to the streets—to urinate on houses, and block the entrances to stores. They left threatening telephone messages, and delivered ugly e-mails, and got people fired from their jobs for holding unpopular political views." (Kimberley Strassel, *The Intimidation Game: How the Left Is Silencing Free Speech* (New York: Hachette Book Group, 2016), x–xi.)

links, and video clips of protesters chanting "What do we want? Dead cops! When do we want it? Now!"[12] and "Pigs in a blanket, fry 'em like bacon."[13] But on cable television, they watched their concerns about law and order denounced as racial "dog whistles."

This was especially unfortunate, because the excesses on the Left pushed many small-government conservatives into an unnatural alliance with the authoritarian and nationalistic right. In her 2005 book *The Authoritarian Dynamic*, Princeton professor Karen Stenner had noted that authoritarianism and political conservatism "appear to be largely distinct predispositions," and that conservatives, with their abhorrence to government power and radical change "can be a liberal democracy's strongest bulwark against the dangers posed by intolerant social movements."

"Those by nature averse to change" she noted, "should find the 'shining path' to a 'glorious future' far more frightening than exciting, and can be expected to defend faithfully an established order—including one of institutionalized respect for difference and protection of individual freedom—against 'authoritarian revolution.'"[14]

This, however required that status quo conservatives be given "reassurances regarding established brakes on the pace of change, and the settled rules of the game to which all will adhere," as well as "confidence in the leaders and institutions managing social conflict, and regulating the extent and rate of social change." In her 2005 book Stenner had written:

> Liberal democracy would seem least secure when conservatives cannot be persuaded that freedom and diversity are authoritatively supported and institutionally constrained, and when authoritarians can be persuaded that greater sameness and oneness—the "one right way" for the "one true people"—lie just at the other end of the "shining path."[15]

Eleven years later, Conor Friedersdorf noted, we saw that scenario play out in the presidential election.[16] Rather than reassuring conservatives about the "settled rules of the game," Democrats began dismantling the filibuster, while President Obama began issuing executive orders and mandates at a dizzying rate.

Caught in their own bubbles, many on the Left ignored and dismissed the concerns that would explode during the 2016 campaign. As the Democrats became a party dominated by a highly educated urban cultural elite, its traditional blue-collar constituencies felt increasingly disenfranchised and disdained. The term "angry white men" was seldom used in the context of asking whether those white men had any legitimate reason to be angry. Instead it was invariably used to argue that we should pay even less attention to their voices and their issues. It is notable that voices on the Left embraced the notion of "white privilege," even as white working-class America entered a period of acute economic and social decline and blue-collar workers faced the loss of jobs, income, and cohesive communities. Too often, the Left's rhetoric telegraphed the message to white working-class voters that their concerns were not high on the progressive agenda.

Blaming the backlash solely on racism is a tempting, but lazy reflexive retreat to a rhetorical safe zone for the Left. Crying wolf had serious consequences for both sides, because over time our audiences shrugged off the charges, responding to accusations of racism with an eye roll and "Not this again." By the time the real thing came along, the Left had used up its rhetorical ammunition, and the Right had become numb to the realities of the bigots around them.

A MORAL FAILURE

But this does not let conservatives off the hook.

For years, we ignored the birthers, the racists, the truthers, and other conspiracy theorists who indulged fantasies of Obama's secret Muslim plot to subvert Christendom, or who peddled tales of Hillary Clinton's murder victims. We treated them like your obnoxious uncle at Thanksgiving. Rather than confront them, we changed the channel because, after all, they were our friends, whose quirks could be indulged or at least ignored. They could rant and pound the table, we thought, but they were merely postcards from the fringe, right? The hope was that the center would always hold, things would not fall apart, and principled conservatives would rise to the occasion. Except they didn't. That proved to be a moral failure that lies at the heart of the conservative movement, even in its moment of apparent electoral triumph.

It is impossible to say how many conservatives actually harbor racial resentments, but what is undeniable is that a great number of American conservatives have proven themselves willing to tolerate and even accept racism and racial resentment. When Speaker Paul Ryan denounced "textbook racism," after Trump lashed out at the Mexican American judge in his Trump University lawsuit, he was hit with an avalanche of opprobrium from many of his fellow conservatives who believed that winning the election was more important than distinguishing conservatism from racial animus.

The hard fact is that only a political party that had cultivated an indifference and insensitivity to racial issues could have nominated Donald Trump and embraced him so easily.

Blogger Ben Howe has lamented all the signs we ignored, the times we looked away or simply rolled our eyes when one of our "allies" suggested that Obama was from Kenya or that liberals wanted to impose Sharia law on the country. "People would say outlandish things and I would find myself nodding my head and awkwardly walking away, not calling them out for their silliness," Howe wrote, because there were more important issues at stake. So, he said, he lied to himself about who they were.

> I chose peace over principle. I chose to go along with those I disagreed with on core matters because I believed we were jointly fighting for other things that were more important. I ignored my gut and my moral compass.
>
> The result is that, almost to a man, every single person I cringed at or thought twice about, is now a supporter and cheerleader of Donald Trump.[17]

THE ALT REALITY RIGHT

I was, of course, well aware that the Right had created an echo chamber. But as authors Kathleen Jamieson and Joseph Cappella noted in 2008, the conservative media were generally united around Reagan conservativism.[18] I was part of that and flattered myself that we were helping the audience become savvier, more sophisticated analysts of current affairs and well-informed consumers of news. For years, the relationship among on-air, online, and print conservatives was symbiotic and apparently seamless. On my show I frequently shared with my audience the latest column by Charles Krauthammer or set up topics by reading a *Wall Street Journal* editorial on air. Other talk shows did likewise, providing a broad forum for conservative authors, editors, and columnists. As long as this nexus held, conservative ideas could be exposed to a much wider audience than Buckley or his generation ever could have imagined.

But as the volume rose and competition for the outrage market intensified, this morphed into an alternative reality bubble that effectively isolated many conservatives from inconvenient information. "The American Right," Matthew Sheffield writes, "has become willfully disengaged from its fellow citizens thanks to a wonderful virtual-reality machine in which conservatives, both elite and grassroots, can believe anything they wish, no matter how at odds it is with reality."[19] The explosive growth of the Right's new media infrastructure was fueled by well-heeled conservative donors, dramatically changing the shape of the media and political landscape. A study by the *Columbia Journalism Review* (*CJR*) of more than 1.25 million online stories published between April 1, 2015, and Election Day documented the impact of a "right-wing media network anchored around Breitbart" that had "developed as a distinct and insulated media system, using social media as a backbone to transmit a hyper-partisan perspective to the world." In a remarkably short period of time, the *CJR* study found, Breitbart had become "the center of a distinct right-wing media ecosystem, . . ." All of this was a long time coming. For years, conservatives criticized the bias and double standards of the mainstream media and much of that criticism was richly deserved; conservatives may exaggerate media bias, but they do not merely imagine it. The double standards—

something treated as a misdemeanor for a liberal was a felony for a conservative—made for daily fodder. Over the years, I used my own radio show to call out the many failures of the liberal media. What the media has learned (one hopes) is that if you ignore or insult your audience long enough, they will find other sources of information and entertainment. Credibility squandered through bias is not easily restored.

But as we learned in 2016, we had succeeded in convincing our audiences to ignore and discount any information whatsoever from the mainstream media. The cumulative effect of the attacks was to delegitimize those outlets and essentially destroy much of the Right's immunity to false information.

So it should not have come as a surprise when "fake news" became a significant factor in the campaign. After the election, a study by University of Oxford researchers found that "nearly a quarter of web content shared by Twitter users in Michigan during the 10 days before the presidential election was false." They concluded that "not only did such junk news 'outperform' real news, but the proportion of professional news content being shared hit its lowest point the day before the election." The false information was spread by automated "chatbots" powered by software programs that flooded Twitter with anti-Clinton, pro-Trump messages.[20] "The use of automated accounts was deliberate and strategic throughout the election," the researchers concluded.[21] The problem was neither small, nor isolated. University of Washington professor Kate Starbird found that there were dozens of "conspiracy propagating websites," such as "beforeitsnews.com, nodisinfo.com and veteranstoday .com." Starbird was able to catalog eighty-one separate sites, "linked through a huge community of interest connected by shared followers on Twitter, with many of the tweets replicated by automated bots."[22]

The proliferation of hoaxes—and the number of gullible voters who believed them—should have inspired some serious introspection among conservatives, but that now seems highly unlikely.

In the wake of the election, the newly weaponized conservative media genuinely believe that they have changed the paradigm of media coverage. In the new Right media culture, negative information simply no longer penetrates; gaffes and scandals can be snuffed out, ignored, or spun; counternarratives can be launched. Trump has proven that a candidate can be immune to the narratives, criticism, and fact-checking of the mainstream media. This was, after all, a campaign in which a presidential candidate trafficked in "scoops" from the *National Enquirer* and openly suggested that the father of his rival, Senator Ted Cruz, may have been involved in the assassination of JFK. And got away with it.

Indeed, in a stunning demonstration of the power and resiliency of our new postfactual political culture, Trump and his allies in the Right media quickly absorbed, disarmed, and turned the term "fake news" against its critics, draining it of any meaning. Now any news deemed to be biased, annoying, or negative can be labeled "fake news." It was surely a sign of things to come when Trump used his first press conference after the election to refuse to answer a question from a reporter because he was from a "fake news" media outlet (CNN).

Perhaps even more cringe worthy has been the rise of a new class of pro-Trump "intellectuals" who attempt to impose some coherence and substance on Trumpism. Often they strained to attribute to Trump an ideological lucidity that seems little more than a projection of their own wishful thinking. Even so, Trump's defenders were often less pro-Trump than anti-anti-Trump, aiming their polemics against the Left and conservatives who have been slow to shift their allegiances. What may have begun as a policy or a tactic in opposition, has long since become a reflex. The *New York Times*'s James Poniewozik notes that politics today" is attitudinal, not ideological. The reason to be for someone is who is against them. What matters more than policy is your side's winning, and what matters more than your side's winning is the other side's losing."[23] But, as I wrote earlier this year, there is an obvious price to be paid for essentially becoming a party devoted to trolling.[24] As the Right doubles down on anti-anti-Trumpism it will find itself goaded into defending and rationalizing ever more outrageous conduct, just as long as it annoys the Left.

In many ways the new anti-anti-Trumpism mirrors Trump himself, because at its core there are no fixed values, no respect for constitutional government or ideas of personal character, only a free-floating nihilism cloaked in insult, mockery, and bombast. Needless to say, this is not a form of conservatism that Edmund Burke, or even Barry Goldwater, would have recognized.

CHAPTER 2

CONFESSIONS OF A RECOVERING LIBERAL

THROUGHOUT THE 2016 CAMPAIGN, I struggled to understand why I had such a different perspective from many of my one-time allies. Why didn't they recognize what I was seeing? What secret knowledge was I missing? I have to confess that this gap in perceptions grew wider with every passing month, and I had a hard time accounting for it. Perhaps it had something to do with my own background.

For years, I described myself not as a conservative, but as a "recovering liberal."

My father, Jay, was a longtime liberal activist, who was president of the Wisconsin Civil Liberties Union and ran antiwar insurgent Eugene McCarthy's Wisconsin primary campaign in 1968. As an eighth grader I helped open the campaign headquarters and was a page to the

Democratic National Convention in Chicago that year. I went on to become an active member of the Young Democrats, serving for a time on the state executive board while I was in high school.

So I did not come by my conservativism either by birth or by upbringing.

Over the next few years both my father and I drifted away from liberalism, largely because we both felt that it had moved away from us. My father was at various times of his life a lawyer, a newspaper reporter, an editorial writer, and professor of journalism. In all of those roles, he was a curmudgeon and a contrarian. I grew up arguing history and politics around the dinner table, often to the horror of the women in our family. Our worst jibe was to accuse the other of "being predictable." But in the 1960s, we were liberals, because the moral issues of the times seemed so clear to us—the fight for civil rights and opposition to a bloody and costly war.

My father was a World War II veteran who opposed the Vietnam War because he regarded it as reckless and ill-advised, but he was also a deeply patriotic man, who understood what we were asking of the men and women in the military. He admired Eugene McCarthy's courage in standing up for principle and challenging his own party's incumbent president. I think that McCarthy, who wrote poetry and made no effort to tone down his wit or hide his erudition, was my father's ideal politician and I shared his attitude. As a junior high school student he let me travel around the state with the Minnesota senator and his national press entourage, an experience that turned me into a political junkie, a condition from which I haven't yet recovered.

But as the antiwar protests became more strident after Nixon's election, my father became increasingly troubled by the tone of the movement. Opposition to a misguided war was morphing into a virulent anti-Americanism. My father, who had served in North Africa, Sicily, and Italy, was especially disgusted by the vicious treatment of returning Vietnam veterans; the first time I saw him truly angry was when he heard one activist celebrating a Viet Cong victory in a battle that cost more than a hundred American lives.

His disillusionment came to a head in 1970, when students went on strike after the invasion of Cambodia and sought to shut down the university where he taught. Originally launched to protest President Nixon's decision to temporarily expand the Vietnam War into Cambodia, as my father later recalled, "The strike was quickly transformed into a crusade against an authoritarian and insensitive faculty; against irrelevant curricula, racism, sexism, oppression, capitalism; against American imperialism oppressing the revolutionary peoples of the Third World; and against all the assorted global inequities that the university has none of the means or the obligation to fix." He described the scene on his campus:

> Bands of ragged students, heavily infiltrated by off-campus civilians and a few faculty partisans, roamed across the campus, through corridors, and into classrooms, chanting "on strike, shut it down." Outfitted with simulated Che Guevara berets, Fidel Castro jackets, and arm bands, many appeared to be acting out roles in a grade-B adventure melodrama of a Balkan revolution. The guerilla brigades were later joined by truant high school students from nearby suburbs, attracted less by the cause than as a relief from boredom entered classrooms, demanding that the classes disband.[1]

After the shooting of four students at Kent State University, the strike intensified. Several university buildings were padlocked by the strikers who then stormed the university library demanding that it be shut down, threatening to scatter hundreds of thousands of book cataloging cards on the floor, which my father regarded as "a new version of book burning." When strikers tried to shut down the student newspaper, my father, who was faculty adviser, ordered the occupiers to leave the office, he recalled, "upon which a seventeen-year-old Fidelista called me a 'fascist pig.'" The paper was surrendered an hour later when it was discovered that "no one among the new barbarians had the expertise to operate a typewriter."

For my father the climax of the strike came when he tried to drive through a blockade around the campus. A student protester jumped on the hood of his car. "My response, not out of principle but personal anger, was to keep my car rolling forward, shouting at the student to get off my car." The protest was no longer "an abstraction but a violent presence on my car. A potentially dangerous impasse was averted when one of the blockade leaders, remembering me from my affiliation with the McCarthy campaign two years before, told his colleagues to let me pass. 'He's all right,' he said mistakenly. I still had some little credits which I quickly dissipated that week."

Memories of the sixties have been romanticized, but left-wing politics came to be dominated by humorless and strident ideologues, who did little to hide their contempt for the older generation, bourgeois values, and for American culture in general.

During the decade that followed, the excesses of the Left drove millions of former Democrats—families who had voted for Franklin Roosevelt, Harry Truman, and John F. Kennedy—to the right. The Left had seemingly lost its mind and the country seemed to be politically realigning, as were we.

A protest against the stultifying conformity of the 1950s now demanded its own conformism to moral and cultural relativism in which every sort of deviancy and crime could be excused. On civil rights, the Left had shifted from an emphasis on judging one another "by the content of their character," to a demand for racial quotas, which for my father evoked memories of the quotas that limited the number of Jewish students that he faced while trying to get into college in the 1930s.

This was not the liberalism my father had signed up for. Later, he regretted not defecting from the Left sooner, but he noted, "The habit of years blocks out reason, making ideological transformation difficult, like a heart that continues to beat after the brain dies."

I was undergoing my own shift. I left the Young Democrats and, after college, embarked on a career in journalism. As a newspaper reporter, I watched as the good intentions of the Great Society often failed to match the results, creating as many problems as they solved. Covering urban issues, I watched the multiplication of programs that had increasingly abstruse acronyms but seemed to exist for no other purpose than to satisfy a voter bloc and provide employment to various hacks and mediocrities. They did not discernibly improve any lives or fix any problems. As it turned out, bureaucracies made poor substitutes for families and neighborhoods and were often insensitive to the unintended consequences they left in their wake.

My particular interest was education reform, especially in the central city, which I came to regard as the civil rights issue of our time. But it was obvious that the greatest impediment to change was an entrenched status quo that clung to its perks, privileges, and powers. As schools dumbed down their curricula and indulged a series of ill-fated educational fads, the results were increasingly horrible. But it was also obvious that the Democratic Party had become a wholly owned subsidiary of the teachers' unions. Here I found that asking awkward questions often led to charges that I was flirting with the dark forces of the Right but, after a while, I simply stopped caring whether I was becoming a heretic. Even though I would lose a lot of friends (and, naturally, be accused of "selling out"), I found that breaking free of the tribal loyalties and ideological straitjackets was quite liberating. I suppose that was a result of my contrarian upbringing.

That did not mean that I became a conservative right away, however. At the time, conservatism still seemed an exotic and not terribly attractive alternative that often came in repellent packages (this was the era of Nixon, after all). But I became open to alternatives. Conservatism was appealing not only because it was contrarian, but because, at the time, it just seemed smarter.

I was charmed and amused by William F. Buckley's critiques and increasingly open to Milton Friedman's case for free markets. In the late 1970s, George Will and Ludwig von Mises made more sense to me than the pieties and obligatory cant of the Carter era. Norman Podhoretz and Irving Kristol, who had similarly moved to the right, reminded me of my father as he struggled with a liberalism from which he felt increasingly alienated. But most important for me was that conservative ideas simply made more sense; they took the world as it was rather than seeing it through the lens of wishful thinking and ideology.

By the late 1980s, my shift from left to right was complete. I wrote several books about universities, political correctness, and the culture of victimization; edited a public policy magazine; and in the early 1990s became a talk radio host. Those were heady times for the new medium. Conservativism suddenly found an audience, and the movement itself seemed alive with ideas. In Wisconsin I helped advance the careers of conservatives like Paul Ryan, Scott Walker, Reince Priebus, and Ron Johnson. In 2010, conservatives won big majorities in the legislature and I openly supported many of their reforms, including reforms of collective bargaining and expansions of school choice. In short, I was under the impression that conservatives actually believed in concepts such as free trade, balanced budgets, and character, and had respect for constitutional rights.

And then along came this campaign.

Donald Trump suddenly surged in the polls, and a conservative media that had once formed a solid phalanx around Reagan conservatism now began a vertiginous pivot toward the erratic populist.

INTO THE WILDERNESS

When I wrote in August 2015 that Trump was a cartoon version of every leftist/media negative stereotype of the reactionary, nativist, misogynist right, I thought that I was well within the mainstream of conservative thought.[2] In January 2016, former presidential speech writer Peter Wehner recalled that the late Daniel Patrick Moynihan, a Democratic senator from New York, had remarked in 1980, "Of a sudden, the G.O.P. has become a party of ideas." But Wehner wrote that a GOP headed by Donald Trump would "become the party of anti-reason."[3]

Like Peter Wehner I thought the issue was clear for conservatives. Even after Wisconsin failed to be a firewall of rationality, I hoped principled conservatives would draw the necessary lines, and many did. But the months that followed were like a slow-rolling version of *Invasion of the Body Snatchers,* in which one friend and associate after another was taken, or rather chose to change their minds.

In my social media feeds I found myself called a "cuckservative"— a favorite gibe of white nationalists. The soundtrack of my year (or at least the second half) were callers and emailers and social media users telling me they would never listen to me again, calling me a sellout, a traitor, a Judas for failing to get on board the Trump train. Under the withering fire of social media trolls, one GOP politician and commentator after another fell into line. The GOP became the party of Trump.

For the second time in my life, I found myself in the political wilderness, with more questions than answers.

CHAPTER 3

THE ATTACK ON THE
CONSERVATIVE MIND

AMONG THE MANY IRONIES of the conservative implosion was how the Right became what it had once mocked. In 2008, conservatives ridiculed the Left for its adulation of Barack Obama, only to succumb to their own cult of personality eight years later. For years, they scoffed at what Rush Limbaugh called the "low information voters," only to find out that the conservative base was (as one pundit put it) itself decidedly *postliterate.*

Polls suggested that as many as seven in ten Republicans doubted Obama's birth in the United States. A majority thought he was a secret Muslim. A Public Policy Poll of Republican voters in May 2016 found that:

—65 percent thought President Obama is a Muslim; only 13 percent thought he's a Christian

—59 percent thought President Obama was not born in the United States; only 23 percent thought that he was

—27 percent thought vaccines cause autism; 45 percent didn't think they do; another 29 percent were not sure

—24 percent thought Antonin Scalia was murdered; just 42 percent thought he died naturally; another 34 percent are unsure.[1]

This is not to say that the Right had a monopoly on voter ignorance. Surveys have found that only about one third of Americans can even name the three branches of government (executive, legislative, and judiciary). As Ilya Somin, a professor at the George Mason University School of Law, has observed, the problem is not that such knowledge is absolutely essential, it is that "anyone who follows politics even moderately closely is likely to know them. The fact that most people do not know is a strong indication of their ignorance about politics and public policy generally." And, indeed, the ignorance runs quite deep:

Despite years of public controversy over the budget, surveys consistently show that most of the public have very little understanding of how the federal government spends its money. They greatly underestimate the percentage of federal funds allocated to massive entitlement programs such as Medicare and Social Security—which are among the largest federal expenditures—and vastly overestimate the proportion that goes to foreign aid (only about 1 percent of the total).[2]

As its coverage of the last campaign demonstrated, the mainstream media is complicit in dumbing down the electorate. As recently as 2008, the nightly news programs on the three major networks devoted a grand total of less than four hours of airtime *over an entire year* to reporting on actual issues (as opposed to candidate speeches or political horse race coverage). By 2016, the Tyndall Report, which monitors networks' newscasts, estimated issue coverage for the year had fallen to just thirty-six minutes.

"Journalists were confronted with the spectacle of an issues-free campaign," analyst Andrew Tyndall told columnist Nicholas Kristof. "They had to decide how to react: with complicity, since such tactics were easy to shoehorn into the ratings—pleasing entertainment structure of a reality TV show, or with defiance, by delving into what was at stake."[3] The media chose entertainment, and the result was a campaign that was seldom about substance or ideas.

The problem here is obvious: An ignorant electorate is not likely to hold ignorant politicians to account. If voters don't know what they don't know, they will also be unlikely to recognize or care very much about what politicians don't know. So ignorance begets ignorance and the tolerance of it in high places.

As it happens, there is actually a term for this: the Dunning-Kruger Effect. Professor David Dunning, for whom the concept is partly named, coauthored a study entitled "Unskilled and Unaware of It: How Difficulties in Recognizing One's Incompetence Lead to Inflated Self-Assessments," which argued that "people tend to hold overly favorable reviews of their abilities in many social and intellectual domains."[4] This occurs "because people who were unskilled in the domain suffer a dual burden: not only do these people reach erroneous conclusions and make unfortunate choices, but their incompetence robs them of the ability to realize it." During the campaign, Dunning extrapolated the concept to the presidential contest, explaining in *Politico* why so many voters seemed untroubled by Trump's ignorance or gaffes. Many voters, "especially those facing significant distress in their life, might like some of what they hear from Trump," wrote Dunning, "but they do not know enough to hold him accountable for the serious gaffes he makes. They fail to recognize those gaffes as missteps." The problem, he noted, was not simply that voters were ignorant, "it is that they are often misinformed—their heads filled with false data, facts and theories that can lead to misguided conclusions held with tenacious confidence and extreme partisanship. . . ."[5]

THE RISE OF THE ILLITERATI

This was not simply an artifact of the Right's Alt Reality bubble; it was also a reflection of a broader populist anti-intellectualism that rejected expertise and authority alike. Within the Alt Reality silos there was a nagging insistence that everyone's opinions and facts were as good as anyone else's and that claims to the contrary were signs of "elitism." This rejection of reason and evidence was essentially a rejection of Enlightenment values as well as the conservative tradition. But ignorance and anger proved to be a dangerous combination.

"What we missed was that nobody cared about solutions," recalled Sarah Huckabee Sanders, who had worked on her father Mike Huckabee's campaign before signing on with Trump. "They just wanted to burn it all down. They didn't care about building it back up. They wanted to burn it to the ground and then figure out what to do with the ashes afterwards. . . . You may have the best policy in the world to get every single American the best job they've ever had. Nobody cared."[6]

Even before 2016, some critics accused the GOP of self-consciously dumbing itself down. In *Too Dumb to Fail*, Matt Lewis charged that conservatism had become "more personal and less principled—more flippant and less thoughtful. It became mean. It became lazy." As conservatives cultivated their everyman anti-intellectualism, Lewis said, many "deliberately shun erudition, academic excellence, experience, sagaciousness, and expertise in politics."[7] It had become the party of Sarah Palin . . . and Donald Trump.

There was also a time—before the Age of Twitter—when statesmen actually read books. "The American Founders could have a conversation among themselves," *National Review*'s Kevin Williamson wrote, "because they had in the main all consumed the same library of Greek and Roman classics (in the original or in translation), British and Continental literature ranging from fiction to political economy, legal literature, and the like." This did not lead to uniformity of opinion. "What it ensured was literate and enlightened argument," noted Williamson. "From the man of many books to the man of one book, we devolved very quickly to the man of one sentence, the paragraph being too demanding and unwieldy a form."[8]

Williamson saw Trump's election as a sign of our "postliterate politics." Williamson's thesis was that Donald Trump's presidential candidacy is only possible in a society that doesn't read or think much. "Trump is something that could not happen in a nation that could read," he wrote. "But we are not a nation that reads, or a nation that shares a living tradition of serious contemporary literature, fiction or nonfiction."[9]

Television personality Tomi Lahren seemed to embody the unapologetic anti-intellectualism of the new generation of conservative media "thought leaders." She has 3.6 million likes on Facebook and 406,000 followers on Twitter, and some of the YouTube clips from her show, which was streamed on Blaze.com, have gotten more than 2 million hits. (Lahren and The Blaze parted ways in early 2017.) She is known for suggesting that Hillary and Bill Clinton could have been behind the deaths of half a dozen political opponents—and government officials linked to them—who died under questionable circumstances over the years.[10]

When the slim, blonde, twenty-four-year-old Lahren was profiled by the *New York Times*, she was described as "young, vocal and the right's rising media star."[11] But in an interview on *The Jamie Weinstein Show* podcast, she admitted that she was no Edmund Burke:

> I don't like to read long books. I like to read news. So I couldn't tell you that there was a book that I read that changed my life. More so, I love to read . . . but I have a very short attention span, so sitting down with a book is very difficult for me.[12]

Her attitude toward reading was, unfortunately, shared by the forty-fifth president of the United States, who has admitted that he has not read any biographies of former presidents. He has no time to read books, he told the *Washington Post*. "I never have. I'm always busy doing a lot. Now I'm more busy, I guess, than ever before."[13]*

---

* "He said in a series of interviews that he does not need to read extensively because he reaches the right decisions 'with very little knowledge other than the

Throughout the campaign there were strained attempts to compare Trump to Ronald Reagan. But although the media often portrayed the Gipper as an amiable dunce, the discovery of the papers that were published in the book *Reagan, In His Own Hand* forced historians to revise their views of the fortieth president. Reagan wrote out many of his radio commentaries and newspaper articles, as well as many of his own speeches. He wrote poetry, short stories, and letters.[14] Trump, in his own hand, writes 140-character tweets.

TRAGEDY OF THE CONSERVATIVE MIND

The story of the conservative movement in the past sixty years has been the long development of a coherent, principled, often witty and sharp-tongued intellectual worldview that provided devastating critiques of liberal pieties.

At one time, the Left had a monopoly not merely of the media and academia, but also of the world of policy think tanks. Lionel Trilling wrote in 1950 that "liberalism is not only the dominant but even the sole intellectual tradition" in this country. Trilling declared that "it is the plain fact that nowadays there are no conservative or reactionary ideas in general circulation." He conceded that there was an impulse to conservatism, but "the conservative impulse and the reactionary impulse do not, with some isolated and some ecclesiastical exceptions, express themselves in ideas but only in action or in irritable mental gestures which seek to resemble ideas."[15] Clinton Rossiter made the same point in *Conservatism in America*: We were a "progressive country with a liberal tradition," and the ideas of the Right were more or less "irrelevant."[16] This continues to be the attitude of much of academia.

---

knowledge I [already] had, plus the words 'common sense,' because I have a lot of common sense and I have a lot of business ability." —Marc Fisher, "Donald Trump Doesn't Read Much. Being President Probably Wouldn't Change That" *Washington Post*, July 17, 2016.

But the playing field was changed by the development of an intellectual infrastructure—including The Heritage Foundation, the Bradley Foundation, the American Enterprise Institute—that has redefined what was possible for conservatism. It became possible to challenge the Left on policy grounds, win the war of ideas, and win elections. No longer content to stand athwart history and yell, "Stop," conservatives were able to propose reform agendas based on free market, nonstatist principles. There would not have been Reagan, a GOP revolution, or a Tea Party without them.

As a recovering liberal, I remember reading their stuff and realizing that their arguments were stronger and their ideas were better. They made free markets understandable, made the case for constitutional government, and inspired a generation to defend a culture of life and personal freedom. They were voices of reason and common sense.

Throughout 2015–2016, the struggle in the GOP was often characterized as a contest between "outsiders" and the "establishment" or the "elites." But this was lazy punditry, and missed a larger (and more troubling) development.

There was, of course, justifiable disillusionment with the Washington, DC, insider/elite who have been co-opted by the beltway culture, but there was something else going on as well: an assault on intellectual traditions of conservative civility. This went beyond candidate Trump's serial insults of conservatives—Charles Krauthammer was a dummy/loser/clown; George Will was "dopey"; Bill Kristol had "lost all respect", Rich Lowry was the "worst"; and so on.

Trump's targets were unusual because they were not politicians or officeholders. But all of them were heirs to the conservative intellectual tradition and a culture that had once placed a value on thoughtfulness, experience, intelligence, and a coherent philosophy of man and his relationship to the state. What we were seeing was, in effect, a repudiation of the conservative mind.

CHAPTER 4

THE CONSERVATIVE IDEA

CONSERVATIVES HAVE BEEN IN exile before.

In 1964, conservatives had been annihilated in Lyndon Johnson's landslide victory over Barry Goldwater. That campaign had introduced the country to some rising political stars, such as Ronald Reagan, but the consensus was that a chastened GOP would have to shake off the stink of the Right and move to the center. For many Republicans, reeling from the prior year's defeat, the future was embodied by young, charismatic liberal Manhattan congressman John Lindsay, who was running as a Republican for New York City mayor.

In a pivotal moment for the movement, William F. Buckley Jr. decided to stand athwart the GOP's retreat from conservatism. The founder of the nation's premier conservative magazine, Buckley decided to run for mayor of New York in 1965 on the Conservative Party ticket, his colleague Neal Freeman later wrote, as "a right-wing insurgent marching against the citadel of self-satisfied liberalism . . . the denizens of the citadel were not amused."[1]

In 1965, there were few platforms for conservative ideas: no talk radio, cable shows, blogs, or social media. The most important platform was the syndicated newspaper column, and by Freeman's count there were only three that could be described as conservative: David Lawrence, "the grand old man" of U.S. News & World Report, "who was by that stage of his career more old than grand." There was also James Jackson Kilpatrick, whose appeal was somewhat limited by his nostalgia for Southern conservatism. And then there was Buckley.

Buckley had been a "conservative long before conservatism was cool," Freeman wrote, so he was regarded by much of the Left and the media as a "creature of the Hard Right lagoon." But he was also one of the most provocative and lively polemicists in American politics. As a magazine editor, Freeman wrote, "he had been poking Liberal shibboleths through the bars of a cage." By running for New York mayor, "he was poking those shibboleths from inside the cage."[2]

Buckley's 1965 campaign, chronicled in his book The Unmaking of a Mayor, was quixotic with a distinctly New York and Buckleyite twist. When asked if he thought he had any chance of winning, he answered simply, "No." Asked what he would do if he did, in fact, win the election, he quipped that he would "demand a recount."

Flippancy aside, Buckley was on a mission; at arguably the worst political moment (a year after the Goldwater debacle) and certainly in the least hospitable environment (New York City), he set out to make an unapologetic case for conservativism. Buckley wanted to explain what freedom, restrained government, and an ordered society actually looked like in the context of the real world, and specifically in the nation's largest and most challenged city.

While establishment Republicans insisted that conservatives rally around the standard-bearer (Lindsay), Buckley challenged the notion of blind party loyalty, especially if that meant jettisoning the party's bedrock principles. Lindsay's GOP, Buckley said, was "indifferent to the historic role of the Republican Party as standing in opposition to those trends of our time that are championed by the collectivist elements of the Democratic Party. . . ." Buckley was offering voters a chance to cast their ballot "for a candidate who consults without embarrassment, and who is proud to be guided by the root premises of the Republican philosophy of government, the conservative philosophy of government."[3]

Buckley was able to carry that debate into the belly of the beast. During the campaign, Buckley had the chance to sit down with the mandarins of the *New York Times* editorial board. In terms of influence, Freeman later recalled, "There is nothing in contemporary culture with which to compare the dominance of the sixties-era *New York Times*." In his close encounter with the citadel of the established media, Buckley met not just with editorial writers, but also the paper's executives as well as the editors and reporters from the major beats. "Bill was surrounded," Freeman recalled, "by contemporary liberalism's A-Team."

The two-hour-long meeting between Buckley and the *Times* men, Freeman wrote, "would prove to be a real education. For them." That conference, he later surmised, "may have been the first time in their lives that most of the *Times*-men had faced an articulate and informed Conservative in close encounter."[4]

A HOUSE DIVIDED

That meeting was a culmination of Buckley's decade-long effort to make some sense out of American conservatism.

For Buckley, this was a battle of ideas that the Right had been losing badly for decades. "One need only to spend some time on a university campus," declared the "publisher's statement" in the first issue of *National Review* in 1955, "to have a vivid intimation of what has happened. It is there that we see how a number of energetic social innovators, plugging their grand designs, succeeded over the years in capturing the liberal intellectual imagination," wrote Buckley.

And since ideas rule the world, the ideologues, having won
over the intellectual class, simply walked in and started to run
things. Run just about everything. There never was an age of
conformity quite like this one, or a camaraderie quite like the
Liberals'.[5]

In the mid-1950s, conservatives—Buckley called them "radical
conservatives"—were a small, neglected, despised remnant in American politics, "for when they are not being suppressed or mutilated by
Liberals, they are being ignored or humiliated by a great many of
those of the well-fed Right, whose ignorance and amorality have never
been exaggerated for the same reason that one cannot exaggerate
infinity."[6]

But in the 1950s, conservatives were also a house divided. "Conservatives," notes Lee Edwards in a thoughtful history of the movement,
"have always been a disputatious lot." Those disputes have generally
focused on genuine philosophical differences—on ideas. "Far from
being signs of a crackup or a breakdown," Edwards argued, "intense
uninhibited debate among conservatives is an unmistakable sign of intellectual vigor in a national movement whose influence and longevity
continue to surprise many in the political and academic worlds."[7]

In the 1950s those disputes generally pitted traditionalists and
libertarians against one another. One of the leading traditionalists,
Russell Kirk, resisted the classical liberal emphasis on individualism,
saying that it amounted to "social atomism" and was, in any case, incompatible with the traditional Christian view of the world. These
were not easy issues to resolve, as Buckley freely admitted. "The conservative movement in America has got to put its theoretical house in
order." One of the goals of *National Review* was to somehow reconcile
the competing schools of thought by bringing together traditionalists,
libertarians, and anticommunists to hash out their differences.

The resolution came from a somewhat unlikely source. Frank
Meyer was a former communist who had morphed into a radical libertarian of the sort distrusted by the traditionalist wing. But in 1962, he
published *In Defense of Freedom*, which laid the foundations for what

became known as "fusionism," a careful balancing of the disparate elements of the Right. Basing his idea of balance on the conservativism of the founding fathers, Meyer made the case for "reason operating within tradition" and the concept of "ordered liberty," which juxtaposed "freedom of the person" with the "Christian understanding of the nature and destiny of man." Fusionism struck a delicate balance between freedom on the one hand and moral responsibility on the other. The fusionists noted that the Constitutional Convention in 1787 had not embraced either the "libertarian" vision of the Jeffersonians nor the "authoritarian" politics of Alexander Hamilton, but had steered a middle course as laid out by James Madison, who helped craft a system of checks and balances.

In 1964 Meyer gathered a group of conservative thinkers of various ideological hues and asked them to address the question, "What is conservatism?" Lee Edwards summarized the rough consensus that emerged:

> They accept "an objective moral order" of "immutable standards by which human conduct should be judged."
>
> Whether they emphasize human rights and freedoms or duties and responsibilities, they unanimously value "the human person" as the center of political and social thought.
>
> They oppose liberal attempts to use the State "to enforce ideological patterns on human beings."
>
> They reject the centralized power and direction necessary to the "planning" of society.
>
> They join in defense of the Constitution "as originally conceived."
>
> They are devoted to Western civilization and acknowledge the need to defend it against the "messianic" intentions of Communism.[8]

But this was not an easy sell. There were still dissenters on the Right who noted that incompatibility between traditional conservatism (suspicious of reason, anticapitalist, and authoritarian) and the rising libertarian tide on the Right. But despite those inherent tensions, writes Edwards, by the mid-1960s, "the tumult between the disputants had nearly subsided, and fusionism had become, by a process Meyer called 'osmosis,' a fait accompli. . . . They were tired of feuding, of endlessly debating how many traditionalists and libertarians can dance on the head of a pin." As historian George Nash noted, the process was helped by "the cement of anti-communism."[9]

It was also helped along by the rise of Barry Goldwater, whose thinking was imbued with the debates that had been taking place among the conservative intellectuals. Goldwater's 1960 book, *The Conscience of a Conservative*, was an instant bestseller and galvanized much of the nascent but still somewhat inchoate conservative movement. Along with his ghost writer, L. Brent Bozell, Goldwater pulled together all of the major schools of conservative thought from anticommunism to classical liberalism. Deeply informed by years of Buckley's attempt to craft a coherent conservative critique of government, the slim volume was also a primer on both antipopulism and antiauthoritarianism.

Although Goldwater would be long remembered for his 1964 convention speech where he declared that "extremism in the defense of liberty is no vice . . . moderation in the pursuit of justice is no virtue," what is striking about rereading *Conscience* is its attempt at carefully balancing the competing strains of conservative thought. In its opening pages Bozell/Goldwater lay claim to a historical tradition of conservatism that "has regarded man neither as a potential pawn of other men, nor as a part of a general collectivity in which the sacredness and the separate identity of individual human beings are ignored."[10] Conservatives rejected the concentration of power in the state as well as populist demagoguery:

> Throughout history, true Conservatism has been at war equally with autocrats and with "democratic" Jacobins.
>
> The true Conservative was sympathetic with the plight of the hapless peasant under the tyranny of the French monarchy. And he was equally revolted at the attempt to solve that

problem by a mob tyranny that paraded under the banner of egalitarianism.[11]

Bozell/Goldwater then laid out the essential elements of the fusionist settlement that united the disparate wings of the movement:

> The Conservative looks upon politics as the art of achieving the maximum amount of freedom for individuals that is consistent with the maintenance of social order.
>
> The Conservative is the first to understand that the practice of freedom requires the establishment of order: it is impossible for one man to be free if another is able to deny him the exercise of his freedom.
>
> But the Conservative also recognizes that the political power on which order is based is a self-aggrandizing force; that its appetite grows with eating. He knows that the utmost vigilance and care are required to keep political power within its proper bounds.
>
> Thus, for the American Conservative, there is no difficulty in identifying the day's overriding political challenge: it is to *preserve and extend freedom.* [Emphasis in original.][12]

This meant, first and foremost, constraining the role of government as well as our expectations. Echoing Buckley's earlier critique of "modern Republicanism," Bozell/Goldwater challenged the Eisenhower era's approach to the issue, which had been spelled out in the book *A Republican Looks at His Party,* written by a member of the Eisenhower administration named Arthur Larson. Both Buckley and Goldwater zeroed in on Larson's formulation that "if a job has to be done to meet the needs of the people, and no one else can do it, then it is the proper function for the federal government." This was, as columnist and author E. J. Dionne has pointed out, a restatement of Abraham Lincoln's comment that the role of government was "to do for the people what needs to be done, but which they cannot, by individual effort, do at all, or do so well, for themselves." But Goldwater juxtaposed Larson's statement with one from a prominent Democrat, Secretary of State Dean Acheson, who had written that the New Deal "conceived of the federal government as the whole people organized to do what had to be done."[13]

Buckley had directed withering fire on that view of government, and Goldwater followed suit:

> Here we have, by prominent spokesmen of both political parties, an unqualified repudiation of the principle of limited government. There is no reference by either of them to the Constitution, or any attempt to define the legitimate functions of government. The government can do whatever needs to be done; note, too, the implicit but necessary assumption that it is the government itself that determines what needs to be done. We must not, I think underrate the importance of these statements.[14]

Goldwater offered a starkly different approach to how conservatives would henceforth look upon government power. "Government represents power in the hands of some men to control and regulate the lives of other men," he wrote. "And power, as Lord Acton said, corrupts men. 'Absolute power,' he added, 'corrupts absolutely.'"

PURGING THE CRACKPOTS

In the early 1960s, conservatives faced another daunting challenge. Liberalism was the regnant ideology, and the GOP establishment was ideologically tepid and lifeless. But even as conservative ideas began to gain traction at the grassroots level, the Right faced a problem on its fringes.

It was the other estimable nineteenth-century philosopher John Stuart Mill who observed that "Conservatives are not necessarily stupid, but most stupid people are conservatives," and the taunt has stuck. However wrong-headed and unfair, the slur has been a source of comfort to the Left and annoyance to the Right for generations.

But as Buckley recognized, the problem that dogged conservatives was not stupidity; it was crackpotism. And before conservatism could compete effectively on the political battlefield it would have to deal with its vexing problem. Conservatism before the *National Review* was a mess. "The *American Mercury,* for which Buckley worked briefly, was a nest of anti-Semites," conservative writer Matthew Continetti later observed. "The libertarian *Freeman* was beset with infighting, more interested in criticizing the New Deal than in coalition-building. Cranky, conspiratorial, bigoted, frustrated, powerless—this was the conservatism of William F. Buckley's young adulthood."[15]

Buckley admitted as much. "Sometimes the conservative needle appears to be jumping about as on a disoriented compass," Buckley wrote. "My professional life is lived in an office battered by every pressure of contemporary conservatism. Some of the importunities upon a decent American conservatism are outrageous, or appear so to me, at any rate. ('We should have high tariffs because the farmers have high subsidies, and they shouldn't, by the way.') Some are pathological ('Alaska is being prepared as a mammoth concentration camp for pro-McCarthyites.') Some are deeply mystical ('The state can do no good.'). . . ."[16]

Conservatism, Buckley insisted, must "be wiped clean of the parasitic cant that defaces it, and repels so many of those who approach it inquiringly." But that would not be easy. As Buckley knew, crackpotism is not incompatible with intelligence and it is not a matter of ideology alone. Crackpots, whose views are fiercely held as a matter of conviction, may be educated and credentialed. As they will often earnestly point out, their views are supported and reinforced by unique research and logic—the sort that flourish in the hothouse environment of the internet.

Within their own bubble, the crackpots' ideas can seem plausible and insightful. Supporters praise one another for daring to embrace overlooked truths. But ideas that win plaudits and huzzahs within the ideological bubble often turn out to be disqualifying for the general electorate. When crackpots venture out of the bubble, their notions are often exposed as eccentric and daft.

Worst of all: They make it harder for the substantive and thoughtful conservative critiques of these issues to break through the media clutter. Of course, the Left has its own cadre of oddities, but the playing field is not a level one. Because the stupidity and extremism of the Right remains its operating assumption, the mainstream media are more than eager to let the wacky displace and overshadow the sensible. Unfortunately, this circumstance is compounded by an understandable tendency among battered and besieged conservatives to launch embarrassing defenses of inappropriate candidates.

Buckley and the editors, Continetti recalls, "spent an enormous amount of time and energy during the early years of the magazine disassociating their conservatism from its atavistic and gnostic forebears." Acting as gatekeepers for the still embryonic movement, Buckley set out to purge the cranks while providing a forum for new, provocative thinkers (many of them Jewish), who would otherwise have been shut out of the movement. "By denying a platform to quacks and haters," Continetti notes, "they broadened their potential audience."[17]

One of the earliest subjects for excommunication was Ayn Rand, whose novel *Atlas Shrugged* had become a massive bestseller that appealed powerfully to younger conservatives (as it would for several decades). In a brutally derisive review in Buckley's magazine, Whittaker Chambers (himself the iconic bestselling author of *Witness*) savaged Rand's book as "sophomoric," "primitive," and dogmatic. Chambers wrote that the novel was "a remarkably silly book. It is certainly a bumptious one. Its story is preposterous." The former communist turned conservative found its tone disconcerting. "From almost any page of *Atlas Shrugged*," he wrote, "a voice can be heard, from painful necessity, commanding: 'To a gas chamber—go!'"[18] (Rand, whose appeal was not diminished by the attack, later called *National Review* "the worst and most dangerous magazine in America.")

Buckley had more luck with the John Birch Society. The anticommunist group was growing, and its profile and influence posed a challenge to the Right. The group's leader, Robert Welch, claimed that former president Dwight D. Eisenhower was a "dedicated, conscious agent of the communist conspiracy," and that the government of the United States was "under operational control of the Communist Party."

Welch's "influence was near-hypnotic, and his ideas wild," Buckley later wrote. The conservative editor regarded Welch's claims as "paranoid and unpatriotic drivel." Conservative icon Russell Kirk was even blunter. He thought Welch was "loony and should be put away."

But the Birchers were a force to be reckoned with and posed a real problem for soon-to-be presidential candidate Barry Goldwater, whose uphill battle against the GOP establishment would be hindered by any lingering associations with the Birchers. Kirk saw a broader problem for conservatives. By making outlandish claims that Eisenhower had been a secret agent of the communists, Welch "was a great weight on the back of responsible conservative political thinking."

So the decision was made to take on the Birchers directly. Perhaps only Buckley, with his impeccable conservative, anticommunist credentials, could have gotten away with it. In February 1962, *National Review* published a lengthy dissection of Welch's bizarre theories and concluded, "His distortions disqualified him from effective services as an anti-communist leader." Buckley's excommunication was scathing.

> The fact of the matter is [our long analysis concluded] that Mr. Welch, by what Russell Kirk has called "an excess of zeal, intemperance and imprudence, promotes a split in the conservative movement—by asking for the tacit support of men who cannot in good conscience give it, who, moreover, feel that to give it is to damage our chances of success. "Cry wolf often enough," Mr. Kirk wrote to Mr. Welch, "and everyone takes you for an imbecile or a knave, when after all there are wolves in this world." If we are to win the war against communism, we have no less a task before us than to change national policy. Nothing is clearer than that Mr. Welch is not succeeding in doing anything of the sort. Mr. Welch, for all his good intentions, threatens to divert militant conservative action to irrelevance and ineffectuality.[19]

Buckley's excommunication of the Birchers was not a repudiation of anticommunism, nor was it an attempt to bolster the GOP establishment
or make the GOP a less conservative party. (At the time it was Goldwater
who was the "antiestablishment gadfly.") In fact it was precisely the opposite: Buckley understood that conservatism would never be viable as
long as it was associated in the public mind with crackpotism.

Goldwater, who grasped the larger challenge to the movement,
took the opportunity to distance himself from Welch. "We cannot
allow the emblem of irresponsibility to attach to the conservative banner," Goldwater wrote. Ultimately this was not enough to save his
candidacy, which was crushed in the Johnson landslide in 1964. But as
Buckley later observed, "The wound we . . . delivered to the John Birch
Society proved fatal over time. Barry Goldwater did not win the presidency, but he clarified the proper place of anti-communism on the right,
with bright prospects to follow."[20] His point: the purge of the Birchers
paved the way for the robust anticommunism of Ronald Reagan.

THE ADVERSARIANS

The fusion of the 1960s did not, however, resolve the inner tensions
within conservativism. The Nixon years were a painful reminder that,
despite the Goldwater nomination, the GOP was not synonymous with
conservatism. Indeed, although he was loathed by the left, Nixon often
governed as a liberal Republican, creating bureaucracies like the Environmental Protection Agency and imposing wage and price controls.
Anticommunist conservatives felt betrayed when he opened the door
to China; Buckley and *National Review* were outspoken in their opposition to his policies.

But the most significant development in the 1970s was the rise of
what became known as the New Right, a movement that had grown
impatient and frustrated with what they regarded as the "establishment"
or the conservative movement. "If there was a single moment you can
point to as the beginning of the New Right, it came in August 1974,"
direct mail guru Richard Viguerie later wrote, when Gerald Ford named

Nelson Rockefeller, "the very symbol of old, Eastern, liberal establishment Republicanism," as his vice president.

In their attacks on the intellectual "elite" of the time, the New Right activists valued activism and winning elections over intellectual theorizing. From the beginning the new movement seemed intent on burning down the conservative status quo. "The enemies of the New Right were compromise, gradualism, and acquiescence in the corrupt system. Partisan identification had little to do with their antagonisms," Matthew Continetti recalled. "Conservatives and Republicans with Ivy League degrees were sellouts, weak, epiphenomena of the social disease."[21]

For a while in the mid-1970s, leaders even toyed with the idea of backing former Alabama governor George Wallace for president. As Kirkpatrick Sale wrote in his 1975 book *Power Shift*, the New Right was not attracted to Wallace because of any positive agenda he might embrace, but rather because of what he was against: "Wallace has no real policies, plans, or platforms, and no one expects them of him," Sale wrote; "it is sufficient that he is agin and gathers unto him others who are agin, agin the blacks, the intellectuals, the bureaucrats, the students, the journalists, the liberals, the outsiders, the Communists, the changers, above all, agin the Yankee establishment."[22]

Others were attracted to what they saw as his strength. *National Review*'s publisher William Rusher was among those who briefly backed the idea of supporting Wallace in 1976, an idea that also appealed to William Loeb, the influential publisher of the *Manchester Union Leader*, who had doubts about whether Reagan was tough enough. "He's a great salesman and a great talker," Loeb said of Reagan, "but the one who goes to Washington has to be a tough SOB."[23]

In the view of some New Right leaders, noted the historian Nicole Hemmer, there was no "tougher S.O.B. than George Wallace." Ultimately the idea of backing Wallace fizzled out, when some of the calmer heads realized that would have meant an alliance with an unsavory coterie of crackpots, including anti-Semites and Holocaust deniers. But the flirtation with Wallace served to expose a soft underbelly of conservativism.

Unfortunately—and this is one the tragedies of the movement—the conservative message of freedom was often overshadowed by the politics of race. It's worth noting that every GOP member of the U.S. Senate supported the 1957 Civil Rights Bill; in the House, only nineteen voted against the bill. But Buckley's *National Review* remained opposed to the legislation and initially took positions that remain a blot on the conservative legacy. In a 1957 editorial titled, "Why the South Must Prevail," Buckley argued that because whites were the "more advanced race," they were "entitled to rule."[24] In another piece, Buckley cited the backwardness of blacks in the South to argue that whites therefore had a right to "impose superior mores for whatever period it takes to affect a genuine cultural equality between the races."[25] Seven years later, Barry Goldwater, who had supported the 1957 bill, voted against the 1964 Civil Rights Bill.

Over time, Buckley moderated his views and came to regret his stance on civil rights. "I rather wish we had taken a more transcendent position, which might have been done by advocating civil rights legislation with appropriate safeguards," he wrote decades later. In an interview with *Time* magazine, Buckley confessed, "I once believed we could evolve our way up from Jim Crow. I was wrong. Federal intervention was necessary."[26] Unfortunately, however, the battle over civil rights was a defining moment for both the GOP and the conservative movement. Electorally, Republicans scored significant successes in the South and in some traditionally Democratic strongholds by exploiting a "white backlash" against many of the social changes that began in the sixties. In his New York mayoral race, Buckley appealed strongly to working-class white voters in the outer boroughs who were being driven away from their Democratic roots by concerns over crime, bad schools, busing, as well as issues like abortion and school prayer. Those voters, many of whom were to become "Reagan Democrats," were key to the GOP resurgence, reshaping the nature of the party and the conservative movement.

In particular, the New Right sought to capitalize on the shift in the Right's center of gravity. Throughout the 1970s, the campaign against the effete, poetry-quoting Burkean elites of the Buckley era continued apace. Clearly targeting erudite conservatives like George Will, author Kevin Phillips derided "conservatives whose game it is to quote English poetry and utter neo-Madisonian benedictions over the interests and institutions of establishment liberalism." Similar themes would be echoed in the 2016 campaign. "The attacks on *National Review,* on George Will, on conservatives with elite educations, on conservatives granted legitimacy by mainstream institutions is a replay of the New Right rhetoric of the 1970s," notes Continetti. "Names have been added to the list of Republicans in Name Only, of false, cuckolded conservatives, but the battle lines are the same."[27]

The parallels are striking. Writing in the 1970s, Phillips's view of the alternative to conservatism "elitism" bore a strong resemblance to what would become of Trumpism three decades later:

> Then there are other conservatives—many I know—who have more in common with Andrew Jackson than with Edmund Burke. Their hope is to build a cultural siege-cannon out of the populist steel of Idaho, Mississippi, and working-class Milwaukee, and then blast the Eastern liberal establishment to ideo-institutional smithereens.[28]

Many conservatives who advocated a more populist and nationalist vision coalesced around former Reagan communications director Patrick Buchanan, who mounted a searing indictment of what was then the establishment GOP. Years before the Trump campaign, Buchanan appealed to both the nativist Right and lingering isolationist sentiment that had been largely dormant since the 1930s. But Buchanan also brought something more troubling back to the forefront of conservative politics. When the former Nixon speech writer referred to Congress as "Israeli occupied territory," many observers detected a whiff of anti-Semitism.

Once again, Buckley was to play a crucial role as gatekeeper, devoting an issue of the *National Review* to a lengthy critique of Buchananism titled "In Search of Anti-Semitism." Buckley did not argue that Buchanan was an anti-Semite, but said that he was clearly "saying anti-Semitic things."[29] While he did not completely excommunicate

Buchanan from the conservative movement as he had done with the Birchers, Buckley effectively marginalized the new anti-Semites. After one of his writers, Joseph Sobran, was accused of trafficking in "crude and naked" anti-Semitism, Buckley first barred him from writing about Israel in *National Review,* and later fired him.[30]

FOR THE NEXT several decades, there would be a complicated, fraught, and at times awkward alliance between mainstream conservatives and the insurgents of the New Right. But despite the tensions, the movement somehow managed not to split itself asunder for the next several decades. Why not? Why didn't the Right embrace Wallace? Why didn't it reject the establishment Right of the time?

In addition to Buckley's role as gatekeeper, there were three major factors at work here. The first and most obvious was the rise of Ronald Reagan and his role as the great unifier of conservatives. Divisions remained, but they were submerged under his leadership; leading voices of various versions of conservatism were gathered under the aegis of his administration, which included both Pat Buchanan and Jack Kemp. (During the 1980s, I was especially drawn to the type of conservativism espoused by groups like Empower America, which was run by Kemp and Bill Bennett. If there is a direct line from some elements of the New Right to Trump, there is also a straight line from Kemp to Paul Ryan's brand of conservatism.) Not surprisingly, the ideological differences flared after Reagan left office.

The second factor was the decision by leading figures on the New Right to walk away from alliances with the kook fringe. Rusher's conclusion that a Wallace campaign was unworkable meant that the extremists expelled from the movement by Buckley in the 1960s would not be invited back in.

But the third factor is, in some ways, the most intriguing. The Reagan years paradoxically coincided with the relative absence of conservative media voices. Even as the New Right began making its push for conservative purity and laying the groundwork for the election of Ronald Reagan, Nicole Hemmer wrote, the first generation of conservative media (the Manion Forum, *Human Events*, Regnery publishing, even the *National Review*) was in decline, "out of power, out of money, and out of influence." On the eve of conservatism's great triumph, "conservative media activism was largely defunct. The second generation would not rise until Reagan left office."[31]*

The Fairness Doctrine, which paved the way for conservative radio, was not repealed until 1987 (over considerable conservative opposition); Rush Limbaugh did not launch his national talk show until 1988; Fox News did not go on the air until 1996. So for most of Reagan's term, there was no conservative echo chamber, no powerful talk radio, no Fox News or a right-wing infrastructure providing air cover or enforcing ideological purity.

This raises what historian Nicole Hemmer calls "an unresolved and vitally important question: *Why did the political movement attain its greatest success at the very moment conservative media was in decline?*" [Emphasis added.][32] One possibility may be that the lack of a raucous Right media during the 1980s actually gave Reagan the space for maneuver and ideological flexibility that his successors would not enjoy. Imagine, for example, the reaction of the current Right media to Reagan's amnesty for illegal immigrants or his decision to raise taxes later in his administration.

After Reagan, the media landscape changed dramatically. In the 1990s, Hemmer notes, "Republican politicians had become markedly more sensitive to the judgment of media personalities." The post-Reagan conservative media types were very different from their predecessors: they made a lot more money, enjoyed significantly more celebrity and, notes Hemmer, "were entertainers first and conservatives second."[33]

---

* "Not every conservative media outlet was shuttering operation at the end of the 1970s. But as the New Right, the religious right, and Reaganites were gathering steam, conservative media were losing it—crippled by shrinking budgets, tragic losses, and a sense of aimlessness. A conservative resurgence was coming, but they would not be at its helm. For the generation of conservative media activists who had built the movement, it seemed the time for media leadership was over." —Nicole Hemmer, *Messengers of the Right*, 251.

But most important of all, they had far more clout. The balance of power had shifted. "The first generation of conservative media may have snuck one of theirs past the GOP gatekeepers in 1964," Hemmer wrote, "but the second generation were the gatekeepers."[34]

The messengers were about to become more important than the message.

CHAPTER 5

STORM WARNINGS

EVEN BEFORE THE END of George W. Bush's presidency, there were warnings that conservativism was in trouble, isolated from both reality and its own constituencies. Some conservatives were troubled by Bush's decision to engage in nation-building exercises in the wake of the Iraq War. There had always been a deep strain of isolationism on the Right, extending back to the America First movement in the 1930s and articulated by such stalwarts as Senator Robert Taft even after the war. But since the end of World War II, (with occasional dissents from Buchananites) conservative foreign policy was shaped first by the fight against Communism and later by the War on Terror. So the vast majority of conservative voters continued to back the war and were later appalled by what they saw as Obama's less aggressive policies. Only after Trump's appearance on the scene (and his false claim that he had opposed the invasion) did Republican voters turn against the Iraq War in large numbers. But the idea of using the military to "spread democracy," disturbed many conservatives, including Buckley and George Will, both of whom were critical of the Bush policies. Seeds of disillusionment had already been planted.

While the Right seemed more or less united on foreign policy, more ominous cracks appeared on the question of immigration. Although a hard line on dealing with illegal immigrants was to become a litmus test in 2016, there was never a real consensus on the issue among conservatives. In 1986, Ronald Reagan had signed the Simpson-Mazzoli Act, which was effectively a massive amnesty for illegals who had entered the country before January 1, 1982. After the number of illegal immigrants surged again, many GOP leaders including Bush, along with Senator John McCain and Marco Rubio and much of the business community began to push for another shot at immigration reform. For a time, comprehensive reform seemed possible, as polls consistently suggested widespread support among Republican voters for some sort of a path to citizenship.

But beginning in the Bush years, the loudest voices on the Right increasingly railed against policies they labeled "amnesty," and the issue became a flash point between the party's establishment and its insurgent populist base. (In 2013, a comprehensive bill crafted by the so-called Gang of 8, passed the U.S. Senate by a vote of 68 to 32, with 14 GOP senators voting in favor. Faced with fierce opposition from conservative activists, the bill died in the House.) As it turned out, the issue appealed powerfully to the elements of the GOP base that had largely been ignored by party leaders.

In 2005 two leading conservative thinkers, Ross Douthat and Reihan Salam, issued a prescient warning in their widely discussed but sadly ignored critique of conservatism: "The Party of Sam's Club."[1] Their point was that the GOP was intellectually exhausted and out of gas. Despite the Left's taunt that the GOP was the party of the "angry white male," Republicans were actually doing very little for the white working class.

Instead, they wrote, the GOP in Bush's second term "feels increasingly tired and corrupted by power, obsessed with fighting yesterday's battles and unwilling to adapt to the changing political landscape. . . ." So far, the Republicans had not "paid a political price for insider-friendly appropriation bills, Medicare boondoggles, or the smog of semi-corruption rising from the party's cozy relationship with K Street." But conservatives should not delude themselves, they argued, because the "conservative" policies of the Bush years were less "a visionary twist on traditional conservatism, and more and more like an evolutionary dead end."[2]

Author David Frum echoed many of those critiques, accusing Republicans of "losing touch with reality" and suffering something worse than a lack of leadership. Rather, Frum wrote in 2008, the Right was experiencing a "crisis of followership." On the eve of Obama's election, Frum wrote that Republican conservatism was "tired and confused":

> Once the party of limited government, now it is the one that
> enacted the largest new social programme since the 1960s: the
> prescription drug benefit. Once the party of law and order, it
> now offers amnesty in all but name to illegal immigrants. Once
> the party that ran against Washington's special interests, it is
> now run by lobbyists. Once the party of sound management,
> it is now tarred by the managerial disasters of the Iraq war and
> Hurricane Katrina.[3]

This had, unfortunately, become a pattern. Despite electoral victories, conservatives too often failed to deliver, often taking detours into political and ideological cul-de-sacs.

DISTRACTED AND DERAILED

The resiliency of the conservative movement had been vividly on display again in 1994, when Republicans won control of Congress.

The vote was a repudiation of Bill Clinton's health care policies and an apparent ratification of the policy agenda laid out in Newt Gingrich's Contract with America. Over the following six years, the GOP had notable successes, including balancing the budget and reforming welfare, but once again set expectations that were doomed to frustration. Republicans quickly learned the futility of trying to run the country without also controlling the White House. An ill-advised government shutdown over Medicare funding helped Clinton revive his sagging political fortunes and easily win a second term.

In 1997, the Gingrich revolution was both derailed and distracted by the Clinton scandals that culminated in the impeachment of the president. Wonky policy proposals on entitlement reform paled beside the temptation of a roiling sex scandal, complete with a semen-stained dress and presidential perjury. This also marked the coming of age of the Right media, which now included Fox News and the growing power of the new generation of conservative talkers, who were shaped by and in turned helped shape the climate of political discourse. Perhaps inevitably, the new conservative media focused far more on Clinton's foibles than on explaining conservative ideas, even those laid out so hopefully in the "Contract with America." That would also set a pattern for the new media that would have notable consequences two decades later.

PROPHETS IGNORED

In their 2005 essay, Douthat and Salam pinpointed a central but overlooked political reality: the GOP had become "an increasingly working-class party, dependent for its power on supermajorities of the white working-class vote," but that voter base was not particularly conservative in any orthodox sense. Writing a full decade before Trump's ascendency, they noted that white working-class voters were "quite okay with raising the minimum wage, and raising taxes on the wealthy; they were upset about globalization, and skeptical if not hostile both to free trade and to open borders immigration." And yet, they argued, the GOP was offering them very little, content to take their votes for granted. "Therein lies a great political danger for Republicans, because on domestic policy," wrote Douthat and Salam, "the party isn't just out of touch with the country as a whole, it's out of touch with its own base."

They offered up a series of proposals to give "coherence and sustainability" to conservativism, while addressing the economic realities of the middle class and matching government policies to the lip service given to family values. The GOP, they noted, seemed stuck in a time warp: "Like aging hippies who never quite got over Woodstock, many of those young Reaganites, now safely ensconced in the GOP establishment, view across-the-board tax cuts as a permanent ticket to political power." But, they argued, it was time for more aggressive pro-family policies that would "keep taxes lowest for those entering the workforce and preparing to have children."

Later labeled "reformicons," the two insisted that this would not mean eschewing a belief in small, limited government, "but it would mean recognizing that these objectives—individual initiative, social mobility, economic freedom—seem to be slipping away from many less-well-off Americans, and that serving the interests of these voters means talking about economic insecurity as well as about self-reliance." Taking aim at some of the wishful thinking of the Bush years, Douthat and Salam wrote that a new reformist conservatism "would mean recognizing that you can't have an 'ownership society' in a nation where too many Americans owe far more than they own. It would mean matching the culture war rhetoric of family values with an economic policy that places the two-parent family—the institution best capable of providing cultural stability and economic security—at the heart of the GOP agenda."[4]

While some of their ideas would later be embraced by thoughtful policymakers and candidates, most notably Marco Rubio, the suggestion that conservatives pay more attention to the problems of their own voter base were largely ignored. The Right preferred redder meat, which they got from the Tea Party.

RISE OF THE TEA PARTY

While many of its discontents can be traced to the Bush years—unhappiness over Medicare Part D, immigration reform, No Child Left Behind, government spending, and Troubled Asset Relief Program (TARP), the Tea Party did not burst into prominence until after Barack Obama's election. That immediately fed suspicion that the uprising was less about policy than about the identity of the new president, but the Tea Party defied easy categorizations.

What was striking about the early rallies was the number of people who attended that had not previously been active in politics. They were also extraordinarily diverse. Journalist John Avlon described the range of attendees at a typical rally: "libertarians, traditionalists, free-marketers, middle class tax protesters, the more patriotic than thou crowd, conservative shock jocks, frat boys, suit and tie Buckley-ites, and more than a couple of requisite residents of Crazytown."[5] But the rallies were also striking for their normality. Despite the caricatures and repeated attempts by the Left to portray them as dangerous or bigoted, Tea Party rallies were generally orderly events whose attendees developed a well-deserved reputation for neatness.

But it was also hard to determine who and what was meant by the "Tea Party." Was it a genuine grassroots movement? A fringe movement increasingly composed of wing nuts? Or was it a series of Scam PACs set up by an emerging class of ideologically driven political grafters? Over time it was all of those things; the Tea Party was a chimerical construct that changed its focus and agenda depending on its leadership and location.

It also became the face of the conservative movement, firing up a base that had been defeated and demoralized in 2006 and again in 2008. As Avlon noted, the movement marked an aggressive shift in tactics, as some conservatives decided to "mimic the confrontational street theater of the far left they had spent decades despising. Civility was the first calculated casualty."[6] At rallies, signs comparing Obama to Hitler began popping up, while literature appeared skewering "Obama's Nazi health plan." Legitimate concerns over rationing of health care morphed into overheated rhetoric about "death panels." Few on the Right pushed back against the excesses.

"In this environment," Avlon noted, "there are no enemies on the right and no such thing as too extreme—the more outrageous the statement, the more it will be applauded."[7] Even after Congressman Joe Wilson was censured for yelling "You lie!" at Obama during a speech on health care, he was hailed as a truth-telling hero.

Avlon later described Glenn Beck's September 2012 march on Washington as a protest "that celebrated the deepest domestic political divisions we've seen since 9/11, with unhinged accusation of traitors and despots in the White House and talk of resistance and revolution."[8] He took note of many of the signs at the event:

"Obama Lied, Granny Died"

"Muslim Marxist"

"Don't Make the U.S. a Third World Country—Go Back to Kenya"

"Mugabe-Pelosi in '12"

"Barack Obama Supports Abortion, Sodomy, Socialism, and the New World Order!"

"If you are a liberal or Progressive Democrat or Republican you are a Communist. Impeach Obama!"

Such rhetoric became increasingly common, and was often echoed by conservative media celebrities. In August 2010, Ted Nugent denounced Obama's "Islamic, Muslim, Marxist, communist and socialist agenda." Did he think Obama was a secret Muslim? Nugent responded: "You're damn right I do. He says he's a Christian so he can continue his jihad of America-destroying policies."[9]

"YOU'RE F---ING DEAD!"

The rhetorical excesses were not, however, confined to the Tea Party. While the Right has indulged in vituperative language to describe its opponents, it was supposedly tolerant progressives who routinely called supporters of the Tea Party "teabaggers," a sniggering reference to a sexual act. While the right engaged in over-the-top rhetoric over Obamacare's "death panels," some Democrats warned that conservatives like Paul Ryan, who had suggested fixes to Medicaid, wanted to push Granny off the cliff.

When conservatives staged a peaceful lakefront rally in downtown Milwaukee in 2009, Mike Tate, chairman of the Wisconsin Democratic Party, responded by attacking the attendees in inflammatory language, comparing them with the Know Nothings and the KKK. They were not only bigoted and dumb, the chairman of the state party declared, they "frankly don't believe in this country." Who were these citizens (and voters)? "They don't want to see more people have access to quality affordable health care; they don't want clean air and water. They fundamentally don't understand how the American economy and capitalism work."[10] Later, Wisconsin's Democratic Party spokesman tweeted out 'It's Medicare's 45th Birthday, celebrate by punching a Republican." (He was later removed for comparing Wisconsin governor Scott Walker to serial killer Jeffrey Dahmer, which was one of his milder rhetorical forays.) This was frankly unhinged stuff and contributed over the next few years to a series of catastrophic defeats of Democrats at the polls.

During the fight over Act 10, Walker's legislation to drastically restrict the collective bargaining powers of public unions, the extremism of the Left's reactions turned the tide in Walker's favor. Early on in the fight, polls showed that voters did not support the GOP governor's antiunion measures, but the excesses of the protesters—including demonstrators dressed as zombies disrupting a ceremony to honor special Olympians—alienated the general public.

During one of the protests in Madison in 2011 a video captured one demonstrator repeatedly shouting the F-word at a fourteen-year-old girl who was speaking at a pro-Walker rally.[11] On the floor of the State Assembly a Democratic state representative turned to a female Republican colleague and shouted, "You are F---ing dead!" None of his fellow Democrats condemned his conduct.[12] A "progressive talk-show host" mocked the state's female lieutenant governor for having colon cancer and suggested she had only gotten elected because she had performed oral sex on talk show hosts.[13]*

Death threats and obscene letters became commonplace, and the language of Walker's critics was especially toxic. In his book *Unintimidated*, Walker recounted a death threat that had been addressed to his wife, Tonette:

> Has Wisconsin ever had a governor assassinated? Scott's heading that way. Or maybe one of your sons getting killed would hurt him more. I want him to feel the pain. I already follow them when they went to school in Wauwatosa, so it won't be too hard to find them in Mad. Town. Big change from that house by [—] Ave. to what you got now. Just let him know that it's not right to [expletive removed] over all those people. Or maybe I could find one of the Tarantinos [Tonette's parents] back here.[14]

Over the next three years, Walker was reelected twice.

So, conservatives were understandably skeptical of demands that they be held to Marquess of Queensbury standards of civility. Even so, the rhetoric became increasingly toxic and much of it was aimed at the country's first African American president.

Conservative firebrand Michael Savage hardly felt the need to resort to dog whistles or coded language when he declared that "the rage has reached a boil." His radio rant contained an implicit threat:

---

*One activist wrote an email to the grandmotherly cochairman of the legislature's Joint Finance Committee that read:

To Soon to be ex-Senator Darling:
Instead of cajoling you to change your mind, I'm just going to tell you what you are: you're a useless f**king c*nt that has no redeeming value. There are not enough words to describe how much I hate you and the rest of the f**king scum in the Wisconsin GOP.
  You're parasites and you contribute nothing. Enjoy getting recalled you useless f**king dried up c*nt. (www.maciverinstitute.com/2011/06 /notoriously-profane-emailer-had-struck-earlier/.)

> If they keep pushing us around and if we keep having these
> schmucks running for office catering to the multicultural
> people who are destroying the culture of this country, the
> white male—the one without connections, the one without
> money—has nothing to lose. . . . He is still the majority. . . .
> You're gonna find out that if you keep pushing this country
> around, there is an ugly side to the white male that has been
> suppressed for probably thirty years right now but it really has
> never gone away.[15]

"This the tragedy of the Tea Party," critic John Avlon charged. "What
began as fiscal-conservative protests against the generational theft of
deficits and debt became infected by a serious strain of Obama Derange-
ment Syndrome. . . . Constructive civic conversation became almost impossible across that divide." But he also warned that Republicans were
"playing a dangerous game." In the short term, they benefited from
stoking the fires of anti-Obama outrage, he warned, "but they have
tapped into something they can't control."[16]

What happened to the Tea Party? David Frum had his own autopsy:
"A political movement that never took governing seriously was exploited
by a succession of political entrepreneurs uninterested in governing,
but all too interested in merchandising." And, he noted, the GOP was
being overrun by impulses "that were once sublimated by the party
elites, but now roam the land freely: ultralibertarianism, crank mon-
etary theories, populist fury, and paranoid visions of a Democratic Party
controlled by ACORN and the New Black Panthers."[17]

RETURN OF THE CRACKPOTS

Indeed, the Tea Party seemed to open the door for the return of the
sort of crackpots that Buckley had worked so hard to expel from
the conservative movement. In contrast to the 1960s, there were
now far more outlets for the voluble defense of crackpotism and
denunciations of their critics. Talk radio too often succumbed to the

temptation to defend candidates who were in the process of immolating themselves.*

Others on the Right flirted with ideas like nullification, an idea that has enjoyed pretty much complete obscurity since the Civil War. (The idea, repeatedly rejected by the courts, is that states can nullify federal laws they deem unconstitutional.) It was, of course, one thing to oppose the implementation of Obamacare state exchanges and quite another thing to begin channeling your inner John C. Calhoun and embrace the rhetoric of the 1830s. As if this were not bad enough, there was also some buzz about states actually seceding from the United States, despite the fact that we fought a war over that, which ended badly for the advocates.

At the time, my sense was that the vast majority of principled conservatives shared my dismay over the parade of bizarre effusions that have sunk so many opportunities, but that many either were reluctant to speak out or were cowed by the fear that they would be flamed by the defenders. For example, after I pointed out on Facebook the unwisdom of talking about secession, one commenter flamed back:

---

* This was, unfortunately, illustrated in several pre-Trump senate races. In Missouri, senate candidate Todd Akin's bizarre notions about "legitimate rape" provided unnecessary fuel to the Left's claim that the GOP was waging a "war on women." Indiana senate candidate Richard Mourdock's comment that pregnancy from rape was "something that God intended" simply made things worse. Both Akin and Mourdock were widely criticized by other Republicans, but both had enough support to remain in the race and go down to defeat. In 2012, the GOP ended up losing Senate seats in an election in which it was expected to gain several seats and perhaps even take control of the upper chamber.

Two years earlier, Delaware's Christine O'Donnell became a punch line, and Nevada's Sharron Angle squandered a chance to unseat the eminently beatable Harry Reid. As unfair as much of the criticism was—and much of it was quite unfair—Angle made it easy to characterize her as ridiculous with her position on the fluoridation of water and support for Church of Scientology–run Criminon drug-treatment programs. Then there was Michele Bachmann, who briefly led the pack of GOP presidential contenders until she shared her internet-gleaned wisdom about the dangers of a vaccine for human papillomavirus (HPV). Her unsubstantiated claim that the vaccine was linked to mental retardation reinforced the narrative that Republicans were hostile to science.

> You call yourself a conservative, Charlie Sykes? It's "conserva-
> tives" like yourself who have allowed this country to grow to
> the extreme sizes that it is and allowed government to run
> amok. We are just trying to clean up your mess.
>
> Your brand of conservatism is the crackpotism and
> extremism.

Apparently "genuine conservatism" now meant embracing the Con-
federacy. That hardly seemed like a winning message.[18]

Inevitably many of the excesses were blamed on the Tea Party. But
the failures of candidates like Christine O'Donnell and Sharron Angle
need to be juxtaposed with the successes of candidates like Florida's
Marco Rubio, Pennsylvania's Pat Toomey, New Hampshire's Kelly Ayotte,
Utah's Mike Lee, Texas's Ted Cruz, South Carolina's Nikki Haley
and Senator Tim Scott, Kentucky's Rand Paul, and Wisconsin's Ron
Johnson. Not everything that came out of the Tea Party was nutty.

But this was another one of the paradoxes of the Tea Party and its
impact on the conservative movement. Had the GOP simply lurched to
the right, the most conservative candidates—the ones who hewed most
closely to the models of ideological purity—would have moved into
dominant positions in the party. But instead the presidential candidates
most closely aligned with the Tea Party—namely, Cruz, Rubio, and
Walker—were spurned, as Republican voters instead chose a man
who had spent most of his career rejecting their values. That suggests a
deeper problem within the populist insurgency.

DUMPING PRIVATE RYAN

So, too, was the speed with which the right turned on Paul Ryan.

Whatever you might think of his policies, Paul Ryan is inarguably
the most formidable intellectual leader the Republican Party has had
in decades. For years, he was known for his dogged advocacy of budget and entitlement reform in the face of opposition from his party's
establishment. His rise from conservative backbencher to Speaker could

have been seen as one of great success stories of the conservative movement. "I spent more time, I'd say, in the backbench, than I have in leadership," Ryan told me during a conversation on my last radio show. "The party really tried to isolate me a number of years ago and tried to explain to our members, 'do not touch what Ryan is talking about, don't deal with these fiscal issues, these entitlements, it's political suicide.' And I just decided instead of trying to win the argument internally, I tried to win it externally, and that took hold," he explained. "What happened, really, was the 2010 election, I think. The 2010 election brought all these, sort of Tea Party conservative Republicans into office."[19]

And yet by 2016, many conservatives who had lauded him just a few years earlier turned against him. As Matt Lewis noted, Ryan went "from wingnut to RINO (Republican in Name Only)" in a remarkably short period of time.[20]

Back in 2010, Sarah Palin had lavished praise on the young congressman, saying, "I'm very impressed with Paul Ryan." Appearing on Fox News, Palin gave the young congressman her blessing.

CHRIS WALLACE: Congressman from Wisconsin.

PALIN: Yes. He's good. Man, he is sharp, he is smart, articulate, and he is passionate about these common-sense solutions that America has got to adopt to get us on the right road.[21]

When Mitt Romney named Ryan as his running mate, Laura Ingraham praised him as a "fine pick" and Ann Coulter called him a "perfect" choice. But by 2016, Palin was declaring Ryan's political career over and endorsed his pro-Trump primary challenger; Ingraham began calling him "Boehner 2.0," and Coulter and her allies took turns anathematizing Ryan for his political sins.

To be sure, Ryan's record was not without blemish: he had supported the Troubled Asset Relief Program (TARP) and voted for No Child Left Behind and Medicare Part D. But that was true when Palin praised him and the Right's punditocracy celebrated his vice presidential nomination. So what had changed? And why were the gatekeepers of conservative purity willing to overlook Trump's many and sundry ideological foibles (i.e., he opposed both free trade and entitlement reform) but unwilling to cut Ryan slack for his deviations from conservative orthodoxy?

The answer is that Ryan had not changed, but the Right had. "In a very short span of time," Lewis noted, "the conservative movement [had] dramatically shifted in a populist direction, and that means embracing positions on trade, taxes, and entitlements that were thought of as rather left-wing just a few years ago."[22] The new litmus test was immigration, and heresy was not tolerated. (Coulter famously declared that she didn't care if Trump "performed abortions in the White House" as long as he took a hard line on illegal immigration.)[23]

Throughout the 2016 campaign, Trump and Ryan were a study in contrasts, with the young Speaker arguing that the election should be about ideas rather than personalities. As Trump was lashing out at the international cabals he said were conspiring against him, Ryan was laying out a detailed and coherent conservative agenda. And yet, as Election Day neared, it was clear that the conservative electorate had turned against Ryan, whose approval rating among Republicans dropped precipitously.[24] A Bloomberg poll in October 2016 asked Republicans which leader better represents their view of what the Republican Party should stand for: 51 percent of likely voters picked Trump, while 33 percent picked Ryan (15 percent weren't sure).[25]

CHAPTER 6

THE PERPETUAL
OUTRAGE MACHINE

Every great cause begins as a movement, becomes a
business, and eventually degenerates into a racket.

—ERIC HOFFER

BY 2016, THE TEA PARTY was effectively defunct, displaced by
new passions. But its demise had not been pretty. The Tea Party movement, noted attorney Paul H. Jossey, had not died a natural death. "It
was murdered," he wrote, "and it was an inside job." While acknowledging that a number of factors may have contributed to the movement's
collapse—including the targeting of Tea Party groups by the IRS—
Jossey placed the blame on opportunists who saw a chance to cash in on
the angers and anxiety of conservatives. "In a half decade, the spontane-
ous uprising that shook official Washington degenerated into a form of
pyramid scheme that transferred tens of millions of dollars from rural,
poorer Southerners and Midwesterners to bicoastal political operatives."[1]

Despite raising tens of millions of dollars, the Tea Party PACs spent only a tiny fraction of the money on the actual support of conservative candidates. Even so, the onslaught of fund-raising emails was relentless and the number of groups playing on conservative frustration and angst multiplied. There were groups called the "Tea Party Patriots," the "Tea Party Leadership Fund," "Tea Party Express," as well as groups pumping out emails urging donors to "Boot Boehner," "Stop Hillary PAC," "Draft Newt," "Fire Paul Ryan," and "Demand NBC Fire Al Sharpton." Grassroots donors who responded found themselves inundated with more appeals, whose volume was routinely set at apocalypse—"Act now . . . your freedom is at stake . . . send a message before it is too late." As it turned out, the politics of outrage was immensely lucrative. Wrote Jossey:

> What began as an organic, policy-driven grass-roots movement
> was drained of its vitality and resources by national political
> action committees that dunned the movement's true believers
> endlessly for money to support its candidates and causes. The
> PACs used that money first to enrich themselves and their
> vendors and then deployed most of the rest to search for more
> "prospects." In Tea Party world, that meant mostly older,
> technologically unsavvy people willing to divulge personal
> information through "petitions"—which only made them prey
> to further attempts to lighten their wallets for what they
> believed was a good cause. While the solicitations continue,
> the audience has greatly diminished because of a lack of policy
> results and changing political winds.

The transformation of the Tea Party was already evident in 2014, when the *Washington Post* noted that Tea Party PACs had been furiously raising money ahead of the midterm elections, but "have put just a tiny fraction of their money directly into boosting the candidates they've endorsed."[2] The six major Tea Party PACs had raised $37.5 million, but less than $7 million went to helping candidates. Nearly half the money ($18 million) was sucked up by fund-raising and direct mail costs primarily benefiting consultants and firms based in Washington, DC. "Meanwhile," the *Post* reported, "Tea Party leaders and their family members have been paid hundreds of thousands of dollars in consulting fees, while their groups have doled out large sums for airfare, a retirement plan and even interior decorating." Some of the best-known Tea Party groups, including the Tea Party Patriots and the Tea Party Express spent less than 5 percent of the money they raised on "election-related activity" during the 2014 campaign.

The numbers reflected the transformation of what had once been a grassroots movement. "The lavish spending," wrote *Post* reporter Hadas Gold, "underscores how the protest movement has gone professional, with national groups transforming themselves into multimillion-dollar organizations run by activists collecting six-figure salaries."*

A *Politico* analysis of thirty-three Tea Party PACs came to a similar conclusion, calculating that they spent only about 7 percent of their cash "on ads and contributions to boost the long-shot candidates often touted in the appeals."[3]

Some conservative activists sounded the alarm. Talk show host Erick Erickson noted that the fund-raisers "have the pulse of the crowd, and they recognize that they can make a profit off the angst of the conservative base voters who are looking for outsiders." They had become a "blight" on the movement, he wrote, draining cash for idealistic

---

* *Politico*'s Kenneth Vogel did a comprehensive takedown of the Scam PACs in January 2015:

> A POLITICO analysis of reports filed with the Federal Election Commission covering the 2014 cycle found that 33 PACs that court small donors with Tea Party–oriented email and direct-mail appeals raised $43 million—74 percent of which came from small donors. The PACs spent only $3 million on ads and contributions to boost the long-shot candidates often touted in the appeals, compared to $39.5 million on operating expenses, including $6 million to firms owned or managed by the operatives who run the PACs. POLITICO's list is not all-inclusive, and some conservatives fret that it's almost impossible to identify all the groups that are out there, let alone to rein them in (Kenneth Vogel, "The rise of 'scam PACs,'" *Politico*, January 26, 2015.)

donors who would eventually "get burned out and stop giving money, including to the legitimate causes."[4]

Because they knew what would motivate the activists, *Politico* noted, the Scam PACs focused many of their appeals "on politicians who are military veterans, Tea Party activists, African-Americans—or all three." For some reason, some of the sketchiest PACs claimed they were raising money for "African-American conservatives, including former Rep. Allen West, 2012 presidential candidate Herman Cain, fringe 2016 hopeful Ben Carson and two-time unsuccessful House candidate Deborah Honeycutt of Georgia," *Politico* reported. One group, the "Black Republican PAC" spent less than 1 percent of the cash it raised actually backing any candidates.

Amid all of this, one Tea Party entrepreneur stood out from the others: an attorney named Dan Backer, who had a hand in at least forty separate organizations that were raising money from conservative activists. As Media Trackers later pointed out, a look at just five of Backer's groups—Tea Party Forward, Tea Party Leadership Fund, Great America PAC, Conservative Action Fund, and Stop Hillary PAC—"reveals an astonishing amount of money going to vendors and very little going to actual political efforts."[5]*

Politico noted that Backer, who served as a lawyer, treasurer, and strategist for many of the PACs, spent the vast majority of the cash he raised on "overhead," including payments to his own law firm.

> In 2014, Backer's PACs—a roster including Draft Newt (created
> to coax the former House speaker into the Virginia Senate
> race), the Tea Party Leadership Fund (which urged Sarah Palin

---

* "Since its launch, Tea Party Forward has raised $137,477 in contributions (excluding transfers from other organizations) but has only spent $28,365 on election efforts. That means close to 80 cents out of every dollar given by donors is spent on overhead unrelated to actually winning elections for endorsed candidates. . . .

"As an older organization, the Tea Party Leadership Fund has raised nearly $1.02 million since January 2015. But only $98,364 of that total has been spent on candidate efforts. Just over 90% of the organization's donations have gone to fund overhead costs." —Media Trackers.[6]

to run for Senate), Stop Hillary (to oppose the former secretary of state's expected presidential campaign), and Stop Pelosi (which the Federal Election Commission called out for using the House Democratic leader's name)—spent more than 87 percent of the $8 million they raised on operating expenses, including $419,000 to Backer's own law firm, DB Capitol Strategies. By contrast, the amount the PACs spent on donations and ads was about $955,000—or less than 12 percent of their total fundraising haul.[7]

Backer defended the overhead for the groups by insisting that direct mail and phone campaigns are costly. "Email is not as free as people want to pretend like it is. It's really expensive," he told *Politico*. "And there's a lot of money that goes into making these things legal so—I hate to say it—you pay for lawyers."[8]

In 2016, Backer would serve as the treasurer for the long-shot (and ultimately doomed) campaign of Paul Nehlen, who was challenging Speaker Paul Ryan in the campaign. (For more on Nehlen, see chapter 12.)

TURNING UP THE VOLUME

All of this was almost certainly legal, but it had dire political consequences for conservatives. The most obvious damage was the amount of money siphoned away from legitimate conservative causes and candidacies. Conservative blogger John Hawkins calculated that the Tea Party PACs had diverted at least $50 million in contributions that might have done some good had they gone elsewhere. "How many conservative candidates lost in 2014 because of a lack of funds?" he asked. "How many of them came up short in primaries, lost winnable seats. Or desperately tried to fight off better funded challengers?"[9]

But the most damaging fallout may have been the way the PACs escalated the rhetoric of outrage, roiling the already unsettled waters of political anger and alienation on the Right. With their incessant and increasingly shrill appeals and warnings, the PACs pushed the GOP into tactical fights it couldn't win, while fueling a deepening disillusionment with conservatism itself. "They stoked controversies beyond all reason," wrote *National Review*'s David French, "fed the worst sort of conspiracy theories, and led rank and file conservatives to believe that their elected representatives were doing literally nothing to oppose the Obama administration."[10]

This notion that the GOP had capitulated to Obama was an alternative reality at stark variance with the way Democrats and mainstream conservatives saw it. Far from rolling over to Obama, Democrats accused the GOP of waging an unprecedented campaign of obstruction. And more thoughtful conservatives, including *National Review* writer Charles C. W. Cooke, argued that the notion that the GOP has simply caved to Obama was "flat-out wrong. Disastrously wrong. Apocalyptically wrong."

Despite the failures to repeal Obamacare or roll back the Obama legacy while he was still in office, Cooke noted that if the GOP had not resisted Obama, "the United States would look dramatically different than it does today." Instead of a public-private hybrid, Obamacare might have been single payer and "at the very least, the law would have included a "public option."[11]

> Without the GOP manning the barricades, we'd have seen a carbon tax or cap-and-trade—or both. Without the GOP manning the barricades, we'd have got union card check, and possibly an amendment to Taft-Hartley that removed from the states their power to pass "right to work" exemptions. Without the GOP standing in the way, we'd now have an "assault weapons" ban, magazine limits, background checks on all private sales, and a de facto national gun registry. And without the GOP standing in the way in the House, we'd have got the very amnesty that the Trump people so fear. . . .

Cooke goes on to say that:

A similar truth obtains at the state level. Had the GOP not taken over the vast majority of the country's local offices since 2010, we'd have seen significantly less progress on right to work, the protection of life, school choice, and the right to keep and bear arms; we'd have seen a whole host of new sanctuary cities; we'd have had considerably fewer attorneys general rising up against Obama's executive overreach; and, perhaps most importantly, we'd have seen Obamacare entrenched almost everywhere as state after state chose to expand Medicaid.[12]

The congressional GOP also pointed to its efforts to hold down domestic spending, and its success in extending the vast majority of the Bush-era income tax cuts. And yet, the disappointment on the Right was palpable, as the loudest voices in the newly weaponized Right made demands that the GOP could not fulfill because they were politically and fiscally impossible to enact.

Conservative wins were real, but they were often buried under the detritus of special-interest favors, and "go along to get along" compromises, including a series of incomprehensible budget votes—the omnibus, followed by the horrifically named "cromnibus"*—that could be portrayed as packages of horrors, because they largely were. Not for nothing did even representatives who voted for the monstrosities call them "crap sandwiches." But they were too frequently on the menu.

All the while the outrage machine became more heated, with charges that conservatives had not merely been disappointed, but that they had been betrayed by a traitorous "establishment." The lack of a coherent alternative seemed beside the point, and conservative politicians found themselves vilified over tactical issues.

In his thoughtful study, *Why the Right Went Wrong*, E. J. Dionne argued that the history of contemporary conservatism was a story of

---

*The "cromnibus" was a long-term Omnibus spending bill joined to a shorter-term Continuing Resolution (CR). It as a term only Washington insiders could love, and even they hated it.

"disappointment and betrayal," because conservative politicians "have made promises to their supporters that they could not keep," which led to disillusionment and "the sense their leaders had failed them," which created "a cycle of radicalization."[13]

The Tea Party accelerated that process, but it was the shift in focus of the venerable Heritage Foundation that really put the cycle on steroids.

HERITAGE GOES ACTIVIST

It's hard to overstate the importance of The Heritage Foundation in the rise of conservatism. One of the oldest of the conservative think tanks that would spring up to give intellectual heft to the Right, Heritage had handed the incoming Reagan administration in 1981 a blueprint for governing, an 1,100-page briefing book called the *Mandate for Leadership*. One news account described the document as "a blueprint for grabbing the government by its frayed New Deal lapels and shaking out 48 years of liberal policy." The foundation later claimed that nearly two thirds of the document's two thousand recommendations "were adopted or attempted by the Reagan administration."[14] Among the ideas advanced by the think tank and embraced by Reagan included across-the-board tax cuts, the Strategic Defense Initiative, and urban "enterprise zones."

William F. Buckley Jr. hailed Heritage's contribution, stating, "The foundation had a great hour when Ronald Reagan was elected president and found waiting for him three volumes of Heritage material designed to help him chart the nation's course in the right direction."[15] It was not an exaggeration when the foundation claimed that "Heritage was President Reagan's favorite think tank, and Reagan was the embodiment of the ideas and principles Heritage holds dear."*

---

* "In his second term, Reagan turned again to Heritage for ideas, and adopted many of them. He recited twenty-two specific proposals from Mandate for Leadership II in his second inaugural address in 1985, prompting the *New York Times* to state,

But with the rise of the Tea Party, Heritage took a fateful turn from policy wonkery to more overt political activism. There had been growing concern, one insider later told me, that there was too much focus at Heritage on "white papers," and not enough on action. That was about to change, dramatically. Throughout the course of this book, I've tried to identify certain pivotal moments for conservatives (e.g., the selection of Sarah Palin, the Drudge Report's decision to link to conspiracy theorist Alex Jones, Rush Limbaugh's attack on a female law student). But near the top of that list has to be the decision in 2010 to create Heritage Action as a political arm of the foundation and then in 2012 to name South Carolina senator Jim DeMint as Heritage's new president.

DeMint's appointment reflected a tectonic shift in Heritage's culture. The foundation's chairman described DeMint's appointment as "turbocharging our already powerful engine."[16] But the shift in focus was immediate as DeMint escalated the pressure on the GOP for both ideological purity and tactical aggressiveness. In a remarkably short time, the activist Heritage Action had effectively eclipsed the venerable foundation. "As Heritage Action flourishes, Heritage Foundation has become less of a force on Capitol Hill," *Time* magazine later reported, "its role for three decades as an omnipresent voice in hearing rooms and Senate hideaways crafting legislation for Republicans now firmly in the rearview mirror."[17]

As a senator, DeMint had not been shy about attacking other Republicans whom he deemed to be insufficiently aggressive. He created in the Senate the Conservative Fund, a PAC that backed conservatives in primaries, often against candidates backed by the GOP leadership. His track record was decidedly mixed. He had backed successful primary bids by Marco Rubio in Florida, Ted Cruz in Texas, Rand Paul in Kentucky, and Mike Lee in Utah. But he had also thrown his support behind such political dumpster fires as Christine O'Donnell in

---

" 'While the wording of the president's speech and the foundation's document were different, many of the proposals were strikingly similar.' " —Andrew Blasko, *Reagan and Heritage: A Unique Partnership*, June 7, 2004, www.heritage.org/research /commentary/2004/06/reagan-and-heritage-a-unique-partnership.

Delaware, Sharron Angle in Nevada, Richard Mourdock in Indiana, Joe Miller in Alaska, and Ken Buck in Colorado.*

As the new Heritage CEO, DeMint immediately cranked up opposition to any budget deal with President Obama that did not include a full and complete repeal of Obamacare, even if that meant a government shutdown. Heritage Action amped up the pressure on GOP representatives by rating their votes, ranking them, and disseminating targeted attacks on recalcitrant members. The group launched a nine-city bus tour that featured both Ted Cruz and his father Rafael. At one rally in Tampa, Heritage Action's CEO Mike Needham declared: "Politicians don't lead, politicians follow. They need to be forced by you all to do the right thing. They won't do the right thing by themselves."[18] Heritage backed up the rhetoric by spending hundreds of thousands of dollars attacking Republicans who were balking at a government shutdown. Perhaps more important, Heritage and other conservative groups had forged close links with the nation's most prominent talkers, fortified by a strong cash nexus. As *Politico* reported in 2014, conservative groups "spent nearly $22 million to broker and pay for sponsorships with the most influential hosts," including Rush Limbaugh, Glenn Beck, Sean Hannity, Laura Ingraham, and Mark Levin.[19] (*Politico* estimated that The Heritage Foundation had paid more than $9.5 million for its five-year sponsorship of Limbaugh's show.)

The problem, of course, was that Heritage was demanding something that was impossible. Ultimately it came down to numbers, and the political math was stark: to repeal Obamacare, the GOP would need sixty votes in a Senate that was still controlled by Democrats. Even if,

---

*I only spoke to DeMint once, when he called me in 2012 to discuss Wisconsin's upcoming GOP U.S. Senate primary. He was thinking about endorsing former congressman Mark Neumann in the primary over former governor Tommy Thompson and businessman Eric Hovde. DeMint told me that he only intervened on behalf of candidates who had strong support from "the grassroots and from talk radio," and wanted to know if that was the case with Neumann. I told him that was not the case in Wisconsin because Neumann had burned too many bridges with his 2010 primary campaign against now governor Scott Walker. DeMint thanked me for the input and the next week endorsed Neumann, who finished third in the primary.

by some miracle, they would get the requisite votes, a presidential veto was certain, meaning that conservatives would have to muster two thirds of both the House and the Senate to override. No rational observer believed that was remotely possible.

As early as July 2013, it was obvious that Heritage Action's shutdown plan had no real exit strategy. "There is no plan B, there is no 'what if,'" one Republican lawmaker told Roll Call.[20] But Heritage Action and other Tea Party groups continued to hammer their fellow Republicans, and their message was amplified by the megaphones of the Right media, who continued to raise expectations that were doomed to be disappointed. (Amid internal debates over the politicization of Heritage, in early 2017 the foundation's board fired DeMint. But this came six months after the election.)

I was tangentially involved in one particularly heated controversy over the shutdown. As the shutdown loomed, Senator Ted Cruz became the leading advocate and a Tea Party hero for his mini filibuster against Obamacare. But Cruz was unable to explain how a shutdown could actually be successful, given the lack of votes either for passing a repeal of Obamacare or for overriding a veto. During the controversy Wisconsin senator Ron Johnson, one of the Senate's most outspoken fiscal conservatives, came on my radio show and called Cruz's strategy to defund Obamacare "intellectually dishonest." That comment brought down the wrath of the Right media onto Johnson's head.

On his nationally syndicated radio show, Mark Levin hammered Johnson, demanding that he come up with an alternative strategy to repeal Obamacare. In a tense exchange, Johnson tried to explain that the only path to repeal would be to get at least five Democratic senators to cross over. Without defections, he said, the only reasonable alternative would be for the GOP to stick together and elect more allies. Levin was having none of it.

Afterward Peter Dominick, writing in the Daily Beast, described the confrontation as a perfect explanation of the showdown controversy. "The strategy Levin supports is great for ratings," wrote Dominick, "but terrible for the country and the Republican Party."[21]

> Levin and other radio performers, commentators, and columnists
> see it as their responsibility to demand purity on every vote
> and issue. They gain respect and larger audiences the more they
> vent the anger and frustration of their listeners by calling
> people names and hanging up on those who argue with them.
> If there is nothing to be outraged by, it's their job to create
> something. That is how it works in radio. But that isn't how it
> works in Washington, D.C., or any state capital in America.

But Levin was not alone, as various conservative groups used the shutdown controversy to pump up their mail lists, generate clicks, and raise money. Other national talkers cheered them on and criticized members of the GOP "establishment," who had not fallen into line. In October 2013, after the shutdown had failed to accomplish much of anything other than cause Republican support to drop in the polls, Limbaugh framed the failed strategy in "us vs. them" terms. He accused members of the "establishment" of having been "embarrassed" by Cruz, whom he described as "one guy with some supporters" standing up to challenge the status quo. What Republicans needed, Limbaugh insisted, was "45 Ted Cruzes" but that weak-kneed GOP leaders acted as if they were "terrified" of him.[22]

Conservative anger and disappointment had been stoked. But, ultimately, Cruz would not be the beneficiary. And therein lies another story.

THE FLAW

The purists who backed the government shutdown ignored political realities in several ways; not only did they get the legislative numbers wrong, but they overestimated public support for their agenda.

The reality that many conservatives have been unwilling to face is that despite their insistence that America was a center-right country, there has never been a strong constituency for the kind of tough budget cuts that would either limit the size of government or reduce the national debt. A 2013 Pew research poll found that only small minorities of the general electorate were in favor of spending cuts. Even as the deadline for the sequester's spending cuts loomed, fewer than 25 percent of the electorate favored cutting spending on health care, environmental protection, energy, scientific research, agriculture, or "aid to the needy in the United States." Fewer than 20 percent favored retrenchments on roads and infrastructure, Medicare, crime fighting, food and drug inspection, or disaster relief. A mere 10 percent favored decreased spending on education, Social Security, or veteran's benefits.[23]

There were, of course, sharp partisan differences, but few signs that even Republican voters had much appetite for spending cuts. Only 21 percent of Republicans said they wanted cuts in spending for Medicare, 15 percent wanted to decrease spending on education, and just 17 percent favored cuts in Social Security.

The Pew Poll also found that Tea Party supporters made up only 37 percent of Republican and Republican-leaning voters, but had an outsized impact on Republican politics because they tended to be more engaged in the political process and more likely to vote in primaries. Support for the Tea Party peaked in 2010, but declined afterward. By 2015, just 17 percent of Americans said they supported the Tea Party, while a record 54 percent said they were neither supporters nor opponents.[24]

But even at the height of the Tea Party influence in Washington, there was little support for entitlement reform. A *Wall Street Journal/NBC News* poll found that less than a quarter of Americans backed significant cuts to Social Security or Medicare. And even self-declared Tea Party supporters said that significant cuts to Social Security were "unacceptable."[25]*

---

* At the same time, the poll found that more than 60 percent of poll respondents "supported reducing Social Security and Medicare payments to wealthier Americans. And more than half favored bumping the retirement age to 69 by 2075. The age to receive full benefits is 66 now and is scheduled to rise to 67 in 2027." (www .wsj.com/articles/SB10001424052748704728004576176741120691736.)

None of this seemed to matter within the echo chamber that was demanding scorched-earth budget tactics. Long before Donald Trump descended the golden escalator and announced his presidential bid, the narrative had been set: the conservative "establishment" had betrayed conservatives. In the echo chamber, the volume was set at "Outrage." As Caleb Howe later noted, this has become the business model of the Right media. "The problem, obviously, is that the talk/radio/conservative publishing/Fox opinion show model isn't about conservative policy and ideas, or good governance, or increasing our liberty, or social conservative values, or even really about the Constitution," he wrote. "To a great extent, it is essentially about getting the audience outraged. Outrage clicks on links. Outrage tunes in. Outrage buys books."[26]

At the center of this new media ecosystem was Fox News, Rush Limbaugh, Breitbart, and Matt Drudge.

PART II

THE POST-
TRUTH
POLITICS OF
THE RIGHT

CHAPTER 7

THE ALT REALITY MEDIA

THIS IS WHAT IT is like to live in an ideological bubble:

> Throughout the day an American conservative can check out
> stories from Breitbart about crimes committed by illegal aliens
> and the headline "Paul Ryan Betrays America"; former
> congressman Allen B. West promises to tell them, "What
> Obama is doing now may be his most heinous and nefarious
> act yet. . . ." A quick click on the Drudge Report brings up a
> banner headline about "Bill Clinton's Illegitimate Son Danney
> Williams." On Facebook, a friend passes on a story headlined
> "Kellyanne Destroys Obnoxious Rachel Maddow In Her Most

Incredible Interview Yet" (VIDEO). Their Twitter feed is
exploding with attacks on the "lying, corrupt media."
Investigative reports in the media about conflicts of interest in
the new administration are dismissed as "fake news."

  Checking emails, a conservative voter might find several
from friends and family, often written in ALL CAPS, including
links to stories about the UN's plans to confiscate guns; several
emails from groups calling themselves the "Tea Party" offer
deals on gold and silver. On television, the hosts on *Fox &
Friends* are interviewing a Trump surrogate who defends the
Russians against charges that they interfered in the election.
On the way to work they can listen to talk show hosts warning
of plans to impose Sharia law on Americans or Sean Hannity
threatening congressional Republicans who might oppose the
new president.

As the Right has isolated itself from other sources of information,
it has fashioned an alternate universe with its own facts, narratives, and
truths. Of course, its members are not alone in doing so.

Americans have segregated themselves into what the Associated
Press called "intellectual ghettoes," each with their own realities and
narratives "What's big news in one world is ignored in another. Conspiracy theories sprout, anger abounds and the truth becomes ever more
elusive," wrote reporter David Bauder.[1] While conservatives can take
their worldview from Laura Ingraham, Rush Limbaugh, or a host of
other conservative outlets, progressives can dive into their own thought
ghetto by immersing themselves in a world bounded by the *Huffington
Post,* Daily Kos, Talking Points Memo, and Salon. The silos are dis-
crete universes that seldom talk to one another or seek to persuade or
engage those of other viewpoints. As a result, the new media ecosystem rewards the loudest, most reckless voices, so the echo chamber
gets louder and angrier and increasingly shrill.

That echo chamber also has grown dramatically in recent years.
A study by the *Columbia Journalism Review* noted that one of the remarkable features of the right-wing media ecosystem was "how new it

is." The study found that pro-Trump audiences "paid the majority of their attention to polarized outlets that have developed recently, many of them only since the 2008 election season." Of the most voluble pro-Trump sites, the report noted, "only the *New York Post* existed when Ronald Reagan was elected president in 1980. By the election of Bill Clinton in 1992, only the *Washington Times*, Rush Limbaugh, and arguably Sean Hannity had joined the fray. Alex Jones of Infowars started his first outlet on the radio in 1996. Fox News was not founded until 1996. Breitbart was founded in 2007, and most of the other major nodes in the right-wing media system were created even later."[2]

The *CJR* study found that Breitbart sat in the middle of this new network, which effectively "turned the right-wing media system into an internally coherent, relatively insulated knowledge community, reinforcing the shared worldview of readers and shielding them from journalism that challenged it." This media ecosystem did not develop spontaneously or on the cheap. Conservative mega-donors generously funded the new alternative media, with the Mercer family reportedly pumping at least $10 million into Breitbart, which not only boosted Trump's candidacy, but became a shrill enforcer of Trumpist loyalty. (The Mercers also made major donations to the Media Research Center, which documents liberal media bias as well as groups like the free-market Heartland Institute, The Heritage Foundation, Citizens United Foundation, and the Federalist Society.)[3] While other well-heeled donors on the right and left focused on more traditional types of politics, noted the *Washington Post*, "the Mercers have exerted pressure on the political system by helping erect an alternative media ecosystem, whose storylines dominated the 2016 race."[4]

THE WAR ON BIAS

As the University of Virginia's Nicole Hemmer explains in *Messengers of the Right: Conservative Media and the Transformation of American Politics*, the history of the modern Right media is anything but a straight line. What we now see as the multimedia Right is actually the second generation of media activists; the first had its roots in the 1940s and 1950s, and as we have seen, fizzled out by the late 1970s.

Although histories of conservatism tend to focus on Buckley's *National Review* magazine, Hemmer notes that there was a broader network of conservative media activists that emerged as leaders of the nascent conservative movement. "The consequences of their leadership were profound," she notes, because these early activists "crafted and popularized the . . . concept that established media were not neutral but slanted towards liberalism. . . ." At the time this was considered a radical idea, so it is easy to underestimate the impact of those early activists.

Hemmer writes:

> Conservative media activists advanced an alternative way of knowing the world, one that attacked the legitimacy of objectivity and substituted for it ideological integrity. That attack was embodied in their notion of "liberal media bias," which disputed not just the content presented by mainstream journalists but the very claims they made about their objective practices.[5]

This marked the beginnings of what would eventually become the echo chambers of our current media ecosystem, but that lay far in the future. Given the paucity of conservative outlets in the 1970s and the continuing dominance of the mainstream media—most everyone still got their news from the major networks—the first generation of media voices were unable to create anything like the echo chamber of later decades.

Those early efforts to fight media bias, Hemmer writes, represented "a battle over fundamentals, a struggle over how best to gauge the trustworthiness of information." The early conservatives argued that "there was no such thing as non-ideological media, that objectivity was a mask mainstream media used to hide their own ideological projects." This would have profound consequences for the development of the alternative media because the "conservative media activists in mid-century America provided their audiences—readers, listeners, and viewers—

with a different way of weighing evidence: a different network of authorities, a different conception of facts and accuracy, and a different way of evaluating truth claims." The conservative assumption that writers and editors were biased "allowed conservatives to develop a robust approach to observing contrary evidence."[6]

What this analysis misses is how much evidence the conservatives could muster for their complaints of media bias. For many members of the media, conservatives were an exotic and slightly scary new breed—and their coverage reflected it. Buckley's account of his quixotic New York mayoral bid, *The Unmaking of a Mayor,* is replete with examples of slanted, tendentious, often erroneous reporting. As the country split apart during the 1960s and many news outlets opted for more ideologically active advocacy, conservative suspicion and disaffection grew, and was easily exploited by politicians like Vice President Spiro Agnew, who labeled the media "nattering nabobs of negativism."

With more than a little help from the media itself, that campaign has been remarkably successful. Not a single conservative activist I know would tell you they trust the mainstream media to be fair, and many of them have the scars to prove it. (Recall Dan Rather's debunked report on George W. Bush's alleged attempts to avoid the draft.) So the incentive to create alternative media outlets was strong and ultimately quite successful.

In a sense, talk radio filled the gap left by the media's failure to take conservative ideas and values seriously. For many conservatives, turning on talk radio in the late 1980s was the first time they felt the media was taking their ideas—and them—seriously. It was like pouring water onto parched ground.

This tilt is not always apparent to those on the Left or their allies in the media, inasmuch as liberalism is often regarded as the default setting of American politics. Many journalists do not recognize their bias any more than a fish recognizes that it is wet: They swim in an ocean of like-minded professionals. Being pro-choice on abortion was simply the position of everyone they knew, while opposition to abortion rights was, by definition, "controversial." It did not help that no one on journalists' personal or social radar held such "retrograde" ideas.

That explained why it was easy for the *Washington Post* to publish an article dismissing evangelical Christians as "largely poor, uneducated, and easy to command," because evangelical Christians were simply not part of their world. As Ralph Reed, the executive director of the Christian Coalition later noted, the comment revealed the blinkered worldview of members of the elite media, especially when it came to certain kinds of Christians. "They don't rub shoulders with these people," he said. "They don't socialize with them."[7]

While the *Washington Post* backed off its slur of evangelicals, there was a notable lack of introspection in the legacy media at large. Rather than respond to the new media and the evidence that it was drawing an audience, many in the established media reacted with scarcely concealed disdain, defensively denying that there was any legitimacy to the criticisms. This refusal to take the complaints of its own customers seriously served to alienate the conservative base—which was increasingly learning to question and later abandon outlets they no longer trusted—even more. In Wisconsin, when I began my own talk radio show, the local media essentially ignored conservatives, even as they were surging toward electoral victories. So I fully understood why conservatives seek out their own bunkers; they were drawn to safe places, but also pushed.

Conservatives simply gave up hoping that they would be treated with respect and honesty by the mainstream media and turned to their own alternative outlets for support and validation. The process accelerated in the 1990s, with Limbaugh's growing popularity, the rise of Fox News, and the explosion of other conservative outlets. By the time Barack Obama became president, the Alt Reality silo was almost fully operational.

In their 2008 study of the new alternative media, *Echo Chamber: Rush Limbaugh and the Conservative Media Establishment*, Kathleen Hall Jamieson and Joseph N. Cappella argued that the new conservative infrastructure had helped "create a self-protective enclave hospitable to conservative beliefs. This safe haven reinforces the views of these outlets' like-minded audience members, helps them maintain ideological coherence, protects them from counterpersuasion, reinforces conservative values and dispositions, holds Republican candidates and leaders accountable to conservative ideals. . . . It also enwraps them in a world in which facts that are supportive of Democratic claims are contested and those consistent with conservative ones championed."[8]

It was about to get much worse.

THE SOCIAL MEDIA SILOS

The creation of competing bubbles was accelerated by the explosion of social media—a Pew survey found that 44 percent of Americans read or watch "news" on Facebook. The algorithms of social media further magnified the process by driving users deeper into their ideological corners, with other like-minded users. The sorting out process is intensified as readers are fed stories that tend to reinforce their worldviews. An article in the *Economist* noted that on Facebook "algorithms are designed to populate their news feeds with content similar to material they previously 'liked.'" In Britain that meant that during the battle over Brexit, users who supported the exit from the European Union mostly saw pro-Brexit articles; those who wanted to stay in the EU were offered pro-EU material.[9]

The process extended to search engines as well. In its study on the new media, BuzzFeed noted that the more users clicked on hyperpartisan websites, "the more Google will show them search results from these sources. The result is that over time people will likely become more polarized because algorithms and friends continue to feed them information that pushes them further in this direction."[10] In the Alt Reality silos, the feedback loop was also effectively closed, creating a hermetically sealed ideological cul-de-sac. BuzzFeed's study found that right-wing pages "almost never used mainstream news sources, instead pointing to other highly partisan sources of information." So, BuzzFeed noted, a story on a site called "Right Wing News" touting an NFL boycott because players were kneeling during the pledge of allegiance was linked to the site Young Conservatives, which linked to Breitbart, which had put its own spin on a poll by Yahoo!

The result is a cycle of post-truthism. "The more we click, like and share stuff that resonates with our own world views the more Facebook feeds us with similar posts," the British newspaper the *Guardian* noted. "Within Facebook's digital echo chamber, misinformation that aligns with our beliefs spreads like wildfire, thanks to confirmation bias."[11]

8

THE POST-TRUTH
POLITICS OF THE RIGHT

THE EXPLOSION OF FABRICATED stories—and the credulous Trump supporters who believed and forwarded them—probably did not flip the election. But their role in the campaign was a leading indicator of the shape of our new post-truth media/political world.

"Honestly," Paul Horner, one of the creators of fake news, told the *Washington Post* after the election, "people are definitely dumber. They just keep passing stuff around. Nobody fact-checks anything anymore— I mean, that's how Trump got elected. He just said whatever he wanted, and people believed everything, and when the things he said turned out not to be true, people didn't care because they'd already accepted it. It's real scary. I've never seen anything like it."[1]

The problem was especially acute on the Right. "I think Trump is in the White House because of me," Horner confessed. "His followers don't fact-check anything—they'll post everything, believe anything. His campaign manager posted my story about a protester getting paid $3,500 as fact. Like, I made that up. I posted a fake ad on Craigslist."

So when, three days before the presidential election, another fake news site posted "FBI Agent Suspected in Hillary Email Leaks Found Dead," the story would also go viral, getting 560,000 shares on Facebook alone. The story had been posted on a website called the Denver Guardian, a source devoted to disseminating anti-Clinton fake news.* Similar bogus stories were shared millions of times during the campaign.

But this didn't happen in a vacuum: such stories fit easily into the new ecosystem of the Right's alternative reality. To some observers, this new post-truth culture seemed to draw its inspiration from the Russian approach to "truth" and its active use of *dezinformatsiya* (disinformation) to build political support or discredit critics. Journalist Peter Pomerantsev, who has written a book about Putin's Russia entitled, *Nothing Is True and Everything Is Possible,* quoted a political adviser saying of the regime, "Now no one even tries proving 'the truth.' You can just say anything. Create realities."[2] Russian dissident and chess grandmaster Garry Kasparov drew upon long familiarity with the process when he tweeted, "The point of modern propaganda isn't only to misinform or push an agenda. It is to exhaust your critical thinking, to annihilate truth."[3]

Kasparov grasps that the real threat is not merely that a large number of Americans have become accustomed to rejecting factual information, or even that they have become habituated to believing hoaxes.

---

*A study by Washington State University's Mike Caulfield found that the fake story about the dead FBI agent was shared more widely on Facebook "and thus reached a far greater number of people than some concurrently 'trending' articles from respected news sources like the *Boston Globe* and the *Washington Post.* Ultimately, the fake article garnered thousands more shares than several of the real news stories he looked at." ("The scariest part of Facebook's fake news problem: fake news is more viral than real news," Vox, November 16, 2016.)

The real danger is that, inundated with "alternative facts," many voters will simply shrug, ask, "What is truth?" and not wait for an answer. In such a world, the leader becomes the only reliable source of truth, a familiar phenomenon in an authoritarian state, but a radical departure from the norms of a democratic society.[4]

But in American politics, the process has been radically decentralized. As Trump slouched toward the nomination, he was backed by a conservative media that had successfully created an Alt Reality bubble around his candidacy. When Trump claimed that "thousands" of Muslims in New Jersey had celebrated the attacks on 9/11, for instance, callers to my show lined up to provide supporting evidence, the only source of which was an echo chamber of partisan bloggers.

Indeed, what we learned was that the walls are down, the gatekeepers dismissed, the norms and standards of journalism and fact-based discourse trashed. In the alternative reality bubble of the conservative media, fake news—and a candidate who daily made demonstrably false statements—could spread like a noxious weed. But then again, so could Breitbart News, Alex Jones, and Sean Hannity and their legions of internet trolls who found out they could drive the political narrative, regardless of the fact-checkers or other recognizable measures of reality.

Indeed, the new Alt Reality media's proficiency at deflecting negative information and shaping a counternarrative was on full display after the election when it effectively hijacked the term "fake news." Rather than seeing it as a canary in the coal mine, Jeremy Peters wrote in the *New York Times*, "Conservative cable and radio personalities, top Republicans and even Mr. Trump himself . . . have appropriated the term and turned it against any news they see as hostile to their agenda."[5] Having delegitimized much of the mainstream media, the Right had effectively also delegitimized the notion of "fake news." As *Washington Post* fact-checker Glenn Kessler observed, "People seem to confuse reporting mistakes by established news organizations with obviously fraudulent news produced by Macedonian teenagers."[6]

A WORD ABOUT POLITIFACT

No account of the fall of the fact-checkers would be complete without a discussion of the self-inflicted wounds of the gatekeepers of truth. As members of the media have discovered, credibility is a fragile commodity—particularly when it comes to judgments about what is credible. While many of the leading fact-checking operations—including Annenberg's FactCheck.org and the *Washington Post*'s Kessler—do a creditable job, PolitiFact has routinely undermined its own trustworthiness. "When it first began," one Republican government official told me, "we all took it very seriously. When we got an inquiry, we dropped everything; it was all hands on deck. After a while, we stopped paying attention. It had become a joke. Nobody gives a shit anymore."*

"Tendentious PolitiFact ratings are a classic genre of bad journalism," the *Wall Street Journal* editorialized, noting its long record of cherry-picking facts, tortured logic, and double standards.[7] Rather than carefully protecting its status as a neutral and trusted arbiter of truth, PolitiFact effectively set its own pants on fire. In 2008, PolitiFact rated Barack Obama's statement "If you like your health care, you can keep it" as "True." The next year it downgraded the problem to "Half True," and finally in 2013 labeled the statement the "Lie of the Year."†

---

* My own PolitiFact "file" assigned me two "Pants on Fire" and one "False" rating, suggesting that I have never, on any occasion, said anything that is even remotely true.

† "The highlight of [PolitiFact's] 2013 'Lie of the Year' article was that it completely ignored [PolitiFact's] own 'True' rating of the 'keep your plan' claim back in 2008," health care expert Avik Roy noted. "PolitiFact's pronouncements about Obamacare were widely repeated by pro-Obama reporters and pundits, and had a meaningful impact on the outcome of the election," he noted. "Indeed, in 2009, PolitiFact won the Pulitzer Prize for its coverage of the 2008 campaign." Roy's verdict was harsh, but widely shared among conservatives: "PolitiFact is an embarrassment to the world of fact-checking, let alone to the world of prediction-checking to which it actually belongs. Their 2008 Pulitzer Prize—prominently mentioned on every PolitiFact web page—owes itself in part to the group's lazy and inaccurate reporting on Obamacare. If PolitiFact were intellectually honest,

Matt Shapiro, a data analyst for the Paradox Project, ran the numbers on PolitiFact; assigning a point value to the ratings 0 for True and 5 for "Pants on Fire," Shapiro found that Democrats had an average rating of 1.8—somewhere between "Mostly True" and "Half True." Republicans, on the other hand, had an average rating of 2.6, somewhere between "Half True" and "Mostly False." Some of the numbers were skewed by Trump's egregious track record of fabulism, but the pattern seemed to hold even when he was removed from the mix. The most frequent rating for a Republican who was not Donald Trump was still "mostly false," and often employed its customary convoluted logics to reach many of the verdicts.[8]

"PolitiFact often rates statements that are largely true but come from GOP sources as 'mostly false,'" Shapiro noted, "by focusing on sentence alterations, simple misstatements, fact-checking the wrong fact, and even taking a statement, rewording it, and fact-checking the re-worded statement instead of the original quoted statement." Again, this cannot be attributed to the Trump effect alone. Shapiro noted that during the 2012 campaign PolitiFact awarded nineteen "Pants on Fire" ratings to Mitt Romney. He put this in some context: from 2007 to 2016 a grand total of twenty-five Democrats combined were assigned the "Pants on Fire" rating. "This seems to indicate Romney wasn't just a liar, but an insane, raving liar, spewing malicious deceit at every possible opportunity," wrote Shapiro. "In the mere two years he was in the spotlight as a Republican presidential nominee, Romney somehow managed to rival the falsehoods told by the entire party of Democrats over the course of a decade. Or it is possible that PolitiFact has a slant in their coverage." In contrast, he noted that based on PolitiFact's ratings, Hillary Clinton was "the single most honest politician to run for president in the last 10 years."[9]

---

it would acknowledge that it was undeserving of that prize, reflect on how its work has gone astray, and focus in the future on actual fact-checking instead of prediction-checking." (Avik Roy, "Pants On Fire: PolitiFact Tries To Hide That It Rated 'True' in 2008 Obamacare's 'Keep Your Health Plan' Promise," *Forbes,* December 27, 2013.)

Similar stories are legion, as PolitiFact writers often changed their standards or invented new ones to fit their agendas. Suffice it to say that by 2015, few conservatives regarded PolitiFact as a credible source, so it was effectively useless in pushing back against fake news at precisely the moment when credible fact-checkers were most needed.

A STORM OF FAKE NEWS

In August 2016, one of the hottest stories on the internet—and on Facebook, in particular—was a story about Fox News anchor Megyn Kelly: "BREAKING: Fox News Exposes Traitor Megyn Kelly, Kicks Her Out for Backing Hillary." The story reported that Kelly was "on her way out of Fox News" for being "a closet liberal who actually wants Hillary to win." The story, which was fake, had more than two hundred thousand "likes," and was "trending" on Facebook for hours before it was finally removed. The source for the hoax was a website called End the Fed, which trafficked in stories like "What Obama Has to Say About 'White Folks' Will Make Your Blood Boil" and "Eric Bolling Exposes New Dirty Tricks Clintons Used to Escape Jail Time and Become Millionaires."[10]

Much of what appeared on social media took a decidedly dark turn. University of Washington Professor Kate Starbird began noticing the proliferation of conspiracy theories that sprang up after mass shootings or terror attacks. After the Boston Marathon bombing, for example, she noticed a surge in social media traffic "than blamed the Navy SEALs for the bombing." As she delved deeper into the phenomenon, she found that these "strange clusters" were actually part of a network of alternative media sites with a far greater reach than anyone had imagined. "More people are dipping into this stuff than I ever imagined," Starbird told a *Seattle Times* columnist.[11] Her study, titled, "Examining the Alternative Media Ecosystem through the Production of Alternative Narratives of Mass Shooting Events on Twitter," documented more than eighty separate websites devoted to spreading "'fake news'—alternative narratives of man-made crisis events."[12] Over the course of the 2016 election, some of those sites (notably Alex Jones's Infowars) began to shape the political narrative and clearly began to influence many voters on the Right.

One of the most frequently referenced theories in this alternative information universe involved the tragic Sandy Hook shootings, which occurred in 2012. "Though a large portion of those tweets contest or deny that alternative narrative," Starbird noted, "several utilize Sandy Hook 'evidence' to support alternative narratives around more recent events." She cited tweets that claimed, "Orlando shooting was a hoax. Just like Sandy Hook, Boston Bombing, and San Bernandino. Keep believing Rothschild Zionist news companies." Other tweets insisted: "More Orlando shooting Hoax-proof—same actors in Sandy hook & Boston Marathon Fake bombing—gun take away agenda."[13]

Many of the stories went viral in a social media ecosystem that was overrun with antiglobalist and pro-Trump narratives. "We found the same stories on multiple domains," Starbird concluded, "sometimes as exact copies, but also in different forms. This means that an individual using these sites is likely seeing the same messages in different forms and in different places, which may distort their perception of this information as it gives the false appearance of source diversity."[14]

By the end of the campaign, the time lines of social media (especially on the Right) were so clogged with misleading or fabricated stories that a cottage industry of intentionally bogus news sprang up. One practitioner, who went by the Twitter handle MassRafTer, began creating fake stories that were "intentional, immediately obvious disinformation" designed to dupe conservative Trump supporters.[15] MassRafTer was responsible, for instance, for creating a document that appeared to be an expense report allegedly showing the Clinton Foundation siphoning money to a variety of high-profile groups and individuals. The payments were listed under the heading "Voter Suppression" and included Sharia Law Center ($30,000), the Black Panthers ($333,400), conservative talk show host Glenn Beck ($109,000), *Weekly Standard* editor Bill Kristol ($10,000), independent conservative presidential candidate Evan McMullin ($12,000), former domestic terrorist Bill Ayers ($42,300), Black Lives Matter ($203,000), ACORN

($89,000), and to the polling firm Public Policy Polling ($75,000). It was clearly and obviously fake, but as the *Daily Beast* later reported, it was quickly picked up by Trump supporters on social media, at least one Fox News contributor, and a conservative radio host. The fake report created a mini firestorm: "Sharia Law? Glenn Beck? Bill Ayers? Black Lives Matter? ACORN? Public Polling? What exactly is this money being paid out for???" one Trump supporter tweeted.

MassRafTer was also responsible for a fake internal memo from Public Policy Polling that purported to show the Clinton campaign's attempts to rig the results. "Your latest poll is unacceptable," the fake memo declared. "We aren't paying you $760,000 per month to show a FIVE POINT LEAD. Are you trying to make Trump win? We will be ending our contract with your company unless results improve quickly." Again, the memo was clearly bogus—and, according to its author, designed to look as absurd as possible. But many readers took the bait, including Donald Trump Jr., who retweeted the story (he later deleted it).[16]

Other fake news sites appeared to have a more straightforward and partisan political agenda, but were also pumping out false stories at a staggering pace. An in-depth report in the *New York Times Magazine* noted that the new websites "have begun to create and refine a new approach to political news: cherry-picking and reconstituting the most effective tactics and tropes from activism, advocacy and journalism into a potent new mixture."[17] The new sites—with names like Freedom Daily, Right Wing News, Eagle Rising, and Occupy Democrats—occasionally carried legitimate stories, but mixed in among the posts was a heavy dose of misleading information.

Perhaps most striking of all: multiple studies suggested that fake news sold quite well, sometimes actually better than accurate news. In the new media ecosystem, there was simply no incentive to stick to the facts, and social media tended to reward not only the loudest voices, but also the most dishonest.* A BuzzFeed report concluded

---

*An academic study by Filippo Menczer and associates at Indiana University "to see whether there are differences in popularity between articles containing 'mis-

that "the least accurate pages generated some of the highest numbers of shares, reactions, and comments on Facebook—far more than the three large mainstream political news pages analyzed for comparison." This was the new normal: "The best way to attract and grow an audience for political content on the world's biggest social network is to eschew factual reporting and instead play to partisan biases using false or misleading information that simply tells people what they want to hear."[18]

WHAT IS TRUTH?

This raises the question, *Why were so many people willing to believe fake news?* The answer is deceptively simple—they believed fake news because they wanted to and because it was *easy.* We might assume that people naturally want to seek out information that is true, but this turns out to be a basic misunderstanding of the human psyche, which feels more comfortable with familiar information, or stories that confirm their biases. Nobel Prize–winning psychologist Daniel Kahneman refers to this as "cognitive ease," the process by which we avoid and resist inconvenient facts that might make us have to think harder. It is far easier to bask in a flow of information that tells us that we have been right all along and confirms our view of the world.[19]

Social psychologist Jonathan Haidt describes the power of tribalism in shaping our ideas about truth. "Once people join a political team," he wrote in *The Righteous Mind,* "they get ensnared in its moral matrix. They see confirmation of their grand narrative everywhere, and it's difficult—perhaps impossible—to convince them that they are wrong if you argue with them from outside the matrix."[20] In this world, writes political scientist Don Kinder, political opinions become "badges of social membership."[21]

---

information' and those containing 'reliable information'" concluded that there is no advantage to being correct or telling truth. ("Yes, I'd Lie to You," *Economist,* September 10, 2016.)

In other words, many voters use information not to discover what is true, but rather to reinforce their relationship to their group or tribe. They use reason to confirm or justify the outcome they want. Studies have shown that hyper-partisans actually got a hit of dopamine when they hear information that supports their positions or their candidates. "And if that is true," writes Haidt, "then it would explain why extreme partisans are so stubborn, closed-minded, and committed to beliefs that often seem bizarre or paranoid . . . the partisan brain has been reinforced so many times for performing mental contortions that free it from unwanted beliefs. *Extreme partisanship may be literally addictive.*"[Emphasis added.][22]

Haidt also cites the work of fellow social psychologist, Tom Gilovich who studies "the cognitive mechanisms of strange beliefs." If we want to believe something, Gilovich says, we ask, "Can I believe it?" and we need only a single piece of evidence, no matter its provenance, so that "we can stop thinking" because we "now have permission to believe" what we wanted to believe. The flip side is that when we are confronted with uncomfortable or unwanted information that we do not want to believe, we ask "Must I believe?" and look for a reason to reject the argument or fact. Again, only a single piece of data is necessary "to unlock the handcuffs of must."[23]

This process of cherry-picking truths seems to lie at the heart of our post-truth political culture and explains one of the more extraordinary (and revealing quotes) from the campaign, when one of Trump's most visible campaign surrogates declared that there really is no such thing as facts anymore. Scottie Nell Hughes, a frequent talking head on cable television throughout the campaign, was asked after the election to defend Trump's clearly false statement that millions of votes had been cast illegally. Her response is worth quoting in its entirety:

> Well, I think it's also an idea of an opinion. And that's—on one hand, I hear half the media saying that these are lies. But on the other half, there are many people that go, "No, it's true." And so one thing that has been interesting this entire campaign

season to watch, is that people that say facts are facts—they're not really facts. Everybody has a way—it's kind of like looking at ratings, or looking at a glass of half-full water.

Everybody has a way of interpreting them to be the truth, or not truth. *There's no such thing, unfortunately, anymore as facts . . . and so Mr. Trump's tweet, amongst a certain crowd—a large part of the population—are truth. When he says that millions of people illegally voted, he has some—amongst him and his supporters, and people believe they have facts to back that up.* Those that do not like Mr. Trump, they say that those are lies and that there are no facts to back it up. [Emphasis added.][24]

Or as George Orwell might have said, "The very concept of objective truth is fading out of the world. Lies will pass into history." But Hughes's comment was, perhaps, unintentionally insightful: for a large portion of the electorate, facts did not matter and therefore they did not particularly care whether (1) their candidate told demonstrable lies, or (2) that much of the news they got on their news feed was fake. That may sound harsh, but the postfactual culture had penetrated deeply into the political culture. Consider two remarks that appeared in the comment section of the website that published Hughes's "there's no such things as facts" statement. One user named "Bile Gull" quoted the statement that Trump faced "criticism for saying things that are patently untrue—like his insistence that millions of people voted illegally." But he flatly rejected that: "Sorry for not buying the garbage that the wise sages in the MSM are presenting as fact."

Another commenter, "SnakeBeMe," took a somewhat more philosophical postfact view: "Truth matters. Fact matters," he wrote. "But whose truths and whose facts?" He expanded on his point:

To me it's like going to an art gallery. People stand around looking at the pictures hanging there, and they see in the art what they need to see, what they want to see.

This is what truth is. We look at the picture and see what we need to see—what we want to see.

In other words, truth—even statements that purported to be about actual facts—were inherently subjective. Truth is not out there as something that can be verified, but is merely "what we want to see." No postmodern decontructionist professor of literature could have put it better.

More than a decade ago, comedian Stephen Colbert had described what he called "truthiness," which was not to be confused with traditional understandings of accuracy or actual truth. "We're not talking about truth, we're talking about something that seems like truth—the truth we want to exist," he explained. "It used to be, everyone was entitled to their own opinion, but not their own facts. But that's not the case anymore. Facts matter not at all. Perception is everything. It's certainty."[25]

ROB'S EMAILS

During the campaign, I had a front-row seat to what was happening. Throughout the year I received emails from listeners forwarding stories like "Australia Voted to Ban Muslims and Liberals Are Pissed," stories about a Hillary Clinton body double, or reports that Obama had given a speech to the United States in which he said that Americans needed to surrender their freedom as part of a "New World Government." On a daily basis I would get mass emails, passing on the latest stories about "tens of thousands of fraudulent ballots" that had been discovered in an Ohio warehouse.[26] Listeners would often feel compelled to post or pass on articles claiming that Hillary Clinton had said that the gorilla Harambe, who was shot at a Cincinnati zoo, was a victim of "racism," or that Trump's name had mysteriously been removed from primary ballots.

For years, I had tried whenever I could to push back against such hoaxes, often replying with links to fact-checking sites like Snopes.com. But it was hard not to notice that the volume of fake news was rising as the websites proliferated and listeners felt the need to break through what they saw as the mainstream media's cover-up of the "real" news out there. So, I continued to try to knock down the more egregious examples, but it was becoming more difficult to keep up. There was another problem as well: Increasingly, I noticed that conservatives were no longer willing to accept any information from respected news outlets that were debunking the fake stories.

Here is how it worked. As I was writing this book, I tweeted out a link to a story about a U.S. Senate hearing on Russian hacking. The story was straightforward and, as far as I could tell (based on reading multiple accounts) quite accurate. But one of my Twitter followers shot back: "And now after 23 years the NYT is a reliable source? [Your] credibility is evaporating by the day. . . ." Note that he did not object to or take issue with any of the reporting in the story; it was not even clear he had even read the actual article. What he objected to was the source itself. For this follower, nothing, absolutely nothing, from the *New York Times* was credible.

During the campaign, I had one loyal listener whom I will call Rob. Virtually on a daily basis, Rob would send emails to his family and friends commenting on the news and highlighting examples of media bias (which were plentiful). But in 2016, he began linking to stories from some of the new sites that trafficked in conspiracy theories. Because I knew Rob to be a good and decent guy (we had actually worked together on a project involving veterans), I gently tried to nudge him back toward the mainstream, without any discernible effect. Instead, he seemed to move rapidly in the opposite direction, unembarrassed even when I pointed out that he was sending out stories that were clearly erroneous.

In June 2016, he sent me an email, objecting to the fact that during one of my discussions, I had cited an NBC news report. "I never thought I'd hear you referencing NBC information as valid," he wrote. Probably unwisely, I responded that I found his criticisms ironic since he was now routinely linking to "some of the sketchiest, most frequently discredited websites on earth" and I suggested that "you are better than this."

By August, however, Rob had apparently become obsessed with discrediting the parents of a Muslim army officer who had been killed in

Iraq. Khzir Khan's speech at the Democratic National Convention criticizing Trump was an emotional and political highlight of the event, and Trump's subsequent attacks on the Gold Star parents temporarily hurt him in the polls. Following a now-familiar path, many right-wing sites, including Breitbart, launched a furious attack on Khan, alleging his support for Sharia law and his financial ties to the Clintons. Rob was fired up and began sending around multiple stories attacking Khan and his wife, Ghazala. Many of them were misleading, some of them just offensive, but I found that my attempts to correct the record were futile; there was always another source, another website with a questionable "fact" about the couple.

In August, I responded to one of Rob's many emails. I'll include it here because it gives a sense of my frustration:

> This article is a piece of bigoted bilge. I have no idea what makes you think that this attack on the parents is justified, or why you would send it to me. I know you as a patriotic, decent man who admires and respects truth. But you have fallen deeper and deeper into this dark vortex of alt-right misinformation.
>
> Please ask yourself: are you willing to give up your principles, your standards, and basic common decency for . . . Donald Trump.

Rob responded frankly: "Yes," he wrote, "I am willing to set aside some principles to defeat Clinton, for a time, for the sake of my country and future generations. . . ." Choosing Trump "is one helluva lot better than a known anti-American, greedy criminal like Hillary."*

---

*I had Rob, and dozens of others like him, in mind when I spoke with Oliver Darcy in August 2016:

Let's say that Donald Trump basically makes whatever you want to say, whatever claim he wants to make. And everybody knows it's a falsehood. The big question of my audience, it is impossible for me to say that, "By the way, you know it's false." And they'll say, "Why? I saw it on Allen B. West." Or they'll say, "I saw it on a Facebook page." And I'll say, "The *New*

EMPOWERING ALT REALITY NEWS MEDIA

All of this is likely going to get worse.

At an event shortly after President Trump's inauguration, Gateway Pundit's Jim Hoft announced that his blog "is going to have a White House correspondent position," bragging that he "had 1 million readers a day coming in. And the reason was because I was telling the truth and the mainstream media was telling the fake fucking news!" Hoft's audience, which had gathered to "celebrate memeing a president into existence," responded by chanting "Real news! Real news! Real news!"[27]

Irony had already taken a beating during the 2016 campaign, but this was nevertheless an extraordinary moment, given Gateway Pundit's notorious reputation for pushing bogus narratives and outright hoaxes. In the weeks leading up to the election, the *Washington Post* noted, Hoft's website had "regularly published outright false stories that became talking points on the conservative Internet."[28] Media critic Callum Borchers described Hoft as "an appallingly unreliable source of information. . . . If you have a conspiracy theory or a hoax you want to spread, Hoft is your guy."[29]

There was the time that Gateway Pundit featured the headline "WOW! Look at MASSIVE LINE to Trump's Town Hall Event," when the picture was actually a picture from the parade following the Cleveland Cavaliers' NBA Finals victory.[30] Or the breathless story in which Gateway Pundit reported that a San Diego high school had canceled "Obama Invite After Discovering His Birth Certificate Was Fake." Unfortunately for Jim Hoft, the article he cited (and which was widely shared on conservative media) was a satire piece. (Gateway Pundit later removed the post.)[31] Gateway Pundit also disseminated a hoax claiming that an organization called Demand Protest was providing

---

York Times did a fact check." And they'll say, "Oh, that's the New York Times. That's bulls—." There's nobody—you can't go to anybody and say, "Look, here are the facts." (Oliver Darcy, "Donald Trump Broke the Conservative Media," *Business Insider,* August 26, 2016.)

paid anti-Trump protesters. He also eagerly forwarded a fake Facebook page that a mass shooter was an Obama fan.[32]

In the weeks before the election, Gateway Pundit headlined a story about apparent voter fraud in North Carolina, only to have the story exposed as an internet joke.[33] As the controversy over Hillary Clinton's emails dogged her campaign, Gateway Pundit reported in late October that Clinton's campaign manager Robby Mook had deleted all of his tweets because he was "spooked" by an FBI investigation: "MOOK SPOOKED: Hillary Campaign Manager Deletes Twitter Timeline."[34] Fact-checkers quickly debunked the bogus story, with the website Snopes.com referring to Gateway Pundit as "disreputable," and "factually-challenged."

But this did not deter the site from continuing to spread hoaxes about disappearing social media posts. Days before the election, Gateway Pundit falsely reported that "Michelle Obama has scrubbed all references to Hillary Clinton from both of her Twitter accounts" with the headline: "Rats Jump Ship⇒ Michelle Obama Scrubs Hillary Clinton from Twitter History?" This was a story whose veracity could easily have been checked by anyone who cared about that sort of thing, but it was quickly picked up by conservative commentators. On his radio show, Sean Hannity eagerly picked up on the fake story, exclaiming, "That means they know it's huge. You know why? Because Obama's implicated! He's implicated here, and he's pissed. You know what his legacy might be? Jail." When it became apparent the story was a hoax, Hannity was forced to issue a retraction and blamed Gateway Pundit for the error.[35]

Despite having been burned by the fake news site, Hannity continued linking to it. In February 2017, Hoft's site breathlessly reported, "Wikileaks Document Shows John McCain Requested Donations from Russians." Mimicking a Russian propaganda outlet, Gateway's post began with the sentence "John McCain is leading a vicious campaign against the Russian government since the November election."[36]

Nevertheless, Hannity retweeted a link that called the decorated veteran a "globalist war criminal," with the comment, "WOW if True." But as it turned out, nothing in the story was true. There was no

WikiLeaks release and the "request" for campaign money was a report from 2008 about a standard mass fund-raising mailer that had been addressed to "Dear Friend." Once again, Hannity was forced to apologize for sharing what he admitted was an "inaccurate" story he had gotten from the website.[37]

This might not matter all that much, except that Gateway Pundit emerged as a go-to news source for the Trump campaign and Donald Trump himself. One analysis in December 2016 found that Trump had tweeted out links from the site fourteen times during the campaign.[38] Even after the election, newly installed White House Press Secretary Sean Spicer continued to tweet out links to Gateway Pundit—which seemed consistent for an administration that has already introduced Americans to the concept of "alternative facts."[39]

Gateway Pundit was not alone. Social media activist Michael Cernovich also enjoyed friendly ties to the Trump White House, despite his reputation for spreading bizarre conspiracy theories such as "pizzagate," an outlandish story that tried to link members of Hillary's Clinton's campaign to a child-sex-trafficking ring operated out of a pizza parlor in Washington, DC. Cernovich, who once said that he had embraced the Alt Right after realizing that "diversity is code for white genocide," enthusiastically touted the story, which he described as both "worldwide" and "real."[40] The fake news nearly turned deadly when a gunman claiming to "self-investigate" the story fired a shot inside the pizza parlor, Comic Ping Pong, which had been falsely linked to the alleged sex trafficking ring. Days later, Trump fired the son of Lieutenant General Michael Flynn from his transition team for using his Twitter account to spread the "pizzagate" story.[41] (Flynn himself was later fired as national security adviser for lying to Vice President Mike Pence about his conversations with the Russian ambassador during the transition.)

But Cernovich continued to prosper in Trump World. In April 2017, after was he was featured on CBS's *60 Minutes*, White House aide Kellyanne Conway called his appearance a "must-see ratings bonanza" and urged followers to watch the full exchange with CBS anchor Scott Pelley.[42] The next day, the president's son, Donald J. Trump Jr., tweeted out: "Congrats to @Cernovich for breaking the #SusanRice story. In a long gone time of unbiased journalism he'd win the Pulitzer, but not today!"[43]*

Others in the Right's media ecosystem took note, including Fox News, which posted a story headlined: "Pro-Trump blogger Cernovich getting big scoops, mainstream attention." The article described the new alternative reality: "A year ago, Mike Cernovich was a fringe blogger posting a blend of pro-Trump memes and self-help tips from his home base in Southern California. Today, he's beating the mainstream media to some of the Trump era's biggest news stories."[44]

---

* The "Susan Rice story," referred to a report that the former national security adviser to President Obama had been involved in the surveillance of members of the Trump transition team and had asked for some of the names to be "unmasked." The story was touted by Trump, who had accused Obama of "wiretapping" Trump Tower, a claim for which he offered no proof and that was denied by law enforcement and intelligence officials.

CHAPTER 9

DRUDGE AND THE
POLITICS OF PARANOIA

SOMETIME IN THE LAST decade, conservative commentator Matt Drudge began linking to a website run by conspiracy theorist Alex Jones. By doing so, he broke down the wall that separated the full-blown cranks from the mainstream conservative media, injecting a toxic worldview into the Right's bloodstream. The conservative movement never recovered.

If you want to understand the nature of the Right's alternative reality, or its vulnerability to "fake news," you need to start with Jones and Drudge. The Drudge Report consistently ranks as one of the top five media publishers in the country, often drawing more than a billion page views a month.[1] Media critic John Ziegler describes Matt Drudge as effectively the "assignment editor" for much of talk radio, many right-leaning websites, and a significant portion of the Fox News channel. "If Drudge wants a certain narrative to gain traction in conservative circles, he has more power to make that happen than anyone else," he writes. The gravitational pull of the Drudge Report is so powerful, Ziegler notes, "that when it becomes clear what narrative Matt is favoring, a literal 'market' is created for stories which fit that storyline so that they might be linked on the Drudge Report." Conservative media types were also reluctant to cross Drudge. "If . . . you can't get your content linked on Drudge," explains Ziegler, "or appear on Fox News, your career is, at best, stunted and, at worst, over."[2]

Alex Jones is not your garden-variety conspiracy theorist. He is a 9/11 truther, who believes the U.S. government conspired in the attacks to justify the creation of a police state.* On his website, Infowars, Jones has suggested that the government also may have been behind the bombings in Oklahoma City, which killed 168 people, and at the Boston Marathon, which killed 3. Jones claimed that the Oklahoma City bombing was an inside job and "a total false flag." He suggested that the Boston Marathon bombing was a "staged event." The bombers, he said, "are definitely patsies that were set up and they're manipulating our tribalism that, 'Hey, the guys from the other tribe bombed us but we got them.' When the truth is they were young men recruited by

---

*In a 2005 film, *Martial Law 9-11: Rise of the Police State,* Jones laid out his theory of what happened on September 11, 2001:
Once the decoys, known as hijackers, were on board the planes, a gas was released knocking out the occupants of the aircraft. Then a small criminal group in control of remote control systems patented for over 20 years took control of the aircraft and flew them into the World Trade Centers and Pentagon. The CIA controlled drills that morning, confused NORAD for over an hour until it was almost too late for them to shoot down the hijacked planes. I said almost too late. When they did find out, Dick Cheney wouldn't let the planes fly over 350 miles an hour so three of the aircraft were able to hit their targets. The fourth wasn't able to because our sources in the Pentagon have told us generals didn't follow their orders and had Flight 93 shot down. If it would have hit its target, the Capitol, the government would have been completely decapitated and the president could have declared total martial law.

globalist intelligence agencies and set up horribly. And they could do it to any of us. We're all in grave danger."[3]

He has repeatedly suggested that the mass shooting at Sandy Hook was a hoax, calling it "a synthetic completely fake with actors, in my view, manufactured. I couldn't believe it at first. I knew they had actors there, clearly, but I thought they killed some real kids. And it just shows how bold they are, that they clearly used actors. I mean they even ended up using photos of kids killed in mass shootings here in a fake mass shooting in Turkey—so yeah, or Pakistan. The sky is now the limit."[4]

Similarly, Jones has told his audiences that the mass murder at a movie theater in Aurora, Colorado, "was a false flag, mind-control event." He also believes that the Columbine school shootings were "100 percent false flag." Ditto for the attacks at a nightclub in Orlando and San Bernardino.[5]

Jones also has charged that the government wants to use chemicals to turn people gay: "I have the government documents where they said they're going to encourage homosexuality with chemicals so that people don't have children." He has frequently referred to women as "tramps," "whore," and "bitch." In 2016, less than a month before the election, he declared that Hillary Clinton was "a frickin' demon and she stinks and so does Obama." Even by Jones's standards his preelection rant was extraordinary.

I'm never a lesser of two evils person, but with Hillary, there's not even the same universe. She is an abject, psychopathic, demon from Hell that as soon as she gets into power is going to try to destroy the planet. I'm sure of that, and people around her say she's so dark now, and so evil, and so possessed that they are having nightmares, they're freaking out. Folks let me just tell you something, and if media wants to go with this, that's fine. There are dozens of videos and photos of Obama having flies land on him, indoors, at all times of year, and he'll be next to a hundred people and no one has flies on them. Hillary, reportedly, I mean, I was told by people around her that they think she's demon-possessed, okay? I'm just going to go ahead and say it, okay?

[. . .]

Imagine how bad she smells, man? I'm told her and Obama, just stink, stink, stink, stink. You can't wash that evil off, man. Told there's a rotten smell around Hillary. I'm not kidding, people say, they say—folks, I've been told this by high up folks. They say listen, Obama and Hillary both smell like sulfur. I never said this because the media will go crazy with it, but I've talked to people that are in protective details, they're scared of her. And they say listen, she's a frickin' demon and she stinks and so does Obama. I go, like what? Sulfur. They smell like Hell.[6]

In other words, Jones peddles weapons-grade nut jobbery—but he is promoted by one of the most heavily trafficked websites in the country and may have played a key role in the 2016 presidential campaign. Jones has claimed that he has 5 million daily listeners of his radio shows, which he simulcasts on his website and extends through his YouTube channel. During the campaign, Trump appeared on Jones's show and lavished praise on the conspiracy theorist. "Your reputation is amazing, I will not let you down," Trump told Jones in a December 2015 appearance.[7] "I think Alex Jones may be the single most important voice in the alternative conservative media," says Trump whisperer Roger Stone, who describes the conspiracy theorist as "a valuable asset" who will "rally the people around President Trump's legislative program."[8] (During a child custody hearing in 2017, Jones's lawyer insisted that the host was "playing a character," describing him as "a performance artist." Jones himself disputed those characterizations.)[9] On the Monday after the election, Donald Trump called Jones to thank him for his support in the campaign. The newly elected president promised Jones he would return to his show, a pledge that the *Washington Post* called "an extraordinary gesture for an incoming president whose schedule is packed with calls from world leaders and the enormous task of overseeing the transition."[10]

Even more extraordinary was the fact that the leader of the free world actually paid attention to this guy.

THE DRUDGE-JONES NEXUS

By 2013, the year that Drudge once proclaimed would be the "year of Alex Jones," the Drudge Report had become a powerful online conduit for Jones's conspiracy theories. In mid-2011, the Drudge Report featured the link to a story about Texas governor Rick Perry, who was then mulling a presidential bid: "Infowars.com: Bilderberg Approved Perry Set to Become GOP Frontrunner." The first paragraph of the piece was vintage Jones:

> Every indication suggests that Bilderberg-approved Texas Governor Rick Perry is set to become the front runner in the Republican race to challenge Barack Obama for the presidency, illustrating once again *how a shady, secretive and undemocratic global elite holds the reigns [sic] of true power while Americans are distracted by the delusional notion that they have a genuine choice in 2012.* [Emphasis added.][11]

The rant captured Jones's paranoid worldview, questioning whether the electoral process had become a fraud, and positing the existence of a vast and dark global conspiracy in language that would make an appearance on the presidential campaign trail in 2016. A contributor to the conservative blog *RedState* noted that this was apparently not the first time Drudge had linked to "that charlatan Alex Jones," but warned that "Drudge loses credibility by linking such crap on his site."[12]

But the Drudge-Jones relationship was actually ramping up. In a 2011 interview with *New York* magazine, Jones credited Drudge with helping to supercharge Infowars. Jones told the magazine, "If you had to say there was one source who really helped us break out, who took our information, helped to punch it out to an even more effective level, he's the guy." He continued, "Three years ago, there was almost no news coverage of Bilderberg [an elite conference] in this country; there was an electronic Berlin Wall. Drudge, every year, takes our reportage and links to it on our site."[13]

Jones also noted that it was "intensifying how much he links to us and promotes us." During the 2010 Christmas season, for example, all of the links on the Drudge Report were turned green, except links to Infowars, which Drudge published in red. "It was like a Christmas present," says Jones.

By April 2013, an analysis by the left-wing organization Media Matters found that Drudge had linked to Jones at least 244 different times since 2011, including 50 so far in 2013:

> Among the fifty Infowars pieces promoted by Drudge so far in 2013: a story mulling over claims that Venezuelan President Hugo Chavez may have been "surreptitiously" given cancer, possibly by the U.S. government; numerous articles promoting conspiracies about supposedly ominous ammunition purchases made by the Department of Homeland Security; and a story comparing Obama to "other tyrants"—including Stalin, Hitler, and Mao—that have "used kids as props."[14]

But this was relatively modest stuff. Among the stories that Drudge had specifically highlighted, Media Matters for America found:

> —A November 2012 article promoting claims that James Holmes, the man currently on trial for the mass shooting at an Aurora, Colorado, movie theater, may actually have been under the influence of CIA "mind control." The piece was based around a story told by an "alleged inmate" supposedly in jail with Holmes, who claimed Holmes told him he was "programmed" to kill by an "evil" therapist.

> —A July 2012 post highlighting an interview between Jones and Joseph Farah, editor of conspiracy website World Net Daily (WND). During that interview, Farah suggested that if Obama were reelected, people like him and Jones would be "hunted down like dogs."

—A March 2012 piece suggesting that the death of conservative publisher Andrew Breitbart may not have been the result of natural causes, but instead related to a "damning" video about President Obama Breitbart had supposedly planned to release the day of his death.

—An April 2011 article responding to President Obama's release of his long-form birth certificate headlined, "New Obama Birth Certificate is a Forgery." The story states: "Our investigation of the purported Obama birth certificate released by Hawaiian authorities today reveals the document is a shoddily contrived hoax. Infowars.com computer specialists dismissed the document as a fraud soon after examining it."[15]

During this same period, Drudge also regularly promoted stories from World Net Daily, which trafficked heavily in stories questioning Obama's birth certificate. But the relationship with Jones was more personal and, over time, troubling. Or at least it should have been troubling for others in the conservative media. In actuality, though, only a few online commentators chided Drudge—and did so mildly. "I'd love it if Drudge report stopped linking to Infowars," said one.[16] But there is no indication that Drudge suffered any significant backlash or loss of influence from his advocacy for Jones and his bizarre worldview.

A 2015 interview of Drudge on Jones's show revealed the depths of the two men's mutual admiration. Jones admitted he was "star-struck" by seeing Drudge in person, while Drudge lavished the conspiracy theorist with praise:

You're a romantic figure, Alex, in Americana. It's romantic what you do here every day. It just is. This is romance. Because you're an American standing up, tough, facing these headwinds. Wow are they blowing. But you're there. And you're not alone. Limbaugh, Savage, Hannity, Levin. There's a lot of people on the airwaves who are as brave. They are brave, and they are living it. I've met 'em all. I'm friends with them all. They are also operating against the grain in an America that needs to go back to that.[17]

CNN's Dylan Byers wrote that the forty-five-minute interview "oscillated wildly between familiar critiques of the establishment and paranoid conspiracy theories with little basis in reality. At one point, Drudge suggested that the Obama administration came up with the name 'ISIS'—for the Islamic State in Iraq and Syria—because it sounded like the last name of Rep. Darrell Issa, the Chairman of the House Oversight and Government Reform Committee."[18]

The two men also discussed an issue that would come to prominence in the 2016 campaign: Hillary Clinton's health. During that campaign, as part of their advocacy for Trump, both Drudge and Jones would relentlessly push various conspiracy theories about Clinton, which they foreshadowed in the 2015 interview.

DRUDGE: You've got to be the greatest you can be. Now. Now. Before this country is so completely altered and we're left with Hillary's brain in the Oval Office in a jar. 'Cuz that's what we're getting. She is old and she's sick. She is not a contender. They're making her a contender with these propped up Saturday Night Live things. It's like a head on a stick.[19]

THE POLITICS OF PARANOIA

In retrospect, Richard Hofstadter's 1964 essay, "The Paranoid Style in American Politics," seems eerily prescient.[20] Some conservatives have dismissed Hofstadter's argument as a slander of the conservative movement and, indeed, he seemed to be describing the culture of the fringe that was excommunicated during the Buckley-era purges. But rereading it in the age of Trump reminds us that the Right has harbored some darker impulses for decades.

The lengthy piece, which appeared in *Harper's* magazine, created a sensation when it was published in the midst of the Johnson-Goldwater campaign. Hofstadter, a professor of history at Columbia University, was awarded the Pulitzer Prize for his book in 1964. The essay was adapted from a lecture he had delivered at Oxford University in November 1963. In his lecture and the subsequent essay, Hofstadter described the culture, mind-set, and tactics of what he saw as a new style of paranoid politics in the United States.

The paranoid spokesman, he wrote, saw the world "in apocalyptic terms—he traffics in the birth and death of whole worlds, whole political orders, whole systems of human values. He is always manning the barricades of civilization. He constantly lives at a turning point. Like religious millennialists he expresses the anxiety of those who are living through the last days and he is sometimes disposed to set a date for the apocalypse." He quoted John Birch Society's Robert Welch's warning in 1951: "Time is running out. Evidence is piling up on many sides and from many sources that October 1952 is the fatal month when Stalin will attack." (As we'll see later, this style of urgent rhetoric became characteristic of the argument that the 2016 election was an end-of-the-world "binary choice.")

At the center of the paranoid worldview, wrote Hofstadter, was an "appeal to a lost America," a sense on the Right that "America has been largely taken away from them and their kind, though they are determined to try to repossess it and to prevent the final destructive act of subversion." His description could easily have been applied to Donald Trump (or the Tea Party) fifty years later:

> The old American virtues have already been eaten away by cosmopolitans and intellectuals; the old competitive capitalism has been gradually undermined by socialistic and communistic schemers; the old national security and independence have been destroyed by treasonous plots, having as their most powerful agents not merely outsiders and foreigners as of old but major statesmen who are at the very centers of American power.[21]

Since the situation is so dire and the stakes so high, the paranoid spokes-man is not interested in half-measures. "He does not see social conflict as something to be mediated and compromised, in the manner of the working politician," Hofstadter wrote, describing what would become the Right's cycle of disappointment. "This demand for total triumph leads to the formulation of hopelessly unrealistic goals, and since these goals are not even remotely attainable, failure constantly heightens the paranoid's sense of frustration."

All the while, he wrote, the paranoid was striving to create an alternative reality, piling up documentation and evidence to back even its most outlandish fantasies. "The higher paranoid scholarship is noth-ing if not coherent—in fact the paranoid mind is far more coherent than the real world. It is nothing if not scholarly in technique," he wrote. He noted that Robert Welch's attack on Dwight Eisenhower, *The Politician,* had one hundred pages of bibliography and notes. "The entire right-wing movement of our time," Hofstadter wrote in 1964, "is a parade of experts, study groups, monographs, footnotes, and biblio-graphies." The distinctive characteristic of the "evidence" collected by the paranoid was that it was gathered as ammunition to prove a preex-isting point rather than any sort of a search for actual truth. "The par-anoid seems to have little expectation of actually convincing a hostile world," Hofstadter argued, "but he can accumulate evidence in order to protect his cherished convictions from it."[22]

In recent years, Hofstadter's essay has enjoyed a resurgence of in-terest. In 2010, for example, a writer in Salon noted that "The Paranoid Style in American Politics" reads "like a playbook for the career of Glenn Beck, right down to the paranoid's 'quality of pedantry' and 'heroic strivings for 'evidence,' embodied in Beck's chalkboard and piles of books. . . . Is it any wonder, then, that a growing number of Americans insist on believing that Barack Obama is a secret Muslim?"[23]

"CHRISTIANITY'S CRAZY UNCLE"

Even after the excommunication of the John Birch Society from the con-servative movement in the 1960s, this sort of virulent paranoid strain remained alive, including in the newly resurgent religious Right, which proved to be fertile ground for some of the fruitier theories. For decades one of its most prominent figures, Pat Robertson, trafficked in conspiracy theories, sharing with his audience warnings about schemes by the Illuminati, Freemasons, and Jewish bankers to impose a Satanic "New World Order."

Within the rising Christian Right, Robertson was a hugely influential figure; he had founded the Christian Broadcast Network in 1960 and expanded his domain to include Regent University (formerly CBN University), the American Center for Law and Justice, and a network of radio, television, and print outlets. Robertson parlayed his prominence into a GOP presidential bid in 1988, finishing strongly in Iowa and winning in Washington, Nevada, Alaska, and Hawaii. In 1989, he helped launch the Christian Coalition, an organization that would have an enormous impact on Republican politics.

Even as his influence grew, however, Robertson developed a reputation for cringe-inducing commentary on current events. In a 1985 book, he wondered, "Are credit cards associated with the mark of the beast?" Robertson also repeatedly suggested that a variety of disasters, including Hurricane Katrina, were actually God's punishments. He attributed the 2010 earthquake in Haiti to a centuries-old deal in which Haitians "swore a pact to the devil."[24] In 2006, he suggested that a stroke suffered by Israeli prime minister Ariel Sharon might have been punishment for Sharon's decision to disengage from Gaza. "God has enmity against those who, quote 'divide my land,'" Robertson declared. "And I would say, Woe unto any prime minister of Israel who takes a similar course to appease the E.U., the United Nations or the United States of America. God says, This land belongs to me. You better leave it alone." The 1995 assassination of former Israeli prime minister Yitzhak Rabin was, Robertson said, "the same thing."[25]

Robertson's comments earned a rebuke from the Anti-Defamation League:

It is outrageous and shocking, but not surprising, that Pat Robertson once again has suggested that God will punish Israel's leaders for any decision to give up land to the Palestinians. His remarks are un-Christian and a perversion of religion. Unlike Robertson, we don't see God as cruel and vengeful.

We would hope that good Christian leaders would distance themselves from Pat Robertson's remarks. It is pure arrogance for Robertson to suggest that he has divine knowledge of God's intent and purpose based on his interpretation of scripture.

After the September 11, 2001, terrorist attacks that killed thousands of Americans, Robertson implied that America had brought the tragedy on itself. "We have insulted God at the highest level of our government. Then, we say, 'Why does this happen?' It is happening because God Almighty is lifting His protection from us."[26]

Jerry Falwell Sr., the founder of the Moral Majority, echoed his remarks in an appearance on Robertson's television show, *The 700 Club*, suggesting that gays, abortion-rights supporters, and liberal civil-rights activists shared the blame for the horrific attacks: "[T]he pagans and the abortionists and the feminists and the gays and the lesbians who are actively trying to make that an alternative lifestyle, the ACLU, People for the American Way—all of them who have tried to secularize America," Falwell continued, "I point the finger in their face and say 'you helped this happen.'"

"Well, I totally concur," responded Robertson.[27]

But Robertson achieved peak crackpottery with the publication in 1991 of his book *The New World Order*, a comprehensive anthology of paranoid fever dreams.[28] In the book, one reviewer noted, Robertson claimed to be revealing "a global conspiracy, stretching back centuries and financed by Jewish bankers, all aimed at the formation of a one-world dictatorship. The brains behind this conspiracy, Robertson said, was Satan, who at that time was working through his unwitting patsy, President George H. W. Bush." The goal of this vast scheme was to create "a one-world government, a one-world army, a one-world economy under an Anglo-Saxon financial oligarchy, and a world dictator served by a council of twelve faithful men."[29] Among Christian conservatives, the book became an immense bestseller, even making the *New York Times* bestseller list.

Author Daniel Pipes explained Robertson's thesis:

> This tyranny will attempt to "destroy the Christian faith" and "replace it with an occult-inspired world socialist dictatorship." In another place, he foresees nothing less than a world under "the domination of Lucifer and his followers" in which spiritual forces will be set into motion "which no human being will be strong enough to contain." Robertson offers Hitler's attempts at world hegemony as the closest historical parallel to the "giant prison" of the New World Order.[30]

Robertson told his followers that this immense international conspiracy was secretly manipulated by the secretive Order of the Illuminati, Freemasons, the Trilateral Commission, the Council on Foreign Relations and, of course, Jewish bankers. Robertson was later subjected to harsh criticism for citing *The Protocols of the Elders of Zion*, a notorious anti-Semitic bit of fake history to make his case.[31] In his defense, Robertson echoed the paranoid activists described by Hofstadter, insisting that his book had been meticulously researched and documented, claims that were quickly debunked.[32]

As striking as Robertson's descent into conspiracy mongering may have been, the response was equally illuminating. Because the Christian Right had become such a critical part of the conservative coalition, few conservatives were willing to break with Robertson. This remained true long after Robertson had established himself as "Christianity's crazy uncle." After the Anti-Defamation League criticized some elements of the religious Right for dabbling in anti-Semitic tropes, prominent conservatives rushed to the defense, accusing the ADL of "anti-Christian" and "antireligious" bias.[33]

Most conservatives did not, of course, take Robertson's ideas seriously. For the most part, his bizarre notions were met with eye rolls, but seldom with censure. Conservative thought leaders looked the other way. As a result, for years elements of the conservative coalition marinated in a toxic stew of conspiracy theories.

Not surprisingly, that had consequences.

BIRTHER-IN-CHIEF

For many on the Right, the ur-conspiracy theory of the Obama presidency was the notion that Obama had not been born in the United States and was therefore not constitutionally eligible to be president. An entire cottage industry of "birthers" sprang up, complete with elaborate attempts to document the "evidence" that Obama was, in fact, a secret Kenyan. Arguably, Donald Trump launched his successful presidential bid by seizing upon the issue, which he milked for the maximum amount of publicity. Trump would eventually disavow birtherism in the final months of the 2016 campaign, while attempting to blame its origins (falsely) on his rival Hillary Clinton. But for five years, Trump had questioned Obama's birthplace.

In March 2011, Trump appeared on the *Laura Ingraham Show* to declare: "He doesn't have a birth certificate, or if he does, there's something on that certificate that is very bad for him. Now, somebody told me—and I have no idea if this is bad for him or not, but perhaps it would be—that where it says 'religion,' it might have 'Muslim.' And if you're a Muslim, you don't change your religion, by the way."[34] On CNN, he escalated his rhetoric, saying that "if he wasn't born in this country, he shouldn't be the president of the United States." After Obama produced the certificate in April 2011, Trump briefly acknowledged his legitimacy, but quickly seemed to recant, saying "a lot of people do not think it was an authentic certificate."

To be sure, some conservatives with megaphones denounced the birthers. Early on, talk show host Michael Medved called the movement's leaders "crazy, nutburger, demagogue, money-hungry, exploitative, irresponsible, filthy conservative imposters" who had become "the worst enemy of the conservative movement." Birtherism, he said, "makes us look weird. It makes us look crazy. It makes us look demented. It makes us look sick, troubled, and not suitable for civilized company."[35]

But despite repeated attempts to debunk the theory, many leading Republicans either stayed silent or refused to forcefully denounce the theories that were springing up. One reason for their reluctance was that "birtherism" was not a fringe notion in the GOP. A Public Policy Poll in February 2011 found that birthers had become a majority among likely Republican primary voters—51 percent said they did not think Barack Obama was born in the United States. Less than one third of GOP voters—28 percent—said they firmly believed that he was born here, while 21 percent weren't sure.[36]

Those numbers helped explain why so many leading Republicans were reluctant to forcefully denounce the attempt to delegitimize the nation's first African American president. The poll also suggested, as Steve Benen noted in the *Washington Monthly*, that "candidates hoping to run sane campaigns will be at a disadvantage in the coming months." Republican voters who doubted Obama's legitimacy tended to gravitate to candidates like Sarah Palin, Newt Gingrich, and Mike Huckabee (all of whom would play key roles in Trump's 2016 campaign).[37]

Throughout 2012, Trump used Twitter to attack Obama's legitimacy. In one tweet, Trump insisted that "an extremely credible source" had told him that the certificate was "a fraud." Trump continually pressured other Republicans to embrace birtherism. In May 2012, Trump tweeted that Obama "is practically begging" GOP front-runner Mitt Romney "to disavow the place of birth movement, he is afraid of it." But Romney had notably gone out of his way to accept Trump's endorsement. "When he accepted Trump's endorsement during the 2012 Republican primaries," E. J. Dionne noted, "Mitt Romney was positively giddy. . . ."[38]

The mogul continued his birther rants:

In August 2012, he tweeted: "Why do the Republicans keep apologizing on the so called 'birther' issue? No more apologies— take the offensive!"

In September: "Wake Up America! See article: 'Israeli Science: Obama Birth Certificate is a Fake.'"

Even after the election, Trump trafficked in elaborate conspiracy theories. In 2013, he tweeted: "How amazing, the State Health Director who verified copies of Obama's 'birth certificate' died in plane crash today. All others lived."* As late as 2014, Trump invited hackers to "please hack Obama's college records (destroyed?) and check 'place of birth.'"[39]

Throughout his political career, the *New York Times*'s Michael Barbaro wrote, Trump was known for his "casual elasticity with the truth," exhausting "an army of fact-checkers with his mischaracterizations, exaggerations and fabrications." But Barbaro wrote, "This lie was different from the start, an insidious, calculated calumny that sought to undo the embrace of an African American president by the 69 million voters who elected him in 2008."[40] And yet, as they embraced Trump's candidacy, a majority of conservatives clearly did not think that the lie, or its underlying racism, was disqualifying for the presidency. By failing to push back against the birther conspiracy theories, conservatives had faced a moral and intellectual test with significant implications for the future. It was a test they failed.

TRUMP'S GRAND UNIFIED CAMPAIGN CONSPIRACY THEORY

Near the end of his presidential campaign, when Trump laid out his theory of a vast globalist conspiracy it caused barely a ripple on the Right, because the ground had been prepared for years for this kind of rhetoric:

---

* "An autopsy said her cause of death was 'acute cardiac arrhythmia due to hyperventilation.'" —"Hawaii Health Director Killed after Plane Crash Had Infant Life Vest," *Hawaii News Now,* March 5, 2016.

Hillary Clinton meets in secret with international banks to plot the destruction of U.S. sovereignty in order to enrich these global financial powers, her special interest friends and her donors.

It's a global power structure that is responsible for the economic decisions that have robbed our working class, stripped our country of its wealth, and put that money into the pockets of a handful of large corporations and political entities," Trump continued. "We've seen this firsthand in the WikiLeaks documents in which Hillary Clinton meets in secret with international banks to plot the destruction of U.S. sovereignty in order to enrich these global financial powers, her special-interest friends, and her donors.[41]

Time magazine called this his "Grand Unified Campaign Conspiracy Theory" that drew upon "conspiracy theories that have been nurtured for years by far-right-wing outlets like InfoWars, which has been a home for 9/11 'truthers,' and unfounded claims about the Bilderberg Group and the World Economic Forum."[42]

Jewish groups, who recognized the echoes in Trump's language, were alarmed.* Jonathan Greenblatt, the CEO of the Anti-Defamation League, quickly tweeted that Trump "should avoid rhetoric and tropes

---

*Trump's rhetoric inspired comparisons between the language he was deploying and *The Protocols of the Elders of Zion*, the infamous forgery has long been a staple of anti-Semitism—and an early example of the sort of fake news that would plague the campaign. Writer Ron Kampeas called attention to the parallel themes:

> TRUMP: Our great civilization here in America and across the civilized world has come across a moment of reckoning. We've seen it in the United Kingdom, where they voted to liberate themselves from global government and global trade deals and global immigration deals that have destroyed their sovereignty and have destroyed many of those nations. The central base of world political power is right here in America, our corrupt political establishment that is the greatest power behind the efforts at radical globalization and the disenfranchisement of working people.

that historically have been used against Jews and still spur #antisemitism. Let's keep hate out of campaign." He expanded on his concerns:

> We've been troubled by the anti-Semites and racists during this political season, and we've seen a number of so-called Trump supporters peddling some of the worst stereotypes all through this year. And it's been concerning that [Donald Trump] hasn't spoken out forcefully against these people. It is outrageous to think that the candidate is sourcing material from some of the worst elements in our society.[43]

PROTOCOLS (from the introduction, written in the voice of a "scholar" who purports to be revealing a secret Jewish document): The nations of the West are being brought under international control at political, military and economic levels. They are rapidly in process of becoming controlled also on the social level. All alike are being told that their only hope lies in the surrender of national sovereignty.

TRUMP: The corporate media in our country is no longer involved in journalism, they are a political special interest, no different than any other . . . with an agenda, and the agenda is not for you, it's for themselves. . . . The establishment and their media enablers wield control over this nation through means that are very well known.

PROTOCOLS (in the voice of its fabricated Jewish "conspirators"): Through the Press, we have gained the power to influence while remaining ourselves in the shade: thanks to the Press we have got the gold in our hands, notwithstanding that we have had to gather it out of the oceans of blood and tears. (Ron Kampeas, "Donald Trump's 'International Bankers' Speech Leaves Some Uneasy," Jewish Telegraphic Agency, October 14, 2016.)

PART III

THE
TRUMPIAN
TAKEOVER

10

THE FOX NEWS PRIMARY

THERE IS NEITHER WORLD enough nor time here to recount the tangled and fraught relationship between Fox News and Donald Trump. At times, the network and the billionaire appeared to be on a collision course, as Trump berated its hosts, attacked its coverage, and boycotted one of its debates. Fox's initial hesitancy to embrace Trump provoked a heated backlash in the right's new media ecosystem and a graphic demonstration of the new media culture. Fox was effectively brought to heel after a sustained attack against it by Trump and his supporters at Breitbart. While much of the fire was directed at Megyn Kelly, the attacks were broader and deeper, with a specific theme. A report by the *Columbia Journalism Review* noted that "the five most-widely shared stories in which Breitbart refers to Fox are stories aimed to delegitimize Fox as the central arbiter of conservative news, tying it to immigration, terrorism and Muslims, and corruption." A sampling of Breitbart's juicier offerings:

The Anti-Trump Network: Fox News Money Flows into Open Borders Group;

NY Times Bombshell Scoop: Fox News Colluded with Rubio to Give Amnesty to Illegal Aliens;

Google and Fox TV Invite Anti-Trump, Hitler-Citing, Muslim Advocate to Join Next GOP TV-Debate;

Fox, Google Pick 1994 Illegal Immigrant To Ask Question In Iowa GOP Debate;

Fox News At Facebook Meeting Is Misdirection: Murdoch and Zuckerberg Are Deeply Connected Over Immigration.

As the *CJR* report observed: "The repeated theme of conspiracy, corruption, and media betrayal is palpable in these highly shared Breitbart headlines linking Fox News, Rubio, and illegal immigration."[1]

After jousting with Trump early in the campaign, and coming under such intense pressure from the candidate and the trolls, Fox News seemed to come down with an especially severe case of Stockholm Syndrome (in which hostages begin to sympathize with their captors). The network's coverage, especially the fawning treatment from Sean Hannity (who publicly announced his support for Trump), became increasingly friendly. By May 2016, conservative talk show host Mark Levin was accusing the network of acting like a "Donald Trump super PAC."[2]

ROGER AILES'S AMBITION

For conservatives, there were few gatekeepers more influential than Fox News. A 2014 Pew Poll measured the extraordinary influence of Fox News among conservatives. Nearly half of "consistently conservative" voters—47 percent—named Fox News as their "main source" for news about politics and government. No other source came close. Among those voters, 88 percent said they trusted Fox as a source. While media bubbles also exist on the left, no single source of information used by liberals comes close to the clout that Fox had with the right.[3]

"There would not have been a Tea Party without Fox," the cofounder of the national political action committee Tea Party Express later said.[4] Fox News boss Roger Ailes also changed the face and tone of the conservative movement. Ailes gave a platform to and conferred celebrity status on figures like Glenn Beck and, despite his doubts about the former Alaska governor, Sarah Palin. After Ailes's death, commentators noted that he was a transformational figure—perhaps *the* transformational figure—for both latter-day conservative media and Republican politics.

In his book about Ailes and Fox News, Gabriel Sherman quotes one Republican who is close to Ailes as saying that Ailes "thinks Palin is an idiot." Ailes, he said, "thinks she's stupid. He helped boost her up. People like Sarah Palin haven't elevated the conservative movement." Nevertheless, Ailes had reportedly given her a $1 million a year contract and built her a television studio in her home in Wasilla, Alaska, from where she helped set the tone of conservative discourse over the next few years.

Ailes was a pivotal figure in the new conservative media in a number of ways, but primarily for the way he aggressively and skillfully blended his political agenda with his network's programming. Because liberal media bias was considered a given, Fox News and others felt justified in embracing a policy of overt bias. There were notable exceptions, as Fox often did solid reporting ("Fair and Balanced"), featured an impressive cast of contributors, and had a number of credible hosts—including Kelly, Brit Hume, Chris Wallace, and Bret Baier.

But Ailes had an agenda and it was obvious to anyone around him, or anyone who watched his network. Beyond the short skirts and low décolletages for on-air women that Ailes preferred, there were stories that were hyped, narratives advanced, and candidates boosted. Sherman recounts the pressure that some reporters felt. In the 1990s, when reporter David Schuster "pursued Clinton, Ailes personally congratulated him. When he pursued Bush, his bosses questioned not only his objectivity, but his loyalty."[5]

Even as Fox grew its audience and its profits, Ailes had larger ambitions. Shortly after the 2010 midterm elections, according to Sherman, Ailes told network executives that the network was "making a lot of money—that's fine. But I want to elect the next president."[6] While Ailes would often deny that he was a "kingmaker," he actively tried to recruit presidential candidates, including General David Petraeus and New Jersey governor Chris Christie, who "had Fox News television values with a ready-made reel."[7] Not coincidentally, the crowded GOP presidential field in 2011 and the chaotic early debates had a distinctly Fox/Ailes vibe. The network held its first presidential debate in May 2011, featuring a mix of presidential wannabes, but no really big names. The debate, Sherman wrote, "confirmed what a mess the field was—a mess partly created by the loudmouths Ailes had given airtime to and a Tea Party he had nurtured."[8] But his influence was undeniable, and as the 2012 campaign became known as the "Fox News primary," some Republicans were already becoming concerned that it was playing too big a role in the process.

But Fox's influence would be magnified in 2016. Even in a year when much of the media simply abdicated their editorial responsibilities and turned over vast acreages of airtime to Trump, Fox's coverage stood out. Its credibility with the GOP base meant that it played a critical role in normalizing Trump's candidacy and making it acceptable to conservative primary voters. But it was not always easy. One Fox host told *Politico*'s Eliana Johnson that when Trump would lash out at Kelly, Ailes would tell him, "Hey, Donald, settle the fuck down."[9] The results were mixed.

Even so, by the time Trump locked up the GOP nomination in May, he had already decisively won the Fox News primary, getting more than twice as much airtime as any other candidate in the race. A breakdown by Media Matters found that from May 1, 2015, to May 3, 2016, Trump had made 243 appearances on Fox and had appeared on the network for more than 49 hours.[10] His closest rival, Ted Cruz, had only 122 appearances; he keenly felt the disparity. On the day his campaign ended,

Cruz accused Fox chairman Rupert Murdoch and Ailes of making "a decision to get behind Donald Trump and turning Fox News 'into the Donald Trump network 24/7.'" Murdoch, Cruz said, "is used to picking world leaders in Australia and the United Kingdom, running tabloids, and we're seeing it here at home. . . ."[11]

In her memoir, which was published shortly after the election, Megyn Kelly strongly suggested that Roger Ailes was actively colluding with the Trump campaign.[12] Before he was ousted over sexual harassment allegations, Ailes reportedly was advising Trump's campaign, even as he was shaping and directing Fox's coverage.[13] Days before Trump announced in July 2015, he reportedly had a lengthy private lunch with Ailes and the two men met several times over the next year and spoke "frequently" over the phone. According to a report by CNN's Dylan Byers and Dana Bash, "Even when Ailes and Trump appeared to be at war over Trump's treatment of Megyn Kelly, the two men kept the conversation going." (After he was ousted from Fox, Ailes briefly advised Trump directly and helped with his debate prep.)[14]

The two men, as it turned out, had a great deal in common. Indeed the blustery, egotistical, thin-skinned Ailes cultivated and nurtured a style and an ethic at Fox that was uniquely suited to the Age of Trump; or to look at it the other way around, Trump was the ideal candidate for the culture that Roger Ailes was putting on the air.

Throughout the campaign, Trump's attitude toward women was a chronic problem for conservatives. But Trump's behavior was never close to disqualifying for Ailes or for his top-rated host Bill O'Reilly. As reporter and author Gabriel Sherman noted, the network that "played an undeniable role in reshaping American politics over the last 20 years," had its own culture where the sexual harassment of women "was encouraged and protected." It was a culture, Sherman said, "where women felt pressured to participate in sexual activity with their superiors if they wanted to advance inside the company. And it was so—what was shocking to me was not that it occurred but that it was so explicit, that there was no subtext, there was no subtlety to it."[15] So it was perhaps not surprising that after the *Access Hollywood* video surfaced, in which Trump is caught bragging about being able to "grab 'em by the pussy," that Ailes and O'Reilly would provide him with valuable air cover at a pivotal moment in the campaign.

That pattern at Fox News would continue after the election. The appointment of Tucker Carlson to replace Megyn Kelly was a sign "of just how much [Fox Chairman Rupert] Murdoch wants to appease Trump," observed Gabriel Sherman.[16] Along with the decision to drop George Will and hire pro-Trump commentator Mollie Hemingway, the move's were widely interpreted as a signal that Fox will become even more overtly pro-Trump in the future than it was during the campaign. As president, Trump continues to be an avid viewer and often praises and promotes segments on Fox News, creating a remarkable symbiotic relationship between the White House and the network. Even after the abrupt and dramatic fall of Bill O'Reilly, that dynamic is unlikely to change. As Eliana Johnson noted, the network's pro-Trump shift had more to do with ratings than ideology. "If the network, broadly speaking, had ever been a serious venue for interrogating conservative ideas," she wrote, "that mission fell by the wayside as it became clear that Trump-friendly programming meant more viewers."[17]

CHAPTER 11

LIMBAUGH'S FLOP

There go the people. I must follow them, for I am their leader.*

ALTHOUGH HE INSISTED FOR months that he was not supporting Trump's presidential bid, few figures in the Right's media ecosystem did more to enable the billionaire's rise than Rush Limbaugh. There were other, more unhinged voices peddling conspiracy theories and outrage. But along with Fox News, Breitbart, and Drudge, Limbaugh was the loudest and most influential voice setting the table for a voter

---

*Attributed to Alexandre Ledru-Rollin, one of the leaders of the revolution of 1848 in France. Alvin R. Calman, *Ledru-Rollin and the Second French Republic.* Studies in History, Economics and Public Law, vol. 103, no. 2), 374 (1922), says Ledru-Rollin's use of "I am their chief; I must follow them" is probably apocryphal.

insurrection. Repeatedly, he warned his listeners about the dire and imminent threat posed to the nation's liberties by the "elites" of both parties.

In December 2015, Limbaugh stoked the fires of conservative outrage after Republicans agreed to a budget deal that even supporters regarded as a "crap sandwich." Citing the GOP victories of 2010 and 2014, Limbaugh declared that voters had "elected Republicans to stop this." But despite the Republican wins, Limbaugh said, "It hasn't made any difference at all. It is as though Nancy Pelosi's still running the House and Harry Reid is still running the Senate." He continued:

> Betrayed is not even the word here. What has happened here is worse than betrayal, and betrayal's pretty bad, but it's worse than that. This was out and out in our face lying. From the campaigns to individual statements made about the philosophical approach Republicans had to all this spending. There is no Republican Party. You know, we don't even need a Republican Party if they're going to do this. You know just elect Democrats, disband the Republican Party and let the Democrats run it because that's what's happening anyway.[1]

Limbaugh argued that the "betrayal" effectively made the case for Trump's candidacy.

> And these same Republican leaders doing this can't for the life of them figure out why Donald Trump has all the support that he has? They really cannot figure this out? Repeated stabs in the back like this, which have been going on for years, combined with Obama's policy destruction of this country is what has given rise to Donald Trump. If Donald Trump didn't exist and if the Republican Party actually does want to win someday, they'd have to invent him.

This was, of course, the sort of rhetoric that had become familiar from the Right's outrage machines, a mélange of hype and misleading statements about what the GOP had actually accomplished and what was politically possible. But it had also become the accepted narrative in the Limbaugh/Hannity/Fox News/Drudge/Ingraham/Breitbart media echo chamber, as it fueled distrust of the GOP establishment.

Limbaugh's role was decisive here. Since the early 1990s, Limbaugh had been a dominant force in the conservative media. In 1992, with his reelection clearly in trouble, President George H. W. Bush invited Limbaugh and Roger Ailes, who was then the producer of his (now defunct) television show to visit the White House. During the visit, as Limbaugh frequently recounted afterward, the president of the United States had carried his bag. "The scene on the White House lawn," historian Nicole Hemmer observed, "illustrated just how different the second generation of conservative media activists was from the first: they were profitable, popular, and powerful, wielding influence that reached far beyond the conservative movement. . . ."[2]*

After Republicans swept into control of Congress in 1994, Limbaugh was named an honorary member of the GOP House caucus and presented with a button proclaiming him "The Majority Maker." Former congressman Vin Weber declared: "Rush is as responsible for what happened here as much as anyone." Polling data seemed to back that up; voters who listened to talk radio for ten or more hours a week had pulled the lever for Republican candidates by a three-to-one margin.[3]

For years, Limbaugh was a leading enforcer of conservative orthodoxy and ideological purity, which made his ideological pirouette in recent years so remarkable. His reversals also tracked with the ongoing transformation of the conservative movement.

In mid-2015, Limbaugh touted the candidacy of Wisconsin governor Scott Walker, only to dump him (as did Matt Drudge) as he pivoted to Trump. The timing, as media critic John Ziegler noted, was critical. If the conservative gatekeepers had wanted to abort the campaign of

---

*After the election, President George H. W. Bush penned the following note to Limbaugh: "Now that I'm retired from active politics, I don't mind that you've become the number one voice for conservatism in our country." (Nicole Hemmer, *Messengers of the Right: Conservative Media and the Transformation of American Politics* (Philadelphia: University of Pennsylvania Press, 2016), 270.)

the "least conservative Republican presidential aspirant in living memory" (in the words of Yuval Levin, editor of *National Affairs*), this was perhaps the final moment. "Trump's campaign was like a rocket ship where the most perilous moments are during liftoff," Ziegler wrote. "If the conservative base had not accepted him a serious or credible candidate, then he would have quickly crashed and burned because, without traction, the media oxygen which would fuel his flight would have immediately evaporated."[4]

To be sure, Limbaugh continued to insist that he was neutral, and would occasionally say positive things about other candidates, including Ted Cruz and Marco Rubio. Other hosts were more enthusiastic, as Sean Hannity morphed into a gushing fan boy. In contrast, Limbaugh's posture was more nuanced; but from the fall of 2015 onward, Limbaugh became Trump's primary enabler. What followed were months of painful and tortured rationalizations as he defended Trump's gaffes and tried to explain why he—the voice of conservatism for a generation—was now willing to abandon one conservative principle after another.

VULNERABLE RUSH

The obvious questions here are: What happened to Rush Limbaugh? Was he leading or following? And did his vulnerability in the marketplace make it impossible for him to push against the populist tide? These are intriguing questions, because it is possible to argue that Limbaugh's turning point may have come four years earlier, when he took to the airwaves to call a young woman who had testified in favor of free contraceptives "a slut" and "prostitute." By attacking Georgetown student Sandra Fluke in such grotesque terms, said radio analyst Darryl Parks, Limbaugh broke a cardinal rule of radio: "Don't beat up on a woman, and don't beat up on a [young person]." Even four years after the incident, which prompted a large-scale boycott of his show, *Politico* reported that "reams of advertisers still won't touch him."[5]

Limbaugh's performance was tone-deaf on several levels. Fluke had testified before Congress that insurance coverage for birth control should be mandated as a matter of right. This was an argument that conservatives should have relished, pointing out the inflated sense of entitlement on display in Fluke's testimony. Specifically, Fluke was called on by Democrats to argue that her school, Georgetown, should be compelled by law to offer contraceptive drugs without any co-pays, even though the Catholic university was morally opposed to artificial birth control. But then Limbaugh weighed in and turned a potentially teachable moment into a cringe-worthy fiasco. For three days, he mocked and demeaned the young woman. On his February 29, 2012, show, Limbaugh riffed:

> What does it say about the college co-ed Susan Fluke [sic], who goes before a congressional committee and essentially says that she must be paid to have sex, what does that make her? It makes her a slut, right? It makes her a prostitute. She wants to be paid to have sex. She's having so much sex she can't afford the contraception. She wants you and me and the taxpayers to pay her to have sex. What does that make us? We're the pimps. (interruption) The johns? We would be the johns? No! We're not the johns. (interruption) Yeah, that's right. Pimp's not the right word. Okay, so she's not a slut. She's "round heeled." I take it back.[6]

The next day, Limbaugh offered what he said was a "compromise" to contraception coverage: buying "all the women at Georgetown University as much aspirin to put between their knees as possible." On the show, he imitated a crying baby's voice, saying: "I'm going broke having sex. I need government to provide me condoms and contraception. It's not fair."* Limbaugh then doubled down:

---

*In her testimony, Fluke described a friend who had polycystic ovary syndrome, which was treated with contraceptive hormones that cost more than $100 a month. "She has to take prescription birth control to stop cysts from growing on her

Ms. Fluke, have you ever heard of not having sex? Have you ever heard of not having sex so often?

So, Ms. Fluke and the rest of you feminazis, here's the deal. If we are going to pay for your contraceptives, and thus pay for you to have sex, we want something for it, and I'll tell you what it is. We want you to post the videos online so we can all watch.[7]

Limbaugh went on to suggest that the young law student was "having so much sex, it's amazing she can still walk," and continued on to suggest that Georgetown should establish a "Wilt Chamberlain scholarship . . . exclusively for women." Limbaugh told his audience that Fluke was "a woman who is happily presenting herself as an immoral, baseless, no-purpose-to-her-life woman. She wants all the sex in the world whenever she wants it, all the time, no consequences. No responsibility for her behavior."

On March 2, Limbaugh came back to the subject, saying that mandating that insurance companies cover contraception is "no different than if somebody knocked on my door that I don't know and said, 'You know what? I'm out of money. I can't afford birth-control pills, and I'm supposed to have sex with three guys tonight.'"[8]

The reaction to Limbaugh's language was intense and immediate. Sandra Fluke became an instant martyr and Limbaugh's career began to implode. On March 3, President Obama called Fluke personally to offer his support. Realizing that he had gone too far, Limbaugh issued a public apology of sorts, explaining that his shtick was intended to illustrate "the absurd with absurdity," but admitted that he "chose

---

ovaries," Fluke said. "Her prescription is technically covered by Georgetown insurance because it's not intended to prevent pregnancy." But, Fluke said her claim "was denied repeatedly on the assumption that she really wanted the birth control to prevent pregnancy. She's gay, so clearly polycystic ovarian syndrome was a much more urgent concern than accidental pregnancy. After months of paying over $100 out of pocket, she just couldn't afford her medication anymore and had to stop taking it." (Sandra Fluke. Statement to Congress (PDF) (speech). Washington, DC.)

the wrong words." He insisted that he "did not mean a personal attack on Ms. Fluke," despite mocking her as a slut and a prostitute. "My choice of words was not the best," his statement said, "and in the attempt to be humorous, I created a national stir. I sincerely apologize to Ms. Fluke for the insulting word choices."[9]★

Fluke did not accept Limbaugh's apology, saying she didn't think his statement "changes anything, and especially when that statement is issued when he's under significant pressure from his sponsors who have begun to pull their support from the show. I think any woman who has ever been called these types of names is [shocked] at first." She called his attacks "an attempt to silence me, to silence the millions of women and the men who support them who have been speaking out about this issue. . . ."[10]

The aftermath was brutal. Despite his apology, Limbaugh's show was hit with a boycott and a significant loss of revenue. "Dozens of companies, including Netflix, JCPenney and Sears, announced they would boycott Limbaugh's show," reported *Politico* in 2016. "Most have yet to return. And the increasing popularity of platforms like Twitter, which can be used to stoke outrage and promote boycotts, makes it highly unlikely they ever will."[11]

★On March 3, 2016, Limbaugh issued a formal apology. It reads in full: (David Jackson, "Limbaugh Apologizes to Sandra Fluke," *USA Today*, March 3, 2012.) For over 20 years, I have illustrated the absurd with absurdity, three hours a day, five days a week. In this instance, I chose the wrong words in my analogy of the situation. I did not mean a personal attack on Ms. Fluke. I think it is absolutely absurd that during these very serious political times, we are discussing personal sexual recreational activities before members of Congress. I personally do not agree that American citizens should pay for these social activities. What happened to personal responsibility and accountability? Where do we draw the line? If this is accepted as the norm, what will follow? Will we be debating if taxpayers should pay for new sneakers for all students that are interested in running to keep fit? In my monologue, I posited that it is not our business whatsoever to know what is going on in anyone's bedroom nor do I think it is a topic that should reach a Presidential level. My choice of words was not the best, and in the attempt to be humorous, I created a national stir. I sincerely apologize to Ms. Fluke for the insulting word choices.

Limbaugh had crossed a crucial line. "Limbaugh's verbal abuse of Sandra Fluke set a new kind of low," said conservative pundit David Frum. "I can't recall anything as brutal, ugly and deliberate ever being said by such a prominent person and so emphatically repeated. This was not a case of a bad 'word choice.' It was a brutally sexualized accusation, against a specific person, prolonged over three days."[12] But, by and large, the reaction from GOP leaders was muted and formulaic. The incident was an opportunity for conservatives to draw a line, but mostly they refused. It was similar to the tests they would repeatedly fail over the next four years. George Will noted that the lack of reaction "was depressing because what it indicates is that the Republican leaders are afraid of Rush Limbaugh. They want to bomb Iran, but they're afraid of Rush Limbaugh."[13]

All of this was a prelude to what would happen in 2015–2016. Perhaps not surprisingly, neither Limbaugh nor Fox News (which was embroiled in its own sexual harassments scandals) thought allegations that Trump harassed women were politically disqualifying.

How badly was Limbaugh hurt by the firestorm over Sandra Fluke? In 2008, when he renewed his mega-contract with Clear Channel for a staggering $400 million, the size of the deal was widely reported and touted. Four years later, the deal was renewed without fanfare and without financial details.[14] In the meantime, Limbaugh's radio show had been bumped from prime stations in major markets like Boston, New York, Los Angeles, and Indianapolis, often shunted off to smaller, lower-powered and lower-rated spots on the dial.[15] In Boston, Limbaugh's show was demoted to a station that ranked twenty-third in the market, with a paltry 0.2 share of the radio market, "just two tenths of a point away from a DNS or 'did not show,'" according to radio analyst Darryl Parks. In Los Angeles, Rush was pulled from the talk power-house KFI-AM, and moved to a station with a 0.4 share of the market. "Years ago, Rush Limbaugh could make or break a news/talk station," he said. "But, that was many years ago and is no longer the case."[16]

During one awkward period of the 2016 campaign, when Limbaugh admitted that he had actually not believed some of the things he had previously said, he offered this explanation for his mission:

I am a radio guy. I do a radio program. And my success here is
defined by radio and broadcast business metrics, not political. It
never has been defined by political metrics, I've never wanted it to
be. I have always said countless times, my success is not determined by who wins elections. That doesn't mean I'm not interested, doesn't mean I have vested interests, but I'm a radio guy.[17]

As he had repeatedly said over the last two decades, Limbaugh didn't
measure his success by whether or not his side won elections, what
mattered was his "business metrics." It was a remarkably candid
acknowledgment.

But Limbaugh's slide also made him vulnerable, especially to the
many new voices all vying to be the next big thing on the Right. The
dynamic here was market segmentation, as more and more broadcast-
ers fought over a relatively small and perhaps shrinking audience. As
syndicated talk show host Michael Medved explained, talk radio worked
this way: "In this environment, you have something of a rush to be
outrageous, to be on the fringe, because what you're desperately competing for is P-1 listeners [the most regular loyal and hard core portion
of the audience]. And the percentage of people on the fringe who are
P-1 is quite high."[18] The pressure was increased by demographic real-
ties that were well understood by anyone in the business. As influential as talk radio was, its audience skewed older (about two thirds were
older than fifty) and was overwhelmingly white, and now Limbaugh's
show was losing both stations and revenue. Writer John Avlon anticipated Limbaugh's dilemma when he noted that many hosts "become
prisoners of their own shtick," because if they softened or wavered, "they
will be called traitors by the tribe they have cultivated." As competition intensified, they could "only move in one direction: further out
into the extremes."[19]

After the Fluke controversy, Limbaugh was no longer impregnable;
he could not risk being outflanked on the Right by angry populist
voices or labeled a part of the "establishment." In the new media landscape, things move fast and Limbaugh was a savvy enough entrepreneur to understand how quickly media brands can fade or be jostled

aside. With his audience aging and shrinking, the reality from a business perspective was that Limbaugh could simply not afford to stand against the populist tide. So he didn't, and neither did most of the other national hosts.

THE TALK RADIO CANDIDATE

Some of the radio talk hosts who enabled Trump's rise may have waxed enthusiastic about the billionaire simply in order to block an establishment candidate like Jeb Bush (hoping to later pivot again to a more conservative candidate like Cruz). But many were clearly taken with the New York mogul's brash, take-no-prisoners approach. In any case, there was clearly a symbiotic relationship between Trump and the Right media. One of the savviest observers of the phenomenon was Jon Favreau, a former Obama speechwriter who recognized that Trump's candidacy was the apotheosis of right-wing media culture. In an essay entitled "Longtime Listener, First-Time Candidate," Favreau pinpointed Trump's central appeal to the talkers: "He won by doing a fairly good impression of a right-wing media celebrity."[20]

> Every issue, every conspiracy, every applause line has been ripped from their websites, radio shows, and television programs. It's why he became America's most prominent birther. It's why he floated rumors that Ted Cruz's dad killed JFK, and that Hillary Clinton killed Vince Foster. It's why he talks the way he does about Mexicans and Muslims and women and African Americans. It's why he's been able to get away with knowing little to nothing about policy or government or world affairs—because Trump, like any good talking head, only speaks in chyrons and clauses and some-people-are-sayings.

As a talk show host myself, for years I had pushed back against the charge that talk radio was simply about entertainment, outrage, and anger. I made an effort to talk about issues and struggled to find ways to repackage conservative and free-market ideas in fresh and understandable terms. Other hosts did as well, notably Hugh Hewitt, Dennis Prager, Michael Medved, as well as many of the other local hosts. But this was clearly not the norm for many of the loudest voices. Favreau noted that Trump had learned some key lessons from studying the Right media:

These outlets have long been labeled the "conservative media," but they don't spend much time discussing tax cuts, free trade, entitlement reform, or school choice. They're not weighing market-based solutions to urban poverty or debating the future of neoconservative foreign policy. . . . They have a lot more in common with the *National Enquirer* than they do with the *National Review*.

Notably, shows like Limbaugh's also talked a lot about "winning," often claiming without much evidence that the country was over-whelmingly conservative and that conservative ideas would always win if they were given a chance. This always struck me as both circular and lazy thinking. After the GOP's crushing defeat in 2008, I wrote a piece called "The End of Limbaughism," which pointed out that conserva-tism is not the same as populism. By its nature, conservatism flies in the face of popular ideas and culture. Because it has firm, occasionally hard-nosed principles, it has to push against the fierce headwinds of both fashion and history.

Arguing from economic principles is not always easy. Arguing facts and logics is not as popular as arguing from feelings and emotions. Tra-ditional morality is a far less easy sell than the culture of "whatever." In education, "most people" may not choose higher standards or rigorous accountability measures over gold stars and happy faces. It is harder to explain why free markets create wealth than it is to pander to work-ers who have been displaced by global competition. It is an uphill fight to persuade workers that the minimum wage is not in their interest. Those arguments, of course, could be won, and Ronald Reagan and others showed that they could be embraced by electoral majorities.

But the case was made by conservatives who understood the odds against them.

Increasingly, however, as they competed in the new media ecosystem, the talkers eschewed wonkery for the more sensational narratives.* The vast majority of airtime was not taken up by issues or explanations of conservative approaches to markets or need to balance liberty with order. Why bother with such stuff, when there were personalities to be mocked, conspiracy theories to be shared, and left-wing moonbats to be ridiculed?

The "ad hominem" argument—literally "to the person"—is rightly regarded as a logical fallacy because it substitutes personal attacks for discussing the argument someone is making. But on many talk shows, including Limbaugh's, nearly every argument was ad hominem. Instead of offering statistics and building a case, it was simply easier to ridicule House Democratic leader Nancy Pelosi, or shrug off a negative report because it came from the "lamestream media." Arguments via the 140-word characters of Twitter fit easily into this media ecosystem, as did Trump himself.

THE DEFENDER-IN-CHIEF

Even before he dumped Scott Walker, Limbaugh played a key role in maintaining Trump's viability as a candidate. Trump's mockery of for-

---

* "For every story that's critical of an Obama policy or decision, these media outlets run 10 more suggesting he's a Kenyan Muslim with terrorist sympathies. They don't criticize Hillary Clinton as someone with questionable judgment who's made some bad decisions; they tell you she's a criminal who left Americans to die in Benghazi, and probably killed a few others along the way. Immigration isn't a debate about border security or legal status, it's an excuse to talk about the dark hordes of criminals and rapists pouring into our country. Inner-city violence is reduced to stories about black kids in hoodies who hate cops, hate white people, and light cities on fire. Terrorism is an imaginary tale about Muslims dancing on rooftops after 9/11, or the lie that the Muslim neighbors of the San Bernardino shooters saw bombs next door and chose to say nothing." —Jon Favreau, "Longtime Listener, First-Time Candidate," *Ringer*, September 6, 2016.

mer POW John McCain ("I like the ones who weren't captured") could have been a campaign-ending gaffe for other politicians. But Limbaugh provided support at a critical moment.

"The American people haven't seen something like this in a long time," he told his audience in July 2015. "They have not seen an embattled public figure stand up for himself, double down and tell everybody to go to hell."[21] Despite the fact that Trump, who had never served in the military, had questioned McCain's status a war hero, Limbaugh opened his show by declaring: "Trump can survive this, Trump is surviving this." He called Trump's refusal to apologize "a great, great teachable moment here, this whole thing with Trump and McCain."

Months later, he defended Trump's claim that he had seen videos of "thousands and thousands of" people in Jersey City "cheering as that building was coming down. Thousands of people were cheering." Actually no such video exists and officials on the ground have consistently denied the story. But again, Limbaugh set the pattern of providing air cover by defending what Stephen Colbert would call the "truthiness" of the statement.

> And, so here comes Trump saying that he saw Muslims cheer on 9/11, he adds tens of thousands there. The bottom line is that a lot of Americans are well aware that Muslims were cheering. *Maybe not in New Jersey in great numbers,* but around the world they were because we saw the video. On 9/11 and in the aftermath, we saw video on the news, unquote of Muslims all over the world, in certain places, cheering. *So, regardless of the specific details,* the American people and a lot of Trump supporters know, I mean it was militant Islamists who conducted 9/11, it's militant Islamists that make up ISIS. [Emphasis added.][22]

This was vintage Limbaugh, rationalizing Trump's statements while conceding they were false, mixing in criticism of the news media and suggesting that the erroneous statement somehow revealed a more important truth. Limbaugh's defense also ignored the vital distinction between celebrations that might have taken place among Islamist sympathizers in the Middle East—and those that did not take place here in the United States among American Muslims.

As the campaign wore on, Limbaugh also did yeoman service by explaining away some of Trump's more flagrant inconsistencies. When it appeared that Trump was about to flip-flop on the signature issue of his campaign—his pledge to deport illegal immigrants—Limbaugh rationalized the broken promise by saying that he had never taken Trump seriously on the issue anyway, even when he was publicly praising it.[23] This became awkward when a caller to Limbaugh's show expressed concern over the flip-flop.

> LIMBAUGH: Yeah? Well, I guess the difference is—or not the difference. I guess the thing is . . . This is gonna enrage you. You know, I could choose a path here to try to mollify you, but—
>
> CALLER: (chuckles)
>
> LIMBAUGH: *I never took him seriously on this.* [Emphasis added.]
>
> CALLER: But thirty million—or fifteen or ten million . . . Excuse me. Ten million people did.
>
> LIMBAUGH: *Yeah, and they still don't care! My point is they still don't care! They're gonna stick with him no matter what.* [Emphasis added.]

Limbaugh was also quick to jettison conservative ideas like "small government" when Trump endorsed a federal maternity leave plan. "Do you think the argument over big versus small government's still going on, or do you think it's over?" Limbaugh wondered. "And if you think it's over, who won?" He proceeded to offer a convoluted rationalization for the new mandate, insisting that "I am the last person on earth who wants any expansion of the government," but blaming the "mess" in child care on the government and the Left. Limbaugh, then, essentially gave up the game, conceding that since the voters wanted more government spending, why not give it to them, regardless of what small-government conservatives had said in the past?

> Other than an intellectual exercise, you can't say, "Oh, what could have been! Oh, how bad! Oh, I told you!" I know there's a whole bunch of I told you so's out there, but I think politi-cally. . . . You wait. I think just for people that are not ideological—which is a hell of a lot of people in this country. I think they're gonna respond so positively to this, and it's gonna disappoint a lot of people. "Oh, my God, do people not even understand the whole concept of Big Government destroying the country?" They don't, folks. They don't look at it the way you and I do in that regard.[24]

Conservative blogger Allahpundit observed that Limbaugh appeared to have "thrown in the towel on what should be the entire point of his show, trying to convince people smaller government is better."[25] The irony of his pivot to Trump did not go unnoticed. Writing in the *Washington Post,* Michael Gerson noted that for decades "Limbaugh set the tone of popular conservatism by arguing for ideological purity," but that he has now enabled the rise of "a candidate who talks more of personal rule than of limited government. A candidate who praises a single-payer health system, proposes higher taxes on the wealthy, opposes entitle-ment reform and advocates the systematic destruction of Ronald Reagan's foreign policy." Gerson credited Limbaugh with giving Trump "the ideological hall pass of a lifetime."[26]

WHAT IF . . . ?

This raises an interesting question: What would have happened if conservative talk radio had not rallied around Trump?

During the campaign, I was able to watch the process from a unique perspective, as Wisconsin became a laboratory of sorts for the role of talk radio. It turned out that when Trump lacked the air cover provided by friendly radio hosts, he fared poorly. In April 2016, Trump lost the GOP primary in Wisconsin by double digits to Ted Cruz. The vote was more anti-Trump than pro-Cruz, since the Texas senator was not a natural fit for the Badger State. (Wisconsin Republicans would have been more comfortable backing either Walker or Marco Rubio, but they had already exited the race.) Conservative voters made the strategic decision that Cruz was the only candidate with a chance to stop Trump.

The day in late March when Trump called in to my radio show, I had posted an article giving him fair warning: "Donald Trump is about to find out that Wisconsin is different. And one of the reasons is conservative talk radio."[27] Along with five other conservative talk show hosts in the state, I had been critical of Trump for months, and it had taken its toll on the front-runner's popularity. Polls showed that in the vote-rich WOW counties around Milwaukee—Waukesha, Ozaukee, Washington—Trump was viewed positively by only 25 percent of GOP voters; 64 percent said they disapproved of the Manhattan billionaire.*

---

*Shortly before the Wisconsin primary, the *New York Times* captured the media/ political environment in the state:

> Later in the week, as Mr. Trump crossed the state, he seemed to acknowledge the power of Wisconsin's talk radio culture, which has been an anti-Trump force, by railing aloud against it for deceiving voters. "In certain areas—the city areas—I'm not doing well," Mr. Trump told voters in Racine, bemoaning his lack of support on talk radio. "I'm not doing well because nobody knows my message. They were given misinformation." Mr. Sykes, along with a handful of other local radio hosts, has spent his mornings criticizing and castigating Mr. Trump over the airwaves. And if Mr. Trump loses the Wisconsin primary on Tuesday, he will have Mr. Sykes and his merry band of talkers partly to blame.
>
> In a nominating contest that has exposed fissures in the Republican Party, Wisconsin's conservative talk radio apparatus remains remarkably united on at least one point: its deep dislike of Mr. Trump, who for months has been the focus of its fiery attacks.
>
> The Wisconsin talk radio conglomerate, which rallied conservative voters to help Gov. Scott Walker win three elections in four years, has now set its sights on stopping Mr. Trump by deprecating the delegate leader and elevating Senator Ted Cruz. (Ashley Parker and Nick Corasaniti, "6 Talk Radio Hosts, on a Mission to Stop Donald Trump in Wisconsin," *New York Times*, April 4, 2016.)

In other words, when Trump was subjected to a sustained critique, conservative voters responded. But in 2016, Wisconsin's media culture was the exception to the trend in the Right media's ecosystem.

Wisconsin was also an outlier for a number of other reasons, including its Midwestern sensibilities and a culture that valued certain norms of civility (although the concept of "Wisconsin nice" may have been overplayed). Conservative voters there had been exposed to substantive, reform-minded conservatives like Paul Ryan for years, and had been battle-tested by recent political fights, including the high-profile attempt to recall Governor Scott Walker.

A few weeks before the primary, I tried to explain what made Wisconsin different. "There's kind of a fundamental decency about Wisconsinites that you can't downplay," I told the *Washington Post*'s Dave Weigel. "We've never had a huge division between the Tea Party and the establishment. We've got think tanks and radio talk shows that have been through the fire and are really intellectually driven. And you don't get that elsewhere. I was driving here listening to Sean Hannity, and after 15 seconds, I could feel myself getting dumber."[28]

In contrast to Trump, Ryan's approach reflected the distinctive sort of conservatism that had flourished in Wisconsin: principled, pragmatic, reformist, but not afraid of taking on tough, controversial issues. While the GOP in Washington, DC, had been frustrated and blocked, the record in Wisconsin was markedly different. Not only did conservatives dominate all three branches of government in Wisconsin, they used that dominance to enact an impressive array of reforms and initiatives, from Act 10, Right to Work, and prevailing wage reform to tax cuts, tort reform, and the expansion of school choice. (Voters also noticed that Trump had lied about the success of the conservative reforms there.) In other words, conservatives in Wisconsin took ideas seriously, at least during the primary season.*

---

*Many of those conservatives would later come to see the election as a "binary choice," and decide to support Trump over Hillary Clinton in November. But Trump still significantly underperformed Mitt Romney in southeastern Wisconsin.

Perhaps most important, though, was what Trump's defeat in Wisconsin suggested about what might have happened if talk radio elsewhere had pushed back against the reality show star. That, of course, didn't happen. So, rather than being a firewall, Wisconsin proved to be merely a speed bump on Trump's road to the nomination.

IT'S NOT ABOUT CONSERVATISM ANYMORE

Limbaugh, meanwhile, continued to adapt himself to the new era. Less than four months into Trump's presidency the one-time conservative guru told his audience that with Trump in the White House, conservative principles were no longer the point.

> How many times a day did I tell people that Donald Trump is not even ideological? Multiple times a day. How many times have I told you, do not expect Trump to be a conservative; he isn't one. . . . I never once talked about conservatism 'cause that isn't what this is about, and I told you back in the campaign that it was not about conservatism. Because that's not who Trump is.

Conservativism had lost in the primary, Limbaugh declared, and his focus on conservative values had been replaced with antiliberalism. That was one of the reasons, he said, that he had changed "the name of my think tank from the Institute for Advanced Conservative Studies to the Institute for Advanced Anti-Leftist Studies." Beneath his bellicose tone, Limbaugh's statement was a declaration of surrender.[29]

CHAPTER 12

THE BIGOTS AMONG US

FOR MUCH OF 2016, Paul Nehlen was the great hope of Breitbart World. A political unknown, Nehlen was the pro-Trump primary challenger to House Speaker Paul Ryan, who had angered Trump supporters with his reluctance to back the GOP nominee and for being willing to criticize Trump's more outrageous statements. Nehlen was backed by pro-Trump luminaries Ann Coulter and Sarah Palin and, at one point, Trump singled out Nehlen for praise before eventually backing Ryan.

Under CEO Steve Bannon, Breitbart and its satellites had not hesitated to use their clout to attack other conservatives who have been insufficiently enthusiastic about embracing Trumpism. Specifically, Bannon declared it was his mission to destroy Speaker Paul Ryan and, even after the public detente between Trump and Ryan, the website relentlessly attacked the conservative Speaker. During Nehlen's campaign, Breitbart kept up a drumbeat of attacks—usually linked on the Drudge Report—on Ryan's choice of a school for his children (it was Catholic), to the fence around his family home (for security). On the day of the election, Nehlen gave an interview to Bannon himself on Breitbart News Daily and called Ryan a "soulless, globalist snake," and bragged that he had "smoked him out of the snake hole."[1]

Readers of Breitbart were repeatedly assured that Nehlen was gaining traction, the site reporting in July that Ryan had "fallen to 43 percent in a new primary poll."[2] Ryan got 84 percent of the primary vote, a result that undoubtedly came as surprise to those who relied on Breitbart's reporting.

But Nehlen's abortive effort to dump Ryan led to one of the more troubling—and revealing—moments of the campaign for me.

Throughout the campaign Nehlen had attempted to out-Trump Trump by enthusiastically backing the GOP nominee's various proposals to ban Muslims from the country and crack down on those who were already here. But in late July, he took it to a new level, suggesting during a Chicago-area radio interview that we should consider *deporting* all Muslims from the country.[3] The radio host asked Nehlen how he would go about vetting refugees or Muslim immigrants. "Then how do you implement, how do you implement the test that you want to implement?" he asked.

PAUL NEHLEN: Well, then, the question is, why do we have Muslims in the country? How can you possibly vet somebody who lies?

DAN CROFT: Well, that said, are you suggesting that we deport all of the Muslims in this country?

PAUL NEHLEN: I'm suggesting that we have a discussion about it. That's for sure. I am absolutely suggesting we figure out how do we, we, here's what we should be doing. We should be monitoring every mosque. We should be monitoring all social media.

The host challenged Nehlen on his proposal:

> DAN CROFT: But what you're talking about is people that are Americans that are here, and whether or not we should deport all of them. Do . . . you see any Constitutional problems with the vetting, the kind that Newt Gingrich wanted to do and apparently you do as well. Much less deporting Americans who have done nothing wrong.
>
> NEHLEN: Well, if somebody supports Sharia that is doing something wrong. It is.

This was, of course, a rather fundamental challenge not merely to conservative principles, but to simple, basic norms of decency. It was also, I thought, a clear test of where we stood as a movement. So that Friday morning, I opened up the phone lines to get my listeners' reactions to the suggestion that we round up and expel Muslims—including American citizens—from the country because of their religion. One of the first callers was Audrey from Oshkosh, who thought it was a great idea. A writer for *Politico* magazine, who was sitting in the studio with me that day, recounted both the call and my reaction.[4]

> "Yeah! Let me make a comparison, and I don't mean this in a bad way," Audrey says. "They're talking about phasing out breeding of pit bulls. Well, not all pit bulls are bad." "You're comparing American citizens, Muslims, to rabid dogs," Sykes responds.
>
> "No, I'm saying, they're talking about phasing out the breed because so many are bad. No one wants to phase out poodles! I mean, there's no Lutherans doing this! We never know when one of these people are going to be radicalized." "One of *these* people," says Sykes. Sykes ends the call. He's silent, broadcasting dead air. He looks upset, like he's stopped breathing. He goes to a commercial break. "OK, that doesn't happen very often," he says off air. "I'm not usually absolutely

speechless." He says his listeners never talked like this until recently. "Were these people that we actually thought were our allies?" he asks.

This was shocking stuff and I was shocked. But the exchange also forced me to ask several hard questions.

He wonders: Did "the faux outrage machine" of Breitbart.com and other right-wing outlets foment the noxious opinions that Trump has stoked so effectively on the trail? "When I would deny that there was a significant racist component in some of the politics on our side, it was because the people I hung out with were certainly not," Sykes says. "When suddenly, this rock is turned over, there is this—'Oh shit, did I not see that?'

"I kind of had that reaction this morning, with that woman: Did we ignore this? There's got to be some serious introspection, because of the things that we either didn't see, or that we ignored, or that we enabled."[5]

Let me stipulate here that critics on the Left will accuse me of naïveté or worse. For years they had warned about the latent racism on the Right, accusing conservatives of engaging in "dog whistles" and coded language to conceal their bias. And indeed, as the base of the GOP shifted to the South after the 1960s, the party became more white and disconnected from minority populations. But in recent years, conservatives had also engaged in concerted efforts to reach out to minority communities, most notably efforts by Ryan along with neighborhood activist Robert Woodson to explore innovative ways to combat poverty.

But it was hard to miss the growing undertow of anti-Muslim sentiment on the Right, and Trump had clearly tapped into it, as he did regarding other anxieties that seemed to target members of minority groups and foreigners—*Brown people were going to take your jobs, your country, and perhaps your women from you.*

THE CURIOUS CASE OF ANN COULTER

The reality was that the Right had become comfortable with racially charged rhetoric. At one time, racist language was a ticket to exile, but that had changed in the new media environment. Now the most extreme language leads not to excommunication, but to celebrity—speaking invitations, cable hits, clicks, bestselling books, and a new level of influence in GOP politics. No one illustrated this phenomenon more clearly than Ann Coulter.

Coulter is both a curious case and a revealing one. Mainstream conservatives had actually drawn a line when Coulter veered from her usual high-pitched (but entertaining) polemics into unhinged xenophobia. In 2002, *National Review* dropped her column after she wrote that the United States should respond to terror attacks by radical Islamists in the following manner: "invade their countries, kill their leaders and convert them to Christianity."*

But this did not dent her continued celebrity on the Right. She wrote bestselling books, was treated like a rock star at the annual Conservative Political Action Conference (once called "the Star Wars bar scene of the conservative movement") and in 2015 actually helped launch Donald Trump's presidential campaign by providing him with one of his defining themes.† In retrospect I should have seen it coming. Early in 2015, she came on my radio show to tout her book, *Adios America*, a

---

*Afterward, Jonah Goldberg explained what happened: "In the wake of her invade-and-Christianize-them column, Coulter wrote a long, rambling rant of a response to her critics that was barely coherent. She's a smart and funny person, but this was Ann at her worst—emoting rather than thinking, and badly needing editing and some self-censorship, or what is commonly referred to as 'judgment.' Running this 'piece' would have been an embarrassment to Ann, and to NRO." (Jonah Goldberg, "L'Affaire Coulter," *National Review*, October 2, 2001.)

† Throughout the 2016 campaign, Coulter and I butted heads, appearing together on MSNBC's *Hardball with Chris Matthews* on several occasions; she appeared on my radio show before the primary and then again at the Republican National Convention in July. During the latter interview, she bet me $100 that Trump would get a larger percentage of the African American vote than any GOP nominee since Richard Nixon. I never collected.

lengthy polemic on Mexican immigrants. For the most part it was standard Coulterism, which was designed to provoke and outrage, but I was taken aback by her emphasis on "Mexican rapists." I remember trying to imagine the reaction if she made the same sort of sweeping generalizations about other ethnic groups. It was the crudest sort of racial stereotyping.

So I was doubly struck when Trump used similar language in announcing his presidential candidacy in June 2015. "When Mexico sends its people, they're not sending their best," he declared. "They're sending people that have lots of problems, and they're bringing those problems with us. They're bringing drugs. They're bringing crime. They're rapists." I instantly recognized the line as Coulter's. The *New York Times Magazine* later reported that then-Trump campaign manager Corey Lewandowski "had reached out to Coulter for advice in the run-up to Trump's announcement speech." Trump's prepared text had touched only lightly on immigration. "Instead, he ad-libbed what Coulter today calls 'the Mexican rapist speech that won my heart.' "[6]

In retrospect I regret that I did not push back on Coulter harder, confining myself to suggesting that she was "painting with an awfully broad brush." This was, of course, wholly inadequate. Coulter was trafficking in the grossest of racial stereotypes and I should have called her on it more forcefully. I doubt that would have made much of a difference, but the failure of conservatives to police the borders of this sort of raw nativism paved the way for what was about to happen.*

THE DANGERS OF CRYING WOLF

Many on the Left seemed genuinely shocked that their charges of racism, sexism, and xenophobia did not seem to dent Trump's popularity with conservatives. Only belatedly did some of them realize that may

---

*Coulter's adulation of Trump even eclipsed the fan boy enthusiasm of Sean Hannity. In the fall of 2016, she released her latest (quickly written) book: *In Trump We Trust*, with Trump's name notably used in place of the more traditional "God."

have been, at least in part, the price they paid for crying wolf for decades. Conservatives had become accustomed to being called mean, dumb, benighted bigots. So liberally had the epithets been hurled at them that conservatives came to recognize them as merely the Left's code for "I don't like you, shut up."

While many Democrats claimed to be nostalgic for the kinder, gentler, more statesmanlike GOP candidates of the past, they often neglected to remember what they had said about them when they were actually running for office. "By 2000," RealClearPolitics.com's Carl Cannon wrote, "calling George W. Bush a racist was the liberals' standard operating procedure, a tactic used against Romney as well. . . . If Reagan and George W. Bush are routinely portrayed as warmongers, if both Bushes (and Reagan and Romney) are painted as bigots . . . how do we expect rank-and-file conservatives or grassroots independents to respond when Trump is dubbed by the media as an existential threat to democracy?"[7]

In an essay entitled "How the Media's History of Smearing Republicans Now Helps Trump," Jonah Goldberg recounted the serial attempts to paint various Republicans as Nazi sympathizers, racists, and granny killers: "I have no doubt many journalists would defend their smears and professional failures, but that doesn't change the fact that many Americans outside the mainstream media/Democratic bubble find it all indefensible. More important, they find it all ignorable—because the race card and the demagogue card have been played and replayed so often they're little more than scraps of lint."[8]

A handful of Democrats belatedly realized the problem. "There's enough truth to it to compel some self-reflection," Howard Wolfson, who was the communications director for Hillary Clinton's presidential bid in 2008, told New York Times columnist Frank Bruni in September 2016. Bruni noted that the mild-mannered Romney was called a "race-mongering pyromaniac" and accused by a black commentator of the "niggerization" of Obama. Wolfson admitted that he helped use "hyperbolic and inaccurate" language to attack candidates like George W. Bush, John McCain, and Mitt Romney. And he called for some introspection on the Left.

"It's only when you find yourself describing someone who really is the definition of an extremist—who really is, essentially, in my opinion, a fascist—that you recognize that the language that you've used in the past to describe other people was hyperbolic and inappropriate and cheap," Wolfson told Broni.

"It doesn't mean that you somehow retrospectively agree with their positions on issues," he admitted. "But when the system confronts an actual, honest-to-God menace, it should compel some rethinking on our part about how we describe people who are far short of that."[9]

It's fair to say that no one on either side of the political divide anticipated the role that the Alt Right would play in electing the next president.

13

THE RISE OF
THE ALT RIGHT

I'M PRETTY SURE THAT I was called a "cuckservative" before I even knew what the Alt Right was. To be sure, I knew of the existence of anti-Semitic trolls and white nationalists who had long existed on the fringes of the conservative movement. But like the John Birchers before them, they had, by and large, been excommunicated, unwelcome even in the biggest tent version of the rational Right.

Unfortunately, this seemed to change in the last campaign, which became a coming-out party for the denizens of the fever swamp. Even this would rate as hardly more than an asterisk, except for the way that the Trump campaign—and its media allies, including Breitbart, Ann Coulter, and Rush Limbaugh—normalized, promoted, and brought Alt

Right ideas into the 2016 campaign. Steve Bannon, who became CEO of Trump's campaign and later counselor to the new president, has bragged that under his leadership Breitbart had become, in his own words, a "platform for the alt-right."[1]

A somewhat sympathetic description in the *Weekly Standard* described the Alt Right as an amalgam that "includes neo-reactionaries, monarchists, nativists, populists, *and even a few self-declared fascists.*" [Emphasis added.] They are very much a creature of the internet and congregate online in websites ranging "from Breitbart and the libertarian-leaning Taki Mag to Alternative Right—a blog that openly supports white nationalism."[2] Even this tends to understate the Alt Right's open embrace of undiluted racism.

In fact, as one conservative commentator noted, "Racism is not a fringe element of the Alt-Right; it's the movement's central premise."[3] Jared Taylor, the Alt Right editor of *American Renaissance,* explained, "The alt right accepts that race is a biological fact and that it's a significant aspect of individual and group identity and that any attempt to create a society in which race can be made not to matter will fail." The Alt Right also frequently embraces the idea of "white genocide," which sees immigration and civil rights as part of plot to decrease the white population. White nationalist leader Richard Spencer explained that "Immigration is a kind a proxy war—and maybe a last stand—for White Americans, who are undergoing a painful recognition that, unless dramatic action is taken, their grandchildren will live in a country that is alien and hostile." Ann Coulter had also pushed a similar narrative, tweeting out: " 'Diversity' =nonwhite; 'White supremacist' =Not anti-white." In her book *Adios America,* which provided some of the central themes for Trump's anti-immigration campaign, Coulter cited the work of the Alt Right site VDare.com and its editor, Peter Brimelow.[4]

TRUMPKINS VERSUS "CUCKSERVATIVES"

Members of the Alt Right could often be identified by their use of increasingly popular Twitter hashtag #cuckservative to criticize non-

Trumpian conservatives. The hashtag in particular was singled out as one of the "apt displays of why the alternative right has often proven more effective at fighting progressive dogma than the traditional Republican Party. . . . The end result: Trump, the darling of the populist alt right (and its cousin, conservative talk radio), is miles ahead of his challengers. . . ."[5]

As an early target of the epithet, I was naturally curious to discover what a "cuckservative" was.

"Cuck," a derivative of "cuckold," is a noun used by white supremacists to refer to whites who invite destruction of the white race by tolerating other races, which they view as weak whites inviting other races to rape their wives, steal their homes/schools/society, etc.[6]

There is no putting lipstick on this wildebeest; it's ugly stuff. Conservative talk show host Erick Erickson was blunt in his description. The phrase "cuckservative," he wrote, "is a racist slur."

It is used by racists in support of a racialist agenda. The people who use it are not opposed to illegal immigration, but are opposed to immigration in general. They are opposed to evangelical Christians who support interracial adoption. They are opposed to anyone who does not think in terms of the white race.[7]

The attacks were often very personal. *National Review* writer David French was singled out by Alt Right trolls because he had adopted an Ethiopian child. "Many of them are unapologetically white-nationalists, hate interracial adoption and other 'race-mixing' practices, and think about the issue of immigration primarily, if not exclusively, in racial terms." One Twitter troll wrote: "David likes to watch 3 Black men sharing his wife."[8]

What does this have to do with conservative politics or the current debates among the GOP candidates? Matt Lewis tried to explain:

By supporting immigration reform, criminal justice reform, etc., a white conservative is therefore surrendering his honor and masculinity (and it won't be long before his women folk are compromised, as well!). A cuckservative is, therefore, a race traitor.[9]

But the term also has its defenders. Breitbart quickly chimed in, touting "cuckservative" as a Gloriously Effective Insult That Should Not Be Slurred, Demonised, or Ridiculed."[10]

By that point, its use had become so widespread that the *Washington Post* sought out expert commentary on the phenomenon from Richard Spencer, who served as president of the white nationalist National Policy Institute. Spencer helpfully explained that #cuckservative is "a full-scale revolt, by Identitarians and what I've called the 'Alt Right,' against the Republican Party and conservative movement."

According to Spencer, "Trump is a major part of the 'cuckservative' phenomenon—but not because he himself is an Identitarian or traditionalist. His campaign is, in many ways, a backward-looking movement: 'Let's make America great again!' Why Trump is attractive to Identitarians and the alt Right is: a) he is a tougher, superior man than 'conservatives' (which isn't saying much), and b) he seems to grasp the demographic displacement of European-Americans on a visceral level. We see some hope there."[11]

Along with the new right-wing populism, the Identitarian movement has been spreading across the European nationalist stream in the last few years. In some countries this phenomenon is manifested by nationalistic radicals as protest movements, in others using neo-Nazis themes. While the movement is not monolithic (there are many factions and variations) the Alt Right is not only explicitly white nationalist, it is also often explicitly anti-Semitic and comfortable with questioning and even mocking the Holocaust. One white nationalist, Paul Ramsey, produced a video entitled, *Is It Wrong Not to Feel Sad About the Holocaust?* One Alt Right internet hub called the Right Stuff also created a social media meme encouraging followers to identify Jews by placing parentheses around their names, such as ((((Charlie

Sykes)))), highlighting that "all Jewish surnames echo throughout history."[12]*

Not surprisingly, the term "cuckservative" was also popular in social media postings that dwell on the perfidy of Israel and Jewish conspiracies. But that did not seem to bother some prominent conservatives.

LIMBAUGH AND THE "CUCKOLDED GOP"

In July 2015, Rush Limbaugh used the term himself when he labeled Trump critics as "cuckolded Republicans." Months later he was still providing the Alt Right with valuable air cover, even though it was unclear whether he even knew what the term "Alt Right" meant. The *Daily Beast*'s Betsy Woodruff captured one particular exchange in December 2015, when a caller told Limbaugh "about burgeoning excitement among right-wing youth in Europe—and then started promoting the white supremacist alt right movement." Woodruff noted that "As the caller talked, the radio host nodded along, expressing pleasure with the caller's analysis of the alt right and inadvertently lending legitimacy to that movement—which flirts with neo-Nazism."[13]

The caller told Limbaugh about the excitement and the appeal to younger people of the new Alt Right. "They're beginning to get people over here, youngsters between 18, 25, 26, to convert to what they call 'the alt right.' I think it's gonna be pretty intense," he told Limbaugh. "I think you should keep an eye out for it." Woodruff reported:

* As writer Michael Knowles explained:
    The echoes repeat the sad tale as they communicate the emotional lessons of our great white sins, imploring us to Never Forget the 6 GoRillion [sic]. An anonymous Alt Right developer even uploaded a Google Chrome extension called "The Coincidence Detector" to automatically insert the parentheses around Jewish-sounding names and thereby highlight the "coincidence" that so many Jews occupy positions among the global elite, which illustrates another aspect of the movement. . . ." (Michael Knowles, "An Actual Conservative's Guide to the Alt-Right: 8 Things You Need to Know," *Daily Wire*, September 26, 2016.)

Limbaugh sounded pleased.

"Yeah, that's a good thought," he replied. "'The alt right,' like in alternative right?"

"Alternative right," replied Roy from Gurnee.

"Yeah, like in alternative media and so forth," Limbaugh replied. . . .

"In fact, we don't have to wait for this alt whatever it is in Europe," the host continued. "There is a thriving youthful conservative emergence happening in this country. They may be borrowing from what's going on in Europe. But, Roy, there's no question you're right."

But Limbaugh genuinely thrilled the Alt Right when he proclaimed "Nationalism and populism have overtaken conservatism in terms of appeal." Limbaugh's comments drew wide attention because he seemed to be conceding that conservative ideas, including free-market economics, no longer seemed especially important to conservative voters. During the discussion, he read a passage from a column by the late columnist Sam Francis, a notorious and valuable advocate for white nationalism.

The article Limbaugh shared with his listeners had been written by Francis in 1996 and seemed to foreshadow what was happening twenty years later. "Sooner or later," Francis had written, "as the globalist elites seek to drag the country into conflicts and global commitments, preside over the economic pastoralization of the United States, manage the delegitimization of our own culture, and the dispossession of our people, and disregard or diminish our national interests and national sovereignty, a nationalist reaction is almost inevitable and will probably assume populist form when it arrives."[14]

The Alt Right picked up on the signal. Sam Francis, who is perhaps best known for his call for a "white racial consciousness," was not merely talking about the campaigns of Pat Buchanan and foreshadowing Donald Trump; he was laying out a nationalist worldview that fundamentally rejected mainstream conservatism. The day of Limbaugh's broadcast, one leading white supremacist wrote: "Sam Francis was right:

We need to stop pretending we are 'true conservatives' or that we have anything in common with these bow-tied, low-T clowns. We don't support the 'conservative agenda' as articulated by the *National Review*. We are populists and nationalists, which means we are 'tethered' to the well-being of our own people and protecting and advancing their interests, not some abstract ideology."[15]

Francis was also well-known in the Alt Right very specifically as an advocate of white nationalism with a strong whiff of racist eugenics. For example, Francis argued:

> If whites wanted to do so, they could dictate a solution to the racial problem tomorrow—by curtailing immigration and sealing the border, *by imposing adequate fertility controls* on nonwhites and encouraging a higher white birth rate, by refusing to be bullied into enduring "multiculturalism," affirmative action, civil rights laws and policies; and by refusing to submit to cultural dissolution, inter-racial violence and insults, and the guilt that multiracialists inculcate. [Emphasis added.][16]

As the Southern Law and Poverty Center later noted, one frequent contributor to the white supremacist website Stormfront chided Limbaugh for not fully embracing the white nationalist premises of Francis's argument. "Now if only El Rushbo will also acknowledge, that what's at the heart of this Nationalist & Populist movement is Racialism," he wrote. "Come on Limbaugh. Grow a real set of nuts would ya [*sic*]."[17]

EMPOWERING THE ALT RIGHT

A caveat: obviously not everyone who uses the term "cuckservative" or flirts with the Alt Right embraces its nativist, xenophobic, anti-Semitic agenda or even has any clue about its darker etymology. Nor is it fair to impugn guilt by association to those voters who may have other reasons for supporting Trump. But there's no doubt that some white nationalists seized on the opportunity to insert themselves into the current campaign, often claiming to be legitimate—actually, the only legitimate—conservatives.

By tapping into the Trump phenomenon online, Alt Right activists were able to vastly expand their reach, slipstreaming behind hundreds of thousands of other social media users who may not have noticed with whom they were now associating. They emerged from the campaign emboldened and empowered. Trump was notably reluctant to condemn former KKK leader David Duke. The implication was that Trump may have imagined that many of his supporters—later labeled "deplorables" by Hillary Clinton—may have shared some of his views. Some of those around him undoubtedly understood the role that the Alt Right played in social media boosting his candidacy and unleashing waves of vitriol against his opponents and critics.

During the campaign Trump tweeted out fake crime stats from one notorious white nationalist website,[18] and later retweeted an image posted by a Twitter account known as "WhiteGenocideTM." (It was a photoshopped image depicting Jeb Bush as a homeless man outside Trump Tower.) The Twitter account retweeted by the future president used the name "Donald Trumpovitz," and linked to a website containing pro-Hitler propaganda. The users' feed was "largely a collection of retweets about violence allegedly committed by African-American suspects and anti-Arab posts."[19]

The Trump campaign also gave media credentials to *The Political Cesspool*, a white nationalist radio program whose host wants "to revive the White birthrate above replacement level fertility."[20] Earlier in the year, Donald Trump Jr. appeared on the show, dramatically raising its profile.[21]

During the campaign Hillary Clinton tried to make an issue of Trump's relationships with the Alt Right, giving a speech in Reno, that Trump "is taking hate groups mainstream and helping a radical fringe take over the Republican Party."[22] "This is not conservatism as we have known it," she said. "This is not Republicanism as we have known it. These are race-baiting ideas, anti-Muslim and anti-immigrant ideas, antiwoman—all key tenets making up an emerging racist ideology known as the 'Alt-Right.' " She noted the close ties between Breitbart and the Alt Right, saying that the "de facto merger between Breitbart and the Trump Campaign represents a landmark achievement for the 'Alt-Right.' A fringe element has effectively taken over the Republican Party." Although the speech was widely covered (and drew praise from some conservative commentators) it was not enough to derail Trump or to dissuade the vast majority of Republicans from backing him in November.

THE RATIONALIZERS

As the presence of white nationalists on the Right became evident, there were inevitably attempts to "explain" or rationalize the movement. One of the more painful attempts was a lengthy essay entitled "The Intellectual Case for Trump: Why the White Nationalist Support?" written by a writer named Mytheos Holt.[23] A senior fellow at the Institute for Liberty, Holt notes that he is Jewish and was careful to explain that he was not himself a white nationalist, but wanted to understand the perspective of the racialists.

In his essay, he recounted his attempts to reach out to and understand white nationalists, including a young woman he calls Sylvia who inhabited some of the darker reaches of the racist swamp. The young woman, he writes, "had been raised as a member of an infamous white nationalist organization. And I do mean 'infamous.' These weren't the comparatively well-mannered sorts that attend conferences led by Richard Spencer. These were the sorts of people who probably get raided by the FBI."

After spending time talking with Sylvia, whom he suggests may have been a neo-Nazi, Holt wrote that he "came away with an appreciation for how much, and how unfairly, her people really were hurting. I say 'unfairly' for multiple reasons: firstly, because people as brilliant as Sylvia is do not deserve to be written off as incurable white trash." Holt goes on to explain that racialists like Sylvia were motivated by what he calls an "otherwise perfectly respectable, conservative pride in Western culture," which he said had "atrophie[d] into white nationalism when the person holding it comes to believe that respect for liberal Western civilization is inextricably tied to one's race." He was willing to accept their reasons for sharing his enthusiasm for Trump's candidacy, because they saw him as a champion of those Western values. And Holt shared their contempt for softer, more traditional conservatives. "In fact, Trump, and Trump alone, has been willing to say what should have been obvious from the start," Holt wrote, "that the universalism and Whig historical pretensions of Kemp-and-W-style 'bleeding heart conservatism' are dangerous distractions if they leave the American people as wounded prey for anti-American, extremist bottom feeders."

He concluded with a sexualized imagery of the nation-as-cuckold. Unless Trump was empowered to fight back, he concluded, "the people damaged by multicultural, leftist attacks on Western civilization will be thoroughly justified in sneering at us as proverbial 'cuckservatives' forever mentally masturbating with our own empty universalism while barbarism rapes Lady Liberty."[24]

MILO (AND BREITBART) EXPLAINS

Besides defending the use of the term "cuckservatives," Breitbart also emerged as one of the chief explainers of the Alt Right, publishing a lengthy apologia by Milo Yiannopoulos in March 2016.[25]

Occasionally described as an "Alt Right provocateur," Milo quickly became a key figure in the propagation of Alt Right ideas and popularizing them on university campuses, where his flamboyant appearances have sparked sometimes violent backlashes. At the bottom of his appeal is the desire to shock and offend. After the birth of former Breitbart colleague Ben Shapiro's baby, Milo tweeted out, "Prayers to Ben who had to see his kid come out half-black," with a picture of a black infant.[26] The message, Shapiro later wrote, was that "I'm a 'cuck' who wants to see the races mixed."[27] He also traffics in flamboyant anti-Semitism. At one of his campus appearances Milo, who is Jewish himself, referred to a Jewish writer as "a typical example of a sort of thick-as-pig shit media Jew, who has all these sort of right, P.C. politics."[28] In July 2016, Twitter shut down Yiannopoulos's account after he led a harassment campaign against actress Leslie Jones, who is African American. Many of his tweets, reported BuzzFeed, "decried Jones for being black and a woman."[29]

In his Breitbart essay Yiannopoulos attempted to normalize and explain the appeal of the new movement. Like the caller to Limbaugh's show, he emphasized its youth and excitement. "The alt-right has a youthful energy and jarring, taboo-defying rhetoric that have boosted its membership and made it impossible to ignore," he wrote.

He also emphasized the movement's intellectual seriousness. "There are many things that separate the alternative right from old-school racist skinheads (to whom they are often idiotically compared), but one thing stands out above all else: intelligence." While skinheads were often "low-information, low-IQ thugs," he insisted, the "alternative right are a much smarter group of people—which perhaps suggests why the Left hates them so much. They're dangerously bright."*

---

*Writer Michael Knowles noted that virtually all of the thinkers Milo Yiannopoulos had cited here were white nationalists:

Richard Spencer, president of the white nationalist National Policy Institute, former editor of Taki's, and founder of Radix Journal/AlternativeRight.com

Kevin MacDonald, who as editor of the *Occidental Observer* promises to "present original content touching on the themes of white identity, white interests, and the culture of the West

Sam Francis, the late syndicated columnist who famously called for a "white racial consciousness

Theodore Robert Beale, the white nationalist blogger better known by his pen name Vox Day, who counts as a central tenet of the Alt-Right that "we must secure the existence of white people and a future for white children," which represents one half of the white nationalist, neo-Nazi numerical symbol 1488.

—Michael Knowles, "An Actual Conservative's Guide to the Alt-Right: 8 Things You Need To Know," *Daily Wire*, September 26, 2016

While the movement held an attraction for "isolationists, pro-Russians and ex–Ron Paul supporters frustrated with continued neo-conservative domination of the Republican Party," he acknowledged that race consciousness was at the center of the Alt Right. "The alt-right believe that some degree of separation between peoples is necessary for a culture to be preserved," he explained. "A Mosque next to an English street full of houses bearing the flag of St. George, according to alt-righters, is neither an English street nor a Muslim street—separation is necessary for distinctiveness."[30]

But above all, Yiannopoulos argued, the Alt Right was . . . *fun*. Young rebels, he wrote, were "drawn to the alt-right for the same reason that young Baby Boomers were drawn to the New Left in the 1960s: because it promises fun, transgression, and a challenge to social norms they just don't understand." Yiannopoulos explained how the "fun" worked:

> Just as the kids of the 60s shocked their parents with promiscuity, long hair and rock'n'roll, so too do the alt-right's young meme brigades shock older generations with outrageous caricatures, from the Jewish "Shlomo Shekelburg" to "Remove Kebab," an internet in-joke about the Bosnian genocide. These caricatures are often spliced together with Millennial pop culture references, from old 4chan memes like pepe the frog to anime and My Little Pony references.[31]

He then proceeds to celebrate the nastiness of the movement's trolls. When GOP consultant Rick Wilson opined on Twitter that they were "childless single men who jerk off to anime," the Alt Right retaliated. Yiannopoulos reported approvingly:

> Responding in kind, they proceeded to unleash all the weapons of mass trolling that anonymous subcultures are notorious for—and brilliant at. From digging up the most embarrassing parts of his family's internet history to ordering unwanted pizzas to his house and bombarding his feed with anime and

Nazi propaganda, the alt-right's meme team, in typically
juvenile but undeniably hysterical fashion, revealed their true
motivations: not racism, the restoration of monarchy or
traditional gender roles, but lulz.[32]

Lulz is defined as "fun, laughter, or amusement, especially that derived
at another's expense." For Yiannopoulos, the trolling, the Nazi imagery, the raw Jew hatred wasn't about ideology, it was about being "fresh,
daring, and funny."*

AN EXPLOSION OF HATE

But few of the targets of the trolling and harassment found it amusing.

In March 2016, Jewish writer Bethany Mandel wrote that "the sur-
est way to see anti-Semitism flood your mentions column is to tweet
something negative about Donald Trump." She was called a "slimy
Jewess" and told that she "deserved the oven."

Not only was the anti-Semitic deluge scary and graphic, it got
personal. Trump fans began to "dox" me—a term for adversar-
ies' attempt to ferret out private or identifying information
online with malicious intent. My conversion to Judaism was
used as a weapon against me, and I received death threats in my
private Facebook mailbox, prompting me to file a police report.[33]

*There were, however, apparently limits even for the Breitbart editor. One faction
of the Alt Right that made many hangers-on uncomfortable was the group known
as 1488. The "14" referred to the fouteen-word slogan "We Must Secure the Existence of White People and a Future for White Children." The "88" (referring to
the eighth letter of the alphabet, H) is code for "Heil Hitler."

"Not very edifying stuff," Yiannopoulos admits. But he then attempts to
draw a moral equivalency between the Hitler fan boys and movements on the
Left. "1488ers are the equivalent of the Black Lives Matter supporters who call for
the deaths of policemen," he insisted, "or feminists who unironically want to
#KillAllMen." (Milo Yiannopoulos, "An Establishment Conservative's Guide To
The Alt-Right," Breitbart, March 29, 2016.)

It had gotten so bad, she wrote, that she bought a gun: "Over the coming weeks, I plan to learn how to shoot it better." Mandel's case may have been extreme, but it was not unusual. A report by the Anti-Defamation League (ADL) found that hundreds of journalists had been the subject of a cascade of anti-Semitic attacks on Twitter during the presidential campaign.[34] One *New York Times* editor was sent drawings of a "hook-nosed Jew" and an image of a concentration camp with the words "Machen America Great." The report found that former Breitbart writer Ben Shapiro (who resigned and became an outspoken Trump critic) was the most frequently targeted journalistic figure.

The ADL task force tried to quantify the problem, concluding that a "total of 2.6 million tweets containing language frequently found in anti-Semitic speech were posted across Twitter between August 2015 and July 2016." It went on to note:

> Of the 2.6 million total tweets, ADL focused its analysis on tweets directed at 50,000 journalists in the United States. A total of 19,253 anti-Semitic tweets were directed at those journalists, but the total number of anti-Semitic tweets directed at journalists overall could be much higher for a variety of factors noted in the report also shows that more than two-thirds (68 percent) of the anti-Semitic tweets directed at those journalists were sent by 1,600 Twitter accounts (out of 313 million existing Twitter accounts). These aggressors are disproportionately likely to self-identify as Donald Trump supporters, conservatives, or part of the "alt-right," a loosely connected group of extremists, some of whom are white supremacists. The words that appear most frequently in the 1,600 Twitter attackers' bios are "Trump," "nationalist," "conservative," and "white."[35]

The report made it clear that the ADL was not suggesting that the Trump campaign itself either supported or endorsed the attacks, "only that certain self-styled supporters sent these ugly messages. The data also illustrates the connectedness of the attackers: waves of anti-Semitic tweets tend to emerge from closely connected online "communities."*

Many of the worst instances of harassment were connected to a website known as the Daily Stormer and its founder, a neo-Nazi activist named Andrew Anglin. I first became aware of the site when I received, via email, a photoshopped image of my picture inside a gas chamber. A smiling Donald Trump wearing a German military uniform is poised to press the red "gas" button. The photoshopping tool had been created by the website and was widely used to troll both Jewish and non-Jewish critics of the Trump campaign.

The site takes its name from the German Nazi newspaper *Der Stürmer*, which was notorious for the viciousness of its anti-Semitic caricatures of Jews. After World War II, *Der Stürmer's* publisher, Julius Streicher, was executed for crimes against humanity. Anglin created the site in 2013 as an updated version of his previous website, which he called Total Fascism.[36] As of this writing, the new website features pictures of Ronald Reagan and Donald Trump and the slogan "Daily Stormer— The World's Most Goal-Oriented Republican Website."

It is important to emphasize again that the Alt Right is a mansion with many rooms and some very real divisions. Anglin, for example, is not a fan of Milo Yiannopoulos, who is depicted on the Daily Stormer with a cartoon of the Jewish nose superimposed on his face and is referred to as "Filthy Rat Kike Milo." But Anglin is also interested in emphasizing the common ground among the various disparate groups and interests that make up the white nationalist movement. In his own guide to the Alt Right, Anglin notes that the movement included various fac-

---

* "The ADL Task Force study shows that a small cohort of journalists bore the brunt of the online abuse. The Task Force identified that some 19,253 overtly anti-Semitic tweets were sent to at least 800 journalists in the U.S. during the 12 month study. The top 10 most targeted journalists—all of whom are Jewish—received 83 percent of those 19,253 tweets. The top 10 includes conservative columnist Ben Shapiro, Tablet's Yair Rosenberg, the *Atlantic's* Jeffrey Goldberg and the *New York Times'* Jonathan Weisman, and CNN's Sally Kohn and Jake Tapper." —"Anti-Semitic Targeting of Journalists During the 2016 Presidential Campaign; A report from ADL's Task Force on Harassment and Journalism," ADL, October 19, 2016.

tions, but that they had all been led "toward this center-point where we have all met. The campaign of Donald Trump is effectively the nexus of that centerpoint."[37] Impressed by Trump's rhetoric on illegal immigrants, Anglin endorsed Trump in 2015 and urged the readers of the Daily Stormer to "vote for the first time in our lives for the one man who actually represents our interests." After Trump called for barring Muslims from the country, the site declared: "Heil Donald Trump— The Ultimate Savior."

But Anglin's greatest accomplishment was the creation of what he calls his "Troll Army," which he uses to attack political opponents, deployed to great effect in early 2016.

After *GQ* magazine published a profile of Melania Trump by writer Julia Ioffe, the future First Lady took to Facebook to denounce the piece as "yet another example of the dishonest media and their disingenuous reporting."[38] Anglin quickly mobilized his Troll Army, posting an article headlined: "Empress Melania Attacked by Filthy Russian Kike Julia Ioffe in GQ!"[39] The post featured a picture of Ioffe wearing a Nazi-era yellow star with the word "Jude" and a call to action from Anglin: "Please go ahead and send her a tweet and let her know what you think of her dirty kike trickery. Make sure to identify her as a Jew working against White interests, or send her the picture with the Jude star from the top of this article."

The result was a torrent of abuse, including death threats against the journalist. On Twitter, she was sent pictures of Jews being shot in the head and pictures of her wearing concentration camp stripes. When she answered her phone, a caller began playing a recording of a speech by Adolf Hitler.

"The irony of this is that today," Ioffe told the British newspaper the *Guardian*, "I was reminded that 26 years ago today my family came to the US from Russia. We left Russia because we were fleeing antisemitism. It's been a rude shock for everyone."[40]* The response from the GOP nominee

---

*Ioffe was later fired by *Politico* after posting an offensive tweet about Trump and his daughter Ivanka. Iofee later apologized: "It was a tasteless, offensive tweet that I regret and have deleted. I am truly and deeply sorry. It won't happen again."

was also troubling. When Trump was asked by CNN's Wolf Blitzer about the anti-Semitic attacks and death threats, the future president pointedly refused to condemn them, pleading ignorance and saying, "I don't have a message to the fans. A woman wrote an article that was inaccurate."[41] Trump's refusal to denounce the Troll Army was greeted with delight by Anglin, who immediately posted: "Glorious Leader Donald Trump Refuses to Denounce Stormer Troll Army." He exulted:

> Asked by the disgusting and evil Jewish parasite Wolf Blitzer to denounce the Stormer Troll Army, The Glorious Leader declined.
>
> The Jew Wolf was attempting to Stump the Trump, bringing up Stormer attacks on Jew terrorist Julia Ioffe. Trump responded to the request with "I have no message to the fans" which might as well have been "Hail Victory, Comrades!"[42]

Melania Trump was also asked about the attacks on Ioffe by writer Mickey Rapkin of *DuJour* magazine. "So if people put a swastika on my face once this article comes out," Rapkin wondered, "will she denounce them?" Again, she declined to condemn the threats, suggesting instead that Ioffe had brought the ugliness onto herself. "I don't control my fans," she said, "but I don't agree with what they're doing. I understand what you mean, but there are people out there who maybe went too far. She provoked them."[43]

BIRCHING THE ALT RIGHT

The implications for mainstream conservatives should have been obvious. After decades of fending off the Left's smear that conservatives are racists, the Alt Right and its media enablers now seem intent on confirming the worst stereotypes. But this is not simply a matter of

---

(forward.com/fast-forward/357126/julia-ioffe-fired-over-obscene-ivanka-trump-tweet.) She is now a writer for the *Atlantic*.

public relations or even semantics. A conservative movement that embraces the Alt Right—or its candidate—will have forfeited both its intellectual integrity and its political future. No tent can possibly be that big and still remain standing.

There should be no doubt what the Alt Right represents for the Right. On an intellectual level, the Alt Right challenges the conservative belief that America is a nation founded on an idea or a vision of natural and God-given rights. They prefer to see it as defined by its ethnic and racial identities. This goes to the core of their break with the conservative tradition. "We question America's founding myth," Spencer, the white nationalist leader, explained. "If you look at the Declaration of Independence, it's not just the notion of 'all men are created equal' that I would object to. It's also this notion that states come into being as entities for people to defend their inalienable rights. I find that to be total hokum, nonsense. That's not how any state, including the United States, came into being."[44] As a result, the Alt Right is skeptical of the idea of American exceptionalism. For them, it is a white, European enclave in which Jews, immigrants, and other minorities are trespassing. This is not simply a matter of emphasis, it is a fundamental rejection of the conservative view of America; and, in particular, a rejection of what Ronald Reagan meant when he described his vision of the country as a "shining city on a hill." Reagan had borrowed this image from John Winthrop, and in his farewell speech in 1989, he explained what it meant to him:

> But in my mind it was a tall, proud city built on rocks stronger than oceans, windswept, God-blessed, and teeming with people of all kinds living in harmony and peace; a city with free ports that hummed with commerce and creativity. *And if there had to be city walls, the walls had doors and the doors were open to anyone with the will and the heart to get here.* That's how I saw it, and see it still. [Emphasis added.][45]

The Alt Right not only wanted walls; they wanted the doors firmly shut. To their credit, many of the leading voices of the conservative movement spoke out forcefully against both the Alt Right and the winking tolerance of its message. Jonah Goldberg repeatedly insisted that the movement needed to draw a definitive line. In an appearance on Hugh Hewitt's radio show, Goldberg argued: "What we should say is this is not your group to them, too. These are not disaffected Tea Partiers. These are people who we have a fundamental, first principle disagreement with. And any movement that has them in it, doesn't have me in it, and vice versa. . . ."

HH: And they have to be driven out of the Republican Party.

JG: Yes.

HH: I'm speaking as a partisan now. As William F. Buckley led the effort to drive the Birchers out of the party, so must genuine conservatives drive out what you and I agree is the core alt right.

JG: Right.[46]

But Buckley was no longer around and there were no longer any gatekeepers with the authority to issue edicts of condemnation that could be enforced. Writers like Noah Rothman, Ben Shapiro, Peter Wehner, Jonah Goldberg, and others could pen scorching jeremiads about the Alt Right's racism, but none of them had the authority that Buckley once wielded. In the 1960s, Buckley could deny the Birchers access to his magazine, forcing them further to the fringes and denying them the media platform they would need to disseminate their message. But now, in an age when everyone can be their own publisher, that is no longer possible.

None of that would have mattered, however, if Trump had forcefully distanced himself from the Alt Right, or even if he had been defeated. Recall that Barry Goldwater had encouraged and backed Buckley's expulsion of the Birchers. In contrast, Trump's campaign enabled the movement to rise to a prominence it could never otherwise have imagined. As a result, conservative pundit Matthew Continetti wrote, the "Nasty mouth-breathers Buckley expelled from conservatism have returned."[47]

In early 2017, the organizers of the annual CPAC convention initially named Milo Yiannopoulos as one of the event's featured speakers, giving the Alt Right provocateur a platform to be the face of conservatism for a new generation. Organizers defended the choice as a blow for free speech; but that was never the issue because the American Conservative Union (ACU), which ran CPAC, was a private organization that retained the ability to choose its spokesmen and set its own standards. Peter Wehner, who is a senior fellow at the Ethics and Public Policy Center, called the invitation "more evidence of the moral decay of conservatism."

Given the group's history, the decision to invite the Alt Right figure was also ironic. Nicole Hemmer notes that the American Conservative Union had originally been founded in 1964 precisely "to clean up conservatism's image, to make it responsible and respectable." Like Buckley, the founders of the ACU saw extremism on the Right as "an existential problem." The whole point of the ACU was "to police the lines of conservatism, to toss out any groups that might tarnish the right's image."[48]

After a video surfaced in which Milo expressed support for sex between grown men and children as young as thirteen, CPAC rescinded the invitation. But the episode was nonetheless revealing; while the advocacy of pedophilia was a bridge too far, the conservative group had been willing to overlook Yiannopoulos's racism, anti-Semitism, Alt Right Nazi trolling, and his bullying. Lines had been crossed; far from being expelled, the Alt Right had been normalized.

14

THE BINARY CHOICE

[The devil] always sends errors in the world in pairs—pairs of
opposites. He always encourages us to spend a lot of time
thinking about which is the worst. You see why, of course? He
relies on your extra dislike of the one error to draw you
gradually into the opposite one. But do not let us be fooled.
We have to keep our eyes on the goal and go straight through
between both errors. We have no other concern than that with
either of them.

—C. S. LEWIS, *MERE CHRISTIANITY*

AS TRUMP'S CANDIDACY SURGED in February 2016, Rush
Limbaugh laid out the stark choice faced by conservatives. The Left
was not simply wrong about a variety of issues, it was out to destroy
almost everything Americans held dear:

> These people have to be defeated. They have to be over-
> whelmed. And then after they're defeated they cannot be
> allowed to bully whoever wins into cowardice and caving
> in . . . if you believe in a certain cultural America, it's under
> siege. There's nothing to join with on the other side in preserv-
> ing it. They want to tear it down, transform it, and rebuild it.

They have to be defeated. This is why the Republican Party's worthless. They don't even think this way. The Republican Party's thinking about showing they can work together, they can cooperate, make Washington work. . . . [1]

Everything was at stake, he insisted, suggesting that this election might be the Right's very last stand.

We've got people coming at us that are gonna try to wipe us out and eliminate everything and pretend it didn't happen, corrupt, sabotage, undermine. Whoever the next president is, and whoever's running the next Congress, and whoever nominates the Supreme Court justice, if it's a conservative, you have no idea what's gonna be brought to bear! We're gonna need people with such backbone and guts and steel and iron to hold up and to withstand what's gonna come at 'em, you can't even imagine it.

For many conservatives steeped in the Right's alternative reality media ecosystem, politics had come down to a starkly binary choice. This reflects our new politics: As the essential loyalties shift from ideas to parties to individuals, choices are increasingly framed as us vs. them; red vs. blue; good vs. evil.

In this binary world, where everything is at stake, everything is in play, there is no room for quibbles about character, or truth, or principles. If everything—the Supreme Court, the fate of Western civilization, the Constitution, the survival of the planet—depends on tribal victory, then nothing else really matters. In a binary political world, voters are told they must not merely surrender their principles, but must also accept bizarre behavior, dishonesty, crudity, and cruelty. The other side is always worse; the stakes require everything to be sacrificed or subsumed in the service of the greater cause.

With each election, the apocalyptic rhetoric has been ratcheted up and the urgent language of fund-raising letters—ACT NOW! DON'T WAIT—was echoed throughout the Right media. Every election was the tipping point—potentially the end of America. "It's just a win at all cost obsession," wrote blogger Ben Howe. "And throughout all this time Republicans infected their base with that same urgency. Every election was do or die. Every election is 1776 reborn. I know this because I not only fell for it, I took part in spreading the idea."

The key, of course, was the relentless demonization of the opposition, who *literally* (yes, *literally*) wanted to flood the country with criminal refugees and rapist immigrant hordes. Hillary Clinton was not merely an ethically challenged liberal retread, she was evil personified. "We have reached a point of hyperbole where people regularly tell me that Hillary Clinton is literally Satan," Howe wrote. "That in fact, if the actual source of all evil in the universe was running opposite Hillary, they'd vote for the Prince of Darkness."[2]

Appearing on the Christian Broadcasting Network, former congresswoman Michele Bachmann declared: "I don't want to be melodramatic, but I do want to be truthful. I believe without a shadow of a doubt this is the last election. This is it. This is the last election."[3] Appearing on the same network, Trump said essentially the same thing—unless he won, "you're going to have illegal immigrants coming in and they're going to be legalized and they're going to be able to vote and once that all happens you can forget it." Electing Clinton would mean "a whole different church structure. You're going to have a whole different Supreme Court structure . . . we're going to end up with another Venezuela, large-scale version. It would be a disaster for the country."[4]

This argument that the choice was strictly binary had powerful appeal among conservatives, including some conservative intellectuals who insisted that the danger to the country was too ominous to sweat the details about "principles," or questions of "character." One of the more thoughtful conservative talk show hosts, author and ethicist Dennis Prager, argued that a Democratic victory in 2016 meant the country might not "survive as the country it was founded to be. In that regard we are at the most perilous tipping point of American history." More perilous, apparently, than the Civil War, the Great Depression, or two World Wars. "Leftism is a terminal cancer in the American bloodstream and soul," Prager argued. "So our first and greatest principle is to destroy this cancer before it destroys us. We therefore see voting for Donald Trump as political chemotherapy needed to prevent our demise. And at this time, that is, by far, the greatest principle."[5]

Perhaps the most startling reversal was former education secretary and drug czar Bill Bennett, who had once written that it is "our character that supports the promise of our future—far more than particular government programs or policies," but now derided concerns about Trump's character as a sign of "vanity."[6]

Historian Victor Davis Hanson similarly acknowledged that Trump was crude and "mercurial," but argued that his defeat would lead to left-wing control of the Supreme Court and a $40 trillion national debt. Like other West Coast thinkers, he expressed impatience with traditional conservatives who were reluctant to back the nominee. "One does not need lectures about conservatism from Edmund Burke when, at the neighborhood school, English becomes a second language, or when one is rammed by a hit-and-run driver illegally in the United States who flees the scene of the accident," insisted Hanson.[7]*

THE FLIGHT 93 ELECTION?

Capturing the full apocalyptic mood among conservatives, the normally low-profile Claremont Institute published a lengthy article entitled "The Flight 93 Election," which linked the election to the doomed flight on September 11, 2001, on which passengers stormed the airplane's cabin to stop hijackers who planned to ram the plane into the Capitol.[8] Everyone on board died.

The author, Michael Anton, writing under the pseudonym Publius Decius Mus, begins, "2016 is the Flight 93 election: charge the

---

* Full disclosure here: I have known both Bill Bennett and Dennis Prager for years and have frequently appeared on their shows (and they have appeared on mine). I consider both of them to be friends. I regard Victor Davis Hanson as one of the foremost conservative thinkers and writers of his generation. He is on the board of directors of the foundation that formerly employed my wife. So, yes, this broke my heart.

cockpit or you die." He goes on to state: "You may die anyway. You—
or the leader of your party—may make it into the cockpit and not
know how to fly or land the plane. There are no guarantees. Except
one: if you don't try, death is certain. To compound the metaphor: a
Hillary Clinton presidency is Russian roulette with a semiauto. With
Trump, at least you can spin the cylinder and take your chances."*

Despite the warnings against Clinton, the gravamen of the piece
was a root-and-branch denunciation of mainstream conservatism, both
its ideology and its tactics. While ostensibly designed to persuade
wavering conservatives to get on board, Conor Friedersdorf noted,
the essay "doubles as a barely disguised rejection of conservatism itself, stoking panic in hopes that conservatives embrace what is essentially right-leaning authoritarianism."[9]

Indeed, you simply cannot read this essay side by side with Goldwater's *The Conscience of a Conservative,* with its emphasis on freedom
and limited government, and imagine that they represent the same
political philosophy or tradition. Whereas Goldwater's book was a man-
ifesto of antiauthoritarianism, Anton/Decius's call to arms was a
trumpet blast of strongman politics in the service of virtuous causes. It
was precisely the sort of appeal that Goldwater had warned against,
but that was now being embraced by influential voices on the Right.

Perhaps because Anton's article oozed with disdain for constitutional niceties and the conservative tradition of restraint, it appealed
powerfully to Rush Limbaugh. As he read long passages on his radio
show, Limbaugh explained, "The point of this whole piece is that
Donald Trump's the only hope, that conservatism no longer applies."
Anton declared:

> If conservatives are right about the importance of virtue,
> morality, religious faith, stability, character and so on in the

---

*The screed's author, Michael Anton, was later rewarded with a position on the
staff of the National Security Council in Trump's White House. (Michael Warren,
"The Anonymous Pro-Trump 'Decius' Now Works Inside the White House,"
Weekly Standard, February 2, 2017.)

individual; if they are right about sexual morality or what came to be termed "family values"; if they are right about the importance of education to inculcate good character and to teach the fundamentals that have defined knowledge in the West for millennia; if they are right about societal norms and public order; if they are right about the centrality of initiative, enterprise, industry, and thrift to a sound economy and a healthy society; if they are right about the soul-sapping effects of paternalistic Big Government and its cannibalization of civil society and religious institutions; if they are right about the necessity of a strong defense and prudent statesmanship in the international sphere—if they are right about the importance of all this to national health and even survival, then they must believe—mustn't they?—that we are *headed off a cliff.* [Emphasis in original.]

But it's quite obvious that conservatives don't believe any such thing, that they feel no such sense of urgency, of an immediate necessity to change course and avoid the cliff.[10]

Friedersdorf called that over-the-top argument "flagrant sophistry that should embarrass The Claremont Institute," which described itself as being dedicated to restoring the values of the American founding. But Anton's argument was that the ends—the conservative agenda—must be achieved by any means necessary. As legal scholar Greg Weiner later noted, that argument "is what Michael Oakeshott would call telocratic—directed toward substantive ends—rather than classically liberal, which is nomocratic, providing boundaries and rules that allow individuals to choose ends of their own."[11] But, Anton now argued that the crisis was so dire, extinction so close, the only solution was to shake off those impediments and trust our fate to the Man on the White Horse.*

---

*Greg Weiner noted that Anton/Decius was exaggerating a sense of catastrophe to make his point:

Consider: Decius warns that "the tsunami of leftism that still engulfs our every—literal and figurative—shore has receded not a bit but indeed has grown."

Noting Anton's theatrical language, Weiner wrote that he "accepts the anticonstitutional and thus anticonservative proposition that the President straddled the Constitution like the Colossus stood astride the harbor at Rhodes." By accepting the notion of an Imperial president, Weiner wrote that Anton was "rejecting the adequacy of a Constitutional framework that survived a British invasion, slavery, the Civil War, the Great War, the rise of fascism and Communism, Jim Crow—and that will obviously survive four years of Hillary Clinton."[12]

Friedersdorf was not alone in noting that Claremont had published an essay that seemed based on a central Alt Right premise. "As a reader sympathetic to that movement put it, the alt-right 'rejects the procedural fetishism of parliamentary and representative democracies.'" The Anton/Decius essay argued from the same premise: He contended that "conservatism grounded in the principles of the Founding, in the Declaration and the Constitution, should be abandoned," wrote Friedersdorf. "The essay would be more honest if it forthrightly declared its belief that conservatives are wrong and should wake up to their mistake—that the right must abandon cultural, economic, and political conservatism to rally around an authoritarian, because that's the only way to stop what the essayist regards as what's most important."[13]

This is absurd. The Speaker of the House is a thoughtful conservative with an operating majority. The Senate is in Republican hands. Several major countries have governments somewhere right of center.

. . .

Consequently, even granting *arguendo* that the cliff awaits, the essential question Trump presents is whether injecting an already inflamed presidency with political growth hormone is the answer. If that is the answer, the Constitution of the United States is not. It divides authority among three branches of government, led by a deliberative Congress whose will the President executes. Decius, apparently, would deepen the corruption of that regime by handing it to a strongman whose devotion to the Constitution stops at its phantom Article XII. Decius' Constitution is thus far more Wilsonian and Progressive than the original. (Greg Weiner, "The Flight of Fancy Election," Library of Law and Liberty, September 8, 2016.)

Like the Alt Right, Anton characterized mainstream conservatives as feckless losers. "The whole enterprise of Conservatism, Inc., reeks of failure," he writes, ignoring decades of demonstrable successes.

> To the extent that you are ever on the winning side of anything, it's as sophists who help the Davoisie oligarchy rationalize open borders, lower wages, outsourcing, de-industrialization, trade giveaways, and endless, pointless, winless war. . . . Their "opposition" may be in all cases ineffectual and often indistinguishable from support. But they don't dream up inanities like 32 "genders," elective bathrooms, single-payer, Iran sycophancy, "Islamophobia," and Black Lives Matter. They merely help ratify them.

This found a receptive audience in talk radio, but it was errant nonsense. Ben Shapiro noted that there was a legitimate case to be made for voting for Trump, but that "this diarrheic mess of jabbering drivel by a faux intellectual substituting classical references for wisdom ain't it."[14]

Indeed, Anton's rant is a randomized word salad ("open borders, lower wages, outsourcing, de-industrialization, trade giveaways, and endless, pointless, winless war") that described few, if any of the conservatives he was targeting. Like Shapiro, I have never been to Davos, nor do I know any of the "Davoisie oligarchy." I'm from Milwaukee, Wisconsin, so we don't travel in those circles. But the new populism needed an enemy, an "elite" or an "establishment," to blast, even if it had to be fabricated.

WE WERE WARNED ABOUT THIS

Enthusiasm for the strongman has been a fixture in Europe's right wing but, until recently, seldom among American conservatives. Rather, the warnings against demagogues and political bullies run deep in American history. Abraham Lincoln, who did not hesitate to use the broad powers of the presidency when it was warranted, nevertheless in his 1838 Lyceum address had warned against the strongman who would seek to overturn the nation's institutions and laws. Perhaps naïvely, Lincoln imagined that the Napoléon-like figure would be a man of "towering genius" rather than a celebrity entrepreneur. But the warning is still relevant. No foreign enemy would ever be able to subdue the country. Even the most powerful army, he said, "could not by force, take a drink from the Ohio, or make a track on the Blue Ridge, in a trial of a thousand years."

Instead, the danger would "spring up amongst us" Lincoln warned. "If destruction be our lot, we must ourselves be its author and finisher. As a nation of freemen, we must live through all time, or die by suicide. . . ." Lincoln described the "towering genius" as a figure who "thirsts and burns for distinction; and, if possible, it will have it, whether at the expense of emancipating slaves, or enslaving freemen." It seemed likely that such a figure would eventually arise here. "And when such a one does, it will require the people to be united with each other, attached to the government and laws, and generally intelligent, to successfully frustrate his designs." Lincoln anticipated that the great man might be a builder of things, at least for a while. "Distinction will be his paramount object, and although he would as willingly, perhaps more so, acquire it by doing good as harm; yet, that opportunity being past, and nothing left to be done in the way of building up, he would set boldly to the task of pulling down." The only bulwark against such a homegrown tyrant, Lincoln argued, was to cling to the nation's laws and founding documents as "the political religion of the nation."[15]

HAYEK SAW THIS COMING

An even more trenchant warning came from Friedrich Hayek, the Austrian-born economist and classical liberal who played such a central role in the emergence of American free-market conservativism. He had a keen understanding of the temptations of authoritarianism, writing that " 'Emergencies' have always been the pretext on which the safeguards of individual liberty have been eroded." In his chapter on "Why the Worst Get on Top" in his classic work *The Road to Serfdom*, Hayek diagnosed the populist impulse that would lead to the demand for ceding power to a "man of action."* This is "the position which precedes the suppression of democratic institutions and the creation of a totalitarian regime."[16]

At some point in a political or economic crisis, there "is the general demand for quick and determined government action that is the dominating element in the situation, dissatisfaction with the slow and cumbersome course of democratic procedure which makes action for action's sake the goal. It is then the man or the party who seems strong and resolute enough 'to get things done' who exercises the greatest appeal. . . ."

Hayek knew that it was the nature of free societies for people to become dissatisfied "with the ineffectiveness of parliamentary majorities," so they turn to "somebody with such solid support as to inspire confidence that he can carry out whatever he wants."

Hayek then lays out the preconditions for the rise of a demagogic dictator: a dumbed-down populace, a gullible electorate, and a common enemy or group or scapegoats upon which to focus public enmity and anger. The more educated a society is, Hayek says, the more diverse their tastes and values will be, "and the less likely they are to agree on a particular hierarchy of values." The flip side is that "if we wish to find a high degree of uniformity and similarity of outlook, we have to descend to the regions of lower moral and intellectual standards where the more primitive and 'common' instincts and tastes prevail." But in a modern society, potential dictators might be able to rely on there being enough of "those whose uncomplicated and primitive instincts" to

---

*It was Roger Kimball, the editor of the *New Criterion,* who first cited Hayek's warning in connection with the Trump campaign. "For many of us, what is most troubling about Donald Trump is not his particular views or policies—much though we might disagree with them—but rather the aroma of populist demagoguery and menace that surrounds him." (Roger Kimball, "How Hayek Predicted Trump with His 'Why the Worst Get on Top'" PJ Media, May 5, 2016.)

support their efforts. As a result, Hayek said, he "will have to increase their numbers by converting more to the same simple creed."

Here is where propaganda comes into play. The "man of action," Hayek wrote, "will be able to obtain the support of all the docile and gullible, who have no strong convictions of their own but are prepared to accept a ready-made system of values if it is only drummed into their ears sufficiently loudly and frequently." Slogans should be simple and relentless. "It will be those whose vague and imperfectly formed ideas are easily swayed and whose passions and emotions are readily aroused who will thus swell the ranks of the totalitarian party," Hayek predicted.

This led to what Hayek called the third and most important element of the demagogue's program: in order to "weld together a closely coherent and homogeneous body of supporters," he needed to find an enemy.

> It seems to be almost a law of human nature that it is easier for people to agree on a negative programme, on the hatred of an enemy, on the envy of those better off, than on any positive task. The contrast between the "we" and the "they," the common fight against those outside the group, seems to be an essential ingredient in any creed which will solidly knit together a group for common action. It is consequently always employed by those who seek, not merely support of a policy, but the unreserved allegiance of huge masses.[17]

The identification of scapegoats had numerous advantages, not the least of which was that it gave the leader far more leeway than a positive agenda for which he might be held accountable.

> The enemy, whether he be internal like the "Jew" or the "Kulak," or external, seems to be an indispensable requisite in the armoury of a totalitarian leader.

Immigrants, foreigners, refugees, "elites," "international bankers," the Chinese, or the Davoisie oligarchy would work equally as well. For students of history, the "air of populist demagoguery and menace," around the Trump campaign as Roger Kimball put it, was deeply troubling because it seemed to be giving shape to precisely what Hayek had warned against. It was not a path to restored "greatness." It was, in Hayek's terms, the road to *serfdom*.

And it was a radical rejection of values that are central to the conservative tradition.

15

WHAT HAPPENED TO
THE CHRISTIANS?

THE REMARKABLE THING ABOUT the Christian Right in 2016 was not its support of Donald Trump in the general election; it was the genuinely stunning transformation of its value system, and even its core standards of personal conduct.

For decades, a bedrock principle of the Christian Right was that character mattered and that personal morality and ethics were essential requirements of political leadership. Evangelical leaders were especially insistent on this point during the presidency of Bill Clinton, when they argued vigorously that Clinton's conduct and perjury disqualified him from the presidency. Richard John Neuhaus spoke for many Christian leaders when he warned about the damage that would be caused by the national acceptance of a public loss of character. As evangelical theologian Russell Moore would note, "Neuhaus was not alone."

> Jerry Falwell Sr. called for both President Clinton and New York City mayor Rudy Giuliani to step down from political office because their marital infidelities disqualified them from office and "lowered the moral bar for political officeholders in America." We were told that we should not put practical considerations—as important as they may be—above objective moral, transcendent standards. "I don't vote my pocketbook," we were taught to say, "I vote my values."[1]

As recently as 2011, only 30 percent of white evangelicals agreed that "an elected official who commits an immoral act in their personal life can still behave ethically and fulfill their duties in their public life and professional life." But in the era of Trump, evangelical attitudes underwent a stunning, head-snapping transformation. A poll released in October 2016 found that fully 76 percent of white evangelicals had decided that a candidate's morals were no longer that important. While other groups had also become more tolerant of personal immorality, no other group had moved so dramatically. Indeed, as one commentator noted, that "immense shift in opinion means that the same types who made up the former 'Moral Majority' now comprise *the religious group most likely to agree that public and private morality can be separate.*" [Emphasis added.][2]

This followed the full-throated embrace of Trump by many of the best-known leaders of the Christian Right, including Pat Robertson; James Dobson, the founder of Family Talk Radio and Focus on the Family; Tony Perkins of the Family Research Council; Ralph Reed, chairman of the Faith and Freedom Coalition; evangelist Franklin Graham, Billy Graham's son; and Jerry Falwell Jr., president of Liberty University and the son of Jerry Falwell Sr., who had cofounded the Moral Majority and famously called for Clinton's resignation.

Falwell was a particularly interesting case. In a campaign replete with images of exquisite humiliations, one particular photograph stood out. Along with his wife, the evangelical leader posed for a thumbs-up picture with Trump in front of a wall of Trump memorabilia—including a cover of *Playboy* magazine featuring a younger Trump with a pro- vocatively posed model. (At the time the picture was taken, the model in the picture was "in prison for participating in a scheme to transport cocaine from Los Angeles to Sydney—by hiding the drug in airplane toilets.")[3] The irony of the moment did not pass unre- marked. "How perfect," one blogger remarked. "The Evangelical community has whored itself out to Trump in exchange for the promise of power, so why not? Look how perfectly framed that is!! Almost as if it was done on purpose. Diabolical!!"[4] Falwell responded to the online mockery by tweeting out a comparison of himself . . . to Jesus:

> Honored for same hypocrites who accused Jesus of being a friend of publicans and sinners to be targeting me over a decades old mag cover! TY[5]

Falwell had endorsed Trump in January 2016, long before the campaign had become a binary choice of Trump versus Clinton. Falwell explained his support for Trump by saying, "Look at the fruits of his life and . . . people he's provided jobs . . . that's the true test of somebody's Chris- tianity." Conservative commentator Erick Erickson responded: "I did not know the truest test of somebody's Christianity was being an em- ployer. I thought humbling yourself, putting your needs behind those of others, and repenting of sin were more characteristics of faith than putting people on the payroll."[6]

A QUESTION OF FORGIVENESS

The evangelical support for Trump was especially surprising given the evidence that Trump was either indifferent toward or ignorant of the basic tenets of the faith. When he was asked in 2015 at an Iowa Family Leadership Summit whether he had ever asked God for forgiveness, Trump answered: "I am not sure I have. I just go on and try to do a better job from there. I don't think so. I think if I do something wrong, I think, I just try and make it right. I don't bring God into that picture. I don't." He then discussed how he regarded Communion: "When I drink my little wine—which is about the only wine I drink—and have my little cracker, I guess that is a form of asking for forgiveness, and I do that as often as possible because I feel cleansed," he said. "I think in terms of 'Let's go on and let's make it right.' "[7]

In June 2016 he was asked by syndicated columnist and conservative Christian activist Cal Thomas: "You have said you never felt the need to ask for God's forgiveness, and yet repentance for one's sins is a precondition to salvation. I ask you the question Jesus asked of Peter: Who do you say He is?"

> TRUMP: I will be asking for forgiveness, but hopefully I won't have to be asking for much forgiveness.
>
> THOMAS: Who do you say Jesus is?
>
> TRUMP: Jesus to me is somebody I can think about for security and confidence. Somebody I can revere in terms of bravery and in terms of courage and, because I consider the Christian religion so important, somebody I can totally rely on in my own mind.[8]

Good enough, apparently, even for evangelicals who might have hoped that Trump would make some reference to his divinity. But none of this fazed his evangelical cheerleaders.

TRUMP AS KING DAVID

Even after a video surfaced showing Trump bragging about sexually assaulting women, Falwell and other Christian Right leaders stood by him. ("And when you're a star they let you do it," Trump says on the tape. "You can do anything. . . . Grab them by the p—y. You can do anything.") The Family Research Council's Tony Perkins declared: "My personal support for Donald Trump has never been based upon shared values, it is based upon shared concerns about issues . . ."; and then he listed Supreme Court appointments, the War on Terror, and religious liberty as more important than Trump's conduct with women. Pat Robertson, who had famously called Bill Clinton "debauched, debased, and defamed," dismissed Trump's comments as simply "trying to look like he's macho" and praised him for rising "like the phoenix" from the controversy.[9]

Jerry Falwell Jr. was particularly outspoken in Trump's defense, which was not surprising, since he had been offering tortured defenses of Trump's personal conduct for months, including comparing the Manhattan mogul to King David:

> God called King David a man after God's own heart even though he was an adulterer and a murderer. You have to choose the leader that would make the best king or president and not necessarily someone who would be a good pastor. We're not voting for pastor-in-chief. It means sometimes we have to choose a person who has the qualities to lead and who can protect our country and bring us back to economic vitality, and it might not be the person we call when we need somebody to give us spiritual counsel.[10]

Wrote Erick Erickson: "That is flat out mocking God." God had, in fact, punished David for his sins. He continues, "David had to cry out to God for forgiveness. Psalm 51, . . . is David crying out to God, 'For I know my transgressions, and my sin is ever before me. . . . Create in me a clean heart, O God, and renew a right spirit within me. Cast me not away from your presence, and take not your Holy Spirit from me. Restore to me the joy of your salvation, and uphold me with a willing spirit.' "[11] Comparing Trump to David was beyond absurd, because Trump felt no need to repent or seek forgiveness.

196 HOW THE RIGHT LOST ITS MIND

DOBSON'S CHOICE

James Dobson, another influential evangelical leader who backed Trump, did so even though he thought that Trump had been influenced by a decidedly nonmainstream Christian pastor. "I hear," Dobson said, "that Paula White has known Trump for years and that she personally led him to Christ."[12]

White, a thrice-married televangelist, is a controversial figure who has faced IRS investigations, a variety of personal scandals, and financial difficulties. She is best known for emphasizing her wealth in her preaching and for being associated with what is known as the "Prosperity Gospel," which *Politico* described as a doctrine that "says God wants people to be rich—and that more traditional religious leaders frown upon."[13] Russell Moore, the Southern Baptist leader minced no words, calling her a "charlatan" and a "heretic." Even Dobson seemed to express skepticism about the depth of Trump's conversion, choosing instead to cast the election in binary terms: "If anything, this man is a baby Christian who doesn't have a clue about how believers think, talk and act. All I can tell you is that we have only two choices, Hillary or Donald. Hillary scares me to death."*

---

* Dobson's full statement is notable for how low he sets the bar for Trump:
     Only the Lord knows the condition of a person's heart. I can only tell you what I've heard. First, Trump appears to be tender to things of the Spirit. I also hear that Paula White has known Trump for years and that she personally led him to Christ.
     Do I know that for sure? No. Do I know the details of that alleged conversion? I can't say that I do.
     But there are many Christian leaders who are serving on a faith advisory committee for Trump in the future. I am among them. There are about 45 of us that includes Franklin Graham, Robert Jeffress, Jack Graham, Ben Carson, James Robison, Jerry Johnson, and many others whom you would probably know.
     We've all agreed to serve. How will that play out if Trump becomes president? I don't know. It is a good start, I would think.
     If anything, this man is a baby Christian who doesn't have a clue about how believers think, talk and act. All I can tell you is that we have only two choices, Hillary or Donald. Hillary scares me to death.

Dobson's choice provides some insight into how the imperatives of binary choice played out in the evangelical community in ways that were perhaps not immediately apparent to outsiders. For years, some leaders of the religious Right, including Pat Roberston, had conditioned their audiences to apocalyptic visions of politics and to warnings about attempts to assault their faith. But political and legal developments had also sharpened the conviction among many evangelicals that the election was the ultimate binary choice: Christian conservatives were *terrified* of the outcome.

In an essay entitled, "The Uncomfortable Truth about Christian Support for Trump," Jonathan Van Maren explained how so many Christians had come to surrender some of their most deeply held values.[14]

> For eight long years, traditional Christians have fought with the Obama Administration as he tried to force Christian business-owners to pay for birth control and abortifacients, decreed that all schools had to bend to the knee to the brand-new transgender ideology or lose their funding, and began speaking of "freedom of worship" rather than "religious liberty."

What makes Van Maren's article notable is that he concedes every conceivable negative about Trump; he admits that Trump had been pro-abortion until "a very short time ago, and was so unfamiliar with the basic positions held by the pro-life movement that he suggested women be punished for having abortions." He cited Trump's multiple marriages, his infidelities, and his "extraordinary cruelty during the divorce proceedings." Based on his refusal to answer the question, "It seems likely that he's paid for abortions in the past." He was indifferent to the

---

And, if Christians stay home because he isn't a better candidate, Hillary will run the world for perhaps eight years. The very thought of that haunts my nights and days. One thing is sure: we need to be in prayer for our nation at this time of crisis. (Dr. James Dobson on Donald Trump's Christian Faith; drjamesdobson.org/news/dr-james-dobson-on-trumps-christian-faith.)

debate over transgender bathrooms and "shockingly uninformed on many of the issues, as this week's presidential debate highlighted. He's also explosive, thin-skinned, and unable to ignore baiting by opponents."

But, but, but . . . he was not Hillary. Her awfulness compelled even the most orthodox of believers to set aside their doubts. "The media doesn't seem to realize just how loathed Hillary is, and don't seem to recognize why," Van Maren wrote, explaining that for many conservative Christians Clinton "poses a real and imminent threat to Christians who want to live their lives, run their own businesses, go to their own churches, and pass their values on to their children. . . . Hillary, to many Americans, is quite literally a destroyer of worlds." Note the word "literally."

In all likelihood, Maren also conceded, Trump did not care about religious liberty or even the right to life. "But Hillary would explicitly attack it." Maren defined the choice:

> At the end of the day, virtually every criticism of Trump is true. He's a huckster. He doesn't care about most, if any, of the issues that are important to Christians. He's probably just making promises to ensure that Christians show up and vote for him in November. But on the other hand, Hillary Clinton is passionate about these issues. She's passionate about the ongoing destruction of human life by abortion, and she's passionate about furthering the secular progressive agenda that has been backing Christians up against a wall for eight years. So when people point out that Donald Trump will probably do nothing, many Christians respond that yes, that's the point. He probably won't. She definitely will.

THE EVANGELICAL LANDSLIDE

This argument proved to be persuasive to the overwhelming majority of white evangelical voters. After Trump's victory, Franklin Graham declared, "I believe it was God. God showed up. He answered the prayers of hundreds of thousands of people across this land who had been praying for this country."[15]

Exit polls indicated that white evangelicals backed Trump by a staggering margin of 80 to 16 percent, eclipsing George W. Bush's 2004 margin of 78 to 21 percent.[16] The intense gravitational pull of partisanship explains much of the evangelical support for the GOP nominee. But the Christian support for Trump was not inevitable or a given. There were powerful voices from within the church opposing Trump, including the magazine *Christianity Today,* which published a scathing editorial comparing support for Trump to "idolatry."

> He has given no evidence of humility or dependence on others, let alone on God his Maker and Judge. He wantonly celebrates strongmen and takes every opportunity to humiliate and demean the vulnerable. He shows no curiosity or capacity to learn. He is, in short, the very embodiment of what the Bible calls a fool.[17]

But polling data near the end of the campaign suggested that the message was not getting through to evangelicals. Pollsters found that when evangelical leaders spoke out against Trump, they weakened support for the mogul. But, pollsters also found that "few Americans are hearing about the presidential candidates from their clergies."[18] Indeed, only 9 percent of white evangelicals said they had heard their clergy speak about Trump and only 6 percent heard them discuss Clinton. Four political scientists who examined the numbers concluded that support for Trump remained high among evangelicals "in part because local religious elites are not regularly talking about his candidacy. Were those discussions to occur, it's possible that they would highlight concerns that many evangelical leaders might have about his moral character." To test that proposition, evangelicals were read portions of editorials that raised questions about Trump's character and compassion. One suggested that Trump's appeal is "dangerously close to Satan's offer to Jesus in Luke 4:9: 'All this I will give you,' he said, 'if you will bow down and worship me.'" The study found that after being exposed to that argument, white evangelical voter support for Trump dropped sharply. But for the most part, evangelical clergy did not speak up and their flocks did not have to confront the problematic nature of the choice before them.

Of course, not all Christian leaders followed suit. Throughout the campaign Trump would often lash out at them in very personal terms. After Bob Vander Plaats, the CEO of The Family Leader and a prominent conservative in Iowa, endorsed Senator Ted Cruz, Trump attacked him on Twitter, calling him a "phony" and "a bad guy."* Trump also singled out Russell Moore, the president of the Ethics & Religious Liberty Commission, the public-policy arm of the Southern Baptist Convention, calling him "truly a terrible representative of Evangelicals and all of the good they stand for. A nasty guy with no heart!"[19]

---

*For years former Arkansas governor Mike Huckabee had rushed to the defense of Christian leaders who were under attack from politicians. But when Trump slammed his fellow Baptist preacher, Huckabee fell notably silent, which was consistent with his political and moral evolution over the past few years. Consider the progression of Huckabee's book titles over the last decade: In 2005, he published *Quit Digging Your Grave with a Knife and Fork: A 12-Stop Program to End Bad Habits and Begin a Healthy Lifestyle*; ten years later, in 2015, he wrote *God, Guns, Grits, and Gravy*, which seemed more designed to strike a populist political note than offer sound dietary advice. In 2007, his message was *Character Makes a Difference: Where I'm From, Where I've Been, and What I Believe*. However, he spent much of 2016 making the case for Trump.

This naturally led to some awkward moments. Huckabee had criticized the parenting skills of Barack and Michelle Obama because they had allowed his daughter to listen to Beyoncé. But clearly he held Trump to a different standard, offering up fulsome praise: "Donald Trump broke the code, owned the media, and inspired the masses." As Francis J. Beckwith noted in a column in the *American Conservative*, "This comes from the pen of the same hand that published these words just eighteen months ago: 'Most people exhibiting crude behavior or language aren't doing anything illegal, but they're contributing to a culture that is abrasive, rude, obnoxious, and just plain mean.'" (Francis Beckwith, "Huckabee Changes His Tune—He Used to Defend Christian Values, But These Days He Only Sings the Praises of Trump," *American Conservative*, May 13, 2016.)

MOORE'S DISSENT

Even as his fellow evangelists were flocking to Trump's standard, Russell Moore staked out an increasingly lonely position. "I have watched," he wrote in February 2016, "as some of these who gave stem-winding speeches about 'character' in office during the Clinton administration now minimize the spewing of profanities in campaign speeches, race-baiting and courting white supremacists, boasting of adulterous affairs, debauching public morality and justice through the casino and pornography industries."[20]

As important as the political issues were to Christians, Moore wrote, they were confusing means with ends and allowing ideology to overshadow the essential Christian message. "The damage to the movement was not merely political," he later wrote. "What's most at stake here is the integrity of our gospel witness and our moral credibility."[21]

For years, he wrote, critics on the secular Left had accused the evangelical Right of being more concerned with power rather than religious conviction. "They have implied that the goal of the Religious Right is to cynically use the 'moral' to get to the 'majority,' not the other way around," he wrote. "This year, a group of high-profile evangelicals has proven these critics right."

In the weeks before the election, Moore delivered a lengthy critique of the evangelical crack-up in an address entitled, "Can the Religious Right Be Saved?" Conservative columnist Rod Dreher described that speech, delivered as the 2016 Erasmus lecture for *First Things* magazine, a "eulogy for the Religious Right," calling it a "generation-defining speech, a line in the sand between the old Guard and the Next generation."[22]

In the lecture, Moore called out the Right's implicit acceptance of moral relativism.

In the 1990s, Gloria Steinem said that feminists should put up with a little bit of womanizing from Bill Clinton because he would keep abortion legal. Religious conservatives rightly said that this showed the moral hypocrisy of a feminist movement that inveighed against sexual harassment and office power

> dynamics—until it became politically inconvenient. Now, a
> conservative commentator [Ann Coulter] says that she doesn't
> mind if the Republican nominee performs abortions in the
> Oval Office as long as he maintains a hard line against
> immigrants.[23]

But Moore also made it clear that he respected and understood voters who felt they needed to hold their noses in the general election because of the importance of the Supreme Court. He disagreed, but said, "That is a respectable and defensible view." Instead he turned his fire on the hucksters among the "old-guard religious right political establishment" who had "normalized an awful candidate—some offering outright support in theological terms, others hedging their bets and whispering advice behind closed doors."

Moore also noted that the binary choice facing voters in November 2016 did not explain the willingness of evangelical leaders to back Trump during the primaries, choosing him over such other obvious alternatives as Ted Cruz, Marco Rubio, Rick Santorum, Bobby Jindal, or even Mike Huckabee. That suggested to Moore a much deeper crisis in the religious Right.

"To be clear, the 2016 campaign did not provoke this crisis," he said. "This was a pre-existing condition. The religious right turns out to be the people the religious right warned us about."

The essential error of the Christian Right was to give politics primacy over faith. At some point, Moore warned, conservative Christians would have to come to grips with the reality that their values were not always going to be politically popular, that they were no longer a "majority." That meant that they must be prepared to choose between the Gospel and winning elections. If they surrendered their values in order to achieve short-term political successes, he said, they would end up with neither values nor political success. Too many evangelicals were confusing means with ends. "Religious liberty is a means to an end," he reminded his listeners, "and the end is not political." Christianity could not allow itself to be bent and warped to win elections, even important ones.

"A religious right that is not able to tie public action and cultural concern to a theology of Gospel and mission will die, and will deserve to die," he said. "When Christianity is seen as a political project in search of a gospel useful enough to advance its worldly agenda, it will end up pleasing those who make politics primary, while losing those who believe the Gospel," said Moore. "Augustine wrote the City of God in the context of Rome's collapse, and he did not repurpose the Gospel to prop up a failing regime."[24]

Moore was especially pointed in declaring the fundamental incompatibility of Christianity with white nationalism or identity politics:

> We still face racism and nativism and anti-Semitism. The religious right, if it wishes to be genuinely religious, must work toward justice and reconciliation, regardless of whether that means a rebuke to those who are our allies on other issues. White Christians, after all, are not part of the majority culture and never have been, unless they define their primary culture as that of the United States of America. If, instead, my first identity is part of the global Body of Christ, then white middle-class Americans are a tiny sliver indeed.[25]

So, Moore, asked, could the so-called religious Right be saved? Yes, but "not by tinkering around the edges." The Christian Right urgently needed to restore its sense of the first principles of their faith and ultimately what they needed to fight for and conserve. Christians needed to be prepared to stand athwart the onrushing tides of the culture and politics.

> More than that, it will mean a religious conservatism that sees the Church as more important than the state, the conscience as more important than the culture, and one that knows the difference between the temporal and the eternal.[26]

But that would have to wait for another year and another campaign.

PART IV

RESTORING
THE
CONSERVATIVE
MIND

TROLLS AND FLYING MONKEYS: THE RIGHT'S NEW CULTURE OF INTIMIDATION

AS THE AGE OF Trump dawns, conservatives should realize that politics is no longer a binary choice. To be sure, Democrats and their Hollywood allies will continue to overreach and overreact, making them an easy foil. The boycotts, protests, and assorted hysterical tantrums remind us why voters have turned against the fashionable Left. But on a host of issues, the lines will be blurrier. Ideologically, Trump has made it clear that he intends to break with the long-standing conservative consensus over free trade and limited government. (He mentioned the word "freedom" just a single time in his inaugural speech. Reagan had used the word eight times; George W. Bush twenty-seven times in his second inaugural.) That creates room for contrarian

conservatives, who refuse to march in lockstep with the new administration.

But—and this has to be said—one of the most formidable challenges
facing independent conservatives will be the culture of bullying, threats,
and intimidation that has become a feature of the Trumpist Right and
its binary politics.

What role will the conservative media play? Skeptics in the conservative media (*National Review, Weekly Standard, Commentary, Wall
Street Journal*, and even elements of Fox News) will undoubtedly mix
praise for the new regime with censure. But the new era has created
painful professional and personal schisms between Trump skeptics and
those more willing to accommodate the new regime. In the first few
months of the Trump presidency, the editorial board of the *Wall Street
Journal* split over the paper's coverage, leading to the departures of several key players, including Pulitzer Prize–winning columnist Bret
Stephens, a consistent Trump critic who now writes for the *New York
Times*.[1] Before his departure from the *Journal*, Stephens publicly lamented
the capitulation to Trumpism of conservative thought leaders, presum-
ably including some of his own colleagues. "The most painful aspect of
this," he said in the Daniel Pearl Memorial Lecture, "has been to watch
people I previously considered thoughtful and principled conservatives give themselves over to a species of illiberal politics from which
I once thought they were immune." Trump's attacks on the media,
Stephens argued, were not simply critiques of liberal bias, which would
be fair criticism. "His objection is to objectivity itself," Stephens said.
"He's perfectly happy for the media to be disgusting and corrupt—so
long as it's on his side."[2]

The campaign, Stephens told his audience, saw the rise of a pundit
class he called the "TrumpXplainers," who would offer to translate the
candidate's incoherent word salads into something that sounded cogent. "For instance, Trump would give a speech or offer an answer in
a debate that amounted to little more than a word jumble," Stephens
said. "But rather than quote Trump, or point out that what he had said
was grammatically and logically nonsensical, the TrumpXplainers
would tell us what he had allegedly meant to say. They became our

political semioticians, ascribing pattern and meaning to the rune-stones of Trump's mind." This posed a painful dilemma for conservatives who declined to adjust their standards. Said Stephens:

> Watching this process unfold has been particularly painful for me as a conservative columnist. I find myself in the awkward position of having recently become popular among some of my liberal peers—precisely because I haven't changed my opinions about anything.
>
> By contrast, I've become suddenly unpopular among some of my former fans on the right—again, because I've stuck to my views. It is almost amusing to be accused of suffering from something called "Trump Derangement Syndrome" simply because I feel an obligation to raise my voice against, say, the president suggesting a moral equivalency between the U.S. and Vladimir Putin's Russia.[3]

In perhaps the most striking section of his address, Stephens compared the Trumpian apologists to the postwar Polish communists described by Czesław Miłosz in his book, *The Captive Mind*. Miłosz's colleagues were not coerced into becoming Stalinists, but actually made the transition willingly. Said Stephens:

> They wanted to believe. They were willing to adapt. They thought they could do more good from the inside. They convinced themselves that their former principles didn't fit with the march of history, or that to hold fast to one's beliefs was a sign of priggishness and pig-headedness. They felt that to reject the new order of things was to relegate themselves to irrelevance and oblivion. They mocked their former friends who refused to join the new order as morally vain reactionaries.[4]

"I fear," Stephens said, "we are witnessing a similar process unfold among many conservative intellectuals on the right." Indeed, as he watched the process of conversion, Stephens concluded that the "mental pathways by which the new Trumpian conservatives have made their peace with their new political master aren't so different from Miłosz's former colleagues." He described the process of rationalization:

> There's the same desperate desire for political influence; the same belief that Trump represents a historical force to which they ought to belong; the same willingness to bend or discard principles they once considered sacred; the same fear of seeming out-of-touch with the mood of the public; the same tendency to look the other way at comments or actions that they cannot possibly justify; the same belief that you do more good by joining than by opposing; the same Manichean belief that, if Hillary Clinton had been elected, the United States would have all-but ended as a country.[5]

Stephens concluded with a call for "intellectual integrity in the age of Trump." But he seemed to recognize that the tide was running heavily against him. All of the early signs suggest that the centrifugal forces of the newly emboldened Right media are already proving too strong as, one by one, they fall into line, as even erstwhile serious conservative commentators pen pieces of fawning hagiography. Even though there was scattered dissent among some Alt Right outlets after Trump ordered a missile attack on Syria and flip-flopped on some of his nationalist policies, many in the conservative media will be reluctant to break ranks. As writer Eliana Johnson observed "the conservative media have been increasingly pulled by a tractor beam that demands positive coverage of the president regardless of how far he wanders from the ideas they once enforced. Producers and editors have been faced with a choice: Provide that coverage or lose your audience."[6] This created an extraordinary dynamic. In the past, the White House has had to be concerned about a more or less adversarial media, but President Trump will be able to call upon a passionately loyal alternative media—which includes talk radio, much of Fox News, websites like Breitbart, the Drudge Report, and dozens of Scam PACs—to attack his enemies and provide air cover in adversity. Some of his most enthusiastic cheerleaders have been granted White House press credentials, and others are hatching plans to expand their operations.

For years, Rush Limbaugh has gibed about what he calls the "state-controlled media"—the liberal news outlets that Limbaugh has long decried for their lack of critical coverage of President Barack Obama—but we may be about to see what one actually looks like. Since so many in the Right media are too deeply invested to be outraged at any failures or reversals from Trump World, they will inevitably be focused on attacking the Left and launching purges of the saboteurs and dissenters on the Right.

At the conservative website Hotair.com, for instance, writer Jazz Shaw not only defended Trump's pick of Steve Bannon as a top aide, but also lashed out at Trump critic David French, whom Shaw writes, "Makes sure to work in the buzzword 'alt-right,' as so many other Never Trumpers continue to do." He then dismissed concerns about the white nationalist movement, saying that the term was "dredged up from the gutters of the internet and injected into the common parlance as a tool to smear Trump." (Actually, as we've seen, the Alt Right is quite real, as its leaders will tell you themselves.)

But Shaw's larger point is that Trump critics needed to get on board, immediately. Before the election, critics of Trump were accused of trying to elect Clinton because it was a "binary choice." But after the election, the narrative pivoted. If conservatives continue to criticize Trump now, Shaw wrote, "you are working to defeat the GOP agenda and advance the Democrats and the Social Justice Warriors." And he sets out the terms of the purges to come: "And if that's the case you are no longer momentarily estranged friends. You are, to borrow the title of a truly awful Julia Roberts movie, *sleeping with the enemy*." [Emphasis in the original.][7]

The demand that conservatives drop their objections and conform was also taken up by the grassroots. In Wisconsin, even after I stepped down from my daily radio show, there were calls for purges of conservatives (like me) who might dissent from the new regime. The publisher of the *Wisconsin Conservative Digest*, for instance, sent out a blast email excoriating conservatives who had not backed Trump, calling them "Judas goats," suggesting that activists retaliate against them after the election. This was curious, because just months earlier (in August 2016) the same publisher had sent out a similar mass email calling on the GOP to repudiate Trump. "If the top leaders, not the old timers of the party stand up and disavow him and tell him to get out let pence [sic] carry the mail we could at least stop the rest of the bleeding," he wrote on August 15. Within weeks, he had decided to back Trump and began castigating dissidents.

After the election, he ratcheted up the recriminations, which were aimed not merely at me (I was about to go off the air), but at other hosts and conservative activists who had been critical of the new president. He commented:

> We remember those Benedict Arnolds that tried that, in 1964 and 1980. Where are those people? They died alone and unloved?
>
> Be smart, turn off Charlie and relegate him to the trash bin. Same with [Green Bay host Jerry] Bader. . . . Why listen to someone trying to get you to commit suicide?
>
> Can you endorse their backstabbing? Why? . . .
>
> Let them swing slowly, slowly in the wind. Do not be scared of these clowns, call them, kick them in the knees or other places. . . .
>
> Do you think that they got their thirty pieces of Silver?[8]

Another talk show host, Mark Belling, struck a similar note. Belling, who is based in Milwaukee and occasionally fills in for Rush Limbaugh, was also originally a fierce Trump critic, calling him a blowhard, buffoon, clown, fraud, and, a liberal before reluctantly saying that he would vote for him because he was preferable to Clinton.[9]*

---

* The story also quotes me: "But don't expect Milwaukee's other top talker, Charlie Sykes, to join the ranks of Trumpkins. '#NeverTrump means never Trump,' said Sykes, whose show airs on WTMJ-AM (620). 'But I am also #NeverHillary. So

But, after the election, Belling lashed out at "egghead anti-Trumpers," arguing that "the first few months of Trump's presidency will require the full support of all committed conservatives." Belling went on to suggest that conservative nonprofit groups "clean house" of Trump skeptics if they betrayed the "Trump Revolution." If conservative think tanks "allow themselves to be co-opted by spoilsport brats who hop in bed with the enemy," Belling insisted "they are not only no longer needed in this state but will be counter-productive."

Belling insisted that while he was "not suggesting a purge," he was "clearly implying that *treason* against the new conservative cause is possible." [Emphasis added.][10] If "fellow travelers in the 'I Hate Trump Club' use Wisconsin organizations to fight against their own groups' very mission, it is imperative that the organizations' boards clean house."

BULLYING CONGRESS

The demand for retaliation and purges also has implications for elected officials. In December 2016, a month after the election, *Politico* reported that many GOP lawmakers were "loath to say anything remotely critical, fearful they might set off the president-elect or his horde of enforcers." Reporter Rachael Bade described the mood among many conservative legislators: "They're terrified of arousing the ire of their tempestuous new leader—or being labeled a turncoat by his army of followers." When one Texas congressman named Bill Flores made some anodyne comments suggesting that the GOP Congress could work well with the new president even though some of his proposals were "not going to line up very well with our conservative policies," the blowback was explosive and revealing. "Little did Flores realize the hell that would soon rain down from Trump's throng of enforcers," Bade wrote.[11]

I'll probably be spending a lot of time this fall talking about the Packers.'" (Daniel Bice, "Mark Belling Endorses Donald Trump—Reluctantly," *Milwaukee Journal Sentinel,* July 13, 2016.)

Breitbart piled on first, suggesting that Flores's remarks were evidence that the House GOP wanted to "isolate and block President Donald Trump's populist campaign promises." Sean Hannity joined in, featuring the Breitbart story on his radio show. Another conservative site headlined: "BREAKING: Rep. Bill Flores Has CRAFTED a PLAN to BLOCK Trump's Immigration Reform."[12] The Twitter hordes, Bade reported, responded on cue: "@RepBillFlores get in @realDonaldTrump way & we will burn your career down until you are reduced to selling life insurance," tweeted one person. "@RepBillFlores you can go hang yourself!!" another wrote.

Examples had to be made and the attack on Flores was a warning shot for other wavering conservatives.*

---

*The assault on Flores also shed light on an account from former labor secretary Robert Reich, who reported a conversation he had with a former Republican congressman who explained why he was reluctant to criticize Trump publicly. Although Reich is a partisan Democrat and an outspoken liberal, his account of the conversation seemed credible:

ME [Reich]: What do you think of your party's nominee for president?

HE: Trump is a maniac. He's a clear and present danger to America.

ME: Have you said publicly that you won't vote for him?

HE: (sheepishly): No.

ME: Why not?

HE: I'm a coward.

ME: What do you mean?

HE: I live in a state with a lot of Trump voters. Most Republican officials do.

ME: But you're a former official. You're not running for Congress again. What are you afraid of?

HE: I hate to admit it, but I'm afraid of them. Some of those Trumpistas are out of their fu*king minds.

ME: You mean you're afraid for your own physical safety?

HE: All it takes is one of them, you know. [In mid-June a gunman targeted several Republican congressman including House Whip Steve Scalise,

THE CULTURE OF INTIMIDATION

Even before Trump had locked up the GOP nomination, the pattern was set. Writing in the *Federalist*, Robert Tracinski described the emerging style:

> When they're not literally pushing people around, they dabble in blackmail and threats of retaliation: Trump's staff and surrogates smear the reputations of female reporters and campaign staff, he threatens to dig up damaging information on donors to rival campaigns, and Trump threatens to crack down on an insufficiently fawning press.[13]

Breitbart and its former CEO Bannon have openly relished the image of street fighters who take no quarter. "If a guy comes after our audience—starts calling working-class people vulgarians and brown-shirts and Nazis and post-literate—we're going to leave a mark," he explained. "We're not shy about it at all. We've got some lads that like to mix it up."[14]

Indeed, Trump and his lawyers have a long and colorful track record of attempting to intimidate journalists. When the *Daily Beast* was

---

who was seriously wounded. The shooting came six years after the shooting of Democratic congresswoman Gaby Giffords.]

ME: Wait a minute. Isn't this how dictators and fascists have come to power in other nations? Respected leaders don't dare take a stand.

HE: At least I'm no Giuliani or Gingrich or Pence. I'm not a Trump enabler.

ME: I'll give you that.

HE: Let me tell you something. Most current and former Republican members of Congress are exactly like me. I talk with them. They think Trump is deplorable. And they think Giuliani and Gingrich are almost as bad. But they're not gonna speak out. Some don't want to end their political careers. Most don't want to risk their lives. The Trump crowd is just too dangerous. Trump has whipped them up into a g*ddamn frenzy. (Available at: www.facebook.com/RBReich/posts/1349621041717155.)

preparing a story about Trump, one of his lawyers, Michael Cohen, threatened the writer with legal action, telling him: "So I'm warning you, tread very fucking lightly, because what I'm going to do to you is going to be fucking disgusting. You understand me?"[15]

Of course, Breitbart is not omnipotent. The site failed spectacularly in its attempt to beat Speaker Paul Ryan in the August 2016 GOP primary. (Breitbart reporter Julia Hahn, who authored some of the most personal attacks on Ryan, was given a job in Trump's White House.) But other, less powerful Republicans might fear risking a similar attack, knowing that the Trumpists can call out the flying monkeys and trolls of the new media against them.

THE FLYING MONKEYS

All of this had become familiar to Trump's early media critics, including me. On March 28, shortly before the Wisconsin primary, Trump called in to my radio show for what was later described as a contentious interview. The tone was civil throughout, but I challenged Trump on his behavior toward women (in particular, his comments about rival Ted Cruz's wife) and his credentials as a conservative. Even before the show was over, I had an email in my in-box from a Breitbart reporter, noting that I had "hammered [Trump] multiple times on his treatment of women," and then linking to a story on a left-wing news site about my previous marriage. "Would you like to give a comment as to the allegation in this story (link above)?" The threat was hardly subtle.*

I also got a taste of the scope of the online troll armies when I began doing cable news appearances. One night in particular stood out. In early May 2016, after Trump had wrapped up the GOP nomination, I appeared on Megyn Kelly's show on Fox News and explained why I

---

*I responded, "Ah, Breitbart being Breitbart." As far as I know, Breitbart did not pursue the story, which was apparently farmed out to an even darker corner of the fever swamp, a site known for its close ties to Trump adviser Roger Stone. The experience gave me a small taste of what was to become routine for many folks in the media.

was not getting on the Trump train. My comments were blunt and obviously provocative to the legions of Trump supporters in the audience.* (I found it interesting that Fox News posted online the interview that preceded me and the one that followed, but not what I had to say that night. Nonetheless, it was posted by other websites.)[16]

After the show, as usual, I checked my Twitter feed. I had become accustomed to what I came to call my "Hour of Hate," as my social media time lines were clogged by angry, obscene, and occasionally

---

*Here is a transcript of what I said that night:

MEGYN KELLY (HOST): My next guest got national attention when he took on Donald Trump in a fiery radio interview just ahead of the Wisconsin primary. Joining me now, Charlie Sykes. Charlie, good to see you. And sure enough, Trump went on to lose the state of Wisconsin but win the GOP primary. And nonetheless you say you remain never Trump. Before I ask you about Paul Ryan, why? Because you know the argument against that is that's a vote for Hillary Clinton.

CHARLIE SYKES: Yeah, well Donald Trump is a serial liar, a con man who mocks the disabled and women. He's a narcissist and a bully, a man with no fixed principles who has the vocabulary of an emotionally insecure nine-year-old. So no, I don't want to give him control of the IRS, the FBI, and the nuclear codes. That's just me.

KELLY: Tell us how you really feel. It doesn't sound like there's a lot of wiggle room there, Charlie.

SYKES: I do see the rats swimming towards the sinking ship. But at some point—if you understand, and this is not just ideological, it's not just the fact that he's abandoned one position after another or that he has the penchant for internet hoaxes or conspiracy theories. I mean a week ago tonight, remember, he was peddling the notion that Ted Cruz's dad had something to do with the JFK assassination. So there are people who say that just because of party loyalty we're supposed to forget all of that. I just don't buy that. Because I've cautioned my fellow conservatives, you embrace Donald Trump, you embrace it all. You embrace every slur, every insult, every outrage, every falsehood. You're going to spend the next six months defending, rationalizing, evading all that. And afterwards, you come back to women, to minorities, to young people and say, that wasn't us. That's not what we're about. The reality is, if you support him to be president of the United States, that is who you are, and you own it.[17]

threatening messages. But the reaction that night eclipsed anything I had seen before, with well over a thousand responses. Because Megyn Kelly's Twitter address was included in many of the messages, I got a glimpse of the sort of reaction she must have been getting throughout the campaign. I've been at this long enough that I didn't think I could be shocked, but seeing the language directed at Kelly, who had clashed with Trump repeatedly, was genuinely shocking. Who were these people, and what was the point?

The point, obviously, was to browbeat critics into silence or acquiescence. One by one, other radio talk show hosts either modified or abandoned altogether their opposition and skepticism. Considering what they were seeing online, this was not surprising.

Talk show host Erick Erickson launched a new website called The Resurgent, but later had to admit that "the sponsorship model died with opposing Trump." He explained that anyone who showed up as a sponsor of the site "saw an alt-right army go on the attack."[18]

It could get very ugly. In an article headlined, "How Breitbart Unleashes Hate Mobs to Threaten, Dox, and Troll Trump Critics," the *Daily Beast*'s Lloyd Grove recounted what happened to one of Trump's most outspoken and colorful critics, Rick Wilson. After a cable news appearance in which Wilson jibed that Breitbart was Trump's "Pravda" and referred to Trump's "low-information supporters," Bannon went on his radio show to "essentially declare war on the Rubio backer."

"It was a planned deployment," Wilson told Lloyd Grove. "After I criticized Breitbart and criticized Trump, they decided they were going to weaponize themselves and go after me." What followed was chilling, even by the standards of an increasingly uncivil political campaign. The *Daily Beast* reported that it had obtained emails that Bannon and another Breitbart staffer "worked to obtain a comprehensive list of Wilson's political clients (with the intention of making them feel uncomfortable about hiring him, Wilson believes)." Worse was to come.

Someone pulled Wilson's credit report, and online trolls, some of whom were "apparently active on an online forum associated with white supremacists" began posting "photoshopped sexual images of his college-age daughter, claimed she'd had a child with an African American, threatened gang-rape, and claimed Wilson's teenage son was a pimp."

There may be even darker (if that's possible) forms of intimidation directed against critics. During the campaign, several high-profile GOP Trump opponents were targeted in an elaborate "catfishing" scheme in which a con man posing as various fictitious characters online sought details of their efforts to oppose the GOP nominee. Over a period of months a convicted scam artist named Steve Wessel used multiple fake identities and offered salacious gossip, gifts, and free trips, "all in an apparent effort to glean more about the operatives and their intentions regarding Trump," reported *Politico*.*†

Occasionally, the attacks against critics would backfire. In April 2016, nationally syndicated talk show host Mark Levin lashed out at anti-Trump Republicans (including me) in the clearest possible language:

These people are not conservatives. They're not constitutionalists. They're frauds. They're fakes. They're not brave. They're asinine. They're buffoons. . . .

* When officials learned of his activities, a judge revoked his bail and Wessel was sent to prison to serve a fifty-five-month sentence on other charges.
† The targets of the catfishing expedition included Wilson, Liz Mair, and Cheri Jacobus, all of whom had been outspoken in their criticism of Trump. None of them believed that Wessel had acted alone. In August 2016, *Politico* reported that Jacobus, who said she believes Wessel was working in concert with allies of Trump, renewed her efforts to get the FBI to investigate the scheme. (The Trump campaign has denied any involvement in the episode.) Adding another ominous wrinkle to the story, Jacobus's emails appear to have been hacked by person or persons unknown. As *Politico* was preparing to publish its article on Wessel's fraud, and after the publication began asking for comment about the article, "Jacobus said thousands of emails disappeared from her personal account and that her Internet provider, AOL, told her the account had been hacked. Jacobus said the hack targeted only emails she has received, not those she has sent, and she believes it was an attempt to prevent her from tracing the origins of more emails sent to her as part of the scheme." The hack was reported to the FBI's Cyber Division on her behalf.[19]

Two days later, he reversed himself. Even in the annals of classic political flip-flops, Levin's 180-degree pirouette was impressive.[20] Levin announced that he was disgusted by the Trump campaign's "bully dirty tricks Nixonian tactics," after Trump adviser Roger Stone apparently targeted Levin himself by implying that he had somehow been bought off by the "establishment."[21] Levin explained:

> As a result of what the Trump supporters have attempted here, particularly Roger Stone, I am not voting for Donald Trump. Period. . . .
>
> So I want to congratulate Roger Stone. And if anybody has a problem with Donald Trump, you can talk to Roger Stone. These bully dirty tricks Nixonian tactics, they're only going to backfire. So count me as never Trump.
>
> Some point you've got to stand up to it . . . I do not like bullies and I never have.[22]

Levin, eventually, reversed himself again, saying that he would vote for Trump after all. But his temporary apostasy was telling, nevertheless. Levin had been prepared to back Trump despite the fact that Trump had routinely smeared his opponents.

But those were other people. He spread vile gossip about women. But those were other people. He mocked the disabled, and lied with impunity. But until Trump's thugs turned their sights on him, Mark Levin saw none of this as disqualifying the man from the Oval Office. In that respect, he was like so many other conservatives who decided that what was happening to their movement was somebody else's problem.

CHAPTER 17

THE CONTRARIAN
CONSERVATIVE

It profits a man nothing to give his soul for the whole world . . .
but for Wales, Richard?

— *A MAN FOR ALL SEASONS*

BEING A CONTRARIAN CONSERVATIVE comes rather naturally to me (maybe it runs in the family DNA), and I suppose this takes
me full circle. Back in the 1970s, I became a "recovering Liberal," when
I looked around me and decided I know longer wanted to be a part of
what that movement had become. My decision came slowly, but it was
ultimately liberating to break free from the cant of tribal politics and
its tendentious talking points.

Part of that was my affinity for Groucho Marx's sentiment that
"I refuse to join any club that would have me as a member." But I was
also sure that I didn't want to be part of *that* club. So this circumstance
feels familiar. If the conservative movement is defined by the nativist,

authoritarian, post-truth culture of Trump-Bannon-Drudge-Hannity-Palin, then I'm out.

So what does that mean?

As difficult as it may be, conservatives need to stand athwart history once again—this time recognizing that Trumpism poses an existential threat to the conservative vision of ordered liberty.

This will be a complicated undertaking, given the pressures of political tribalism and the reality that conservatives will actually applaud much of the Trump agenda. At times, they will be impelled to mount the barricades against the overreach of the Left and will align themselves with Trump on issues like the judiciary.

But despite the clamorous demands that conservatives now fall into line with the new regime, precisely the opposite is needed. Rather than conformity, conservatism needs dissidents who are willing to push back—in other words, contrarian conservatives, who recognize that conservatism now finds itself reduced to a remnant in the wilderness. But the wilderness is a good place for any movement to rethink its first principles, rediscover its forgotten values, and ask: Who are we, really?

Contrarian conservatives will answer as follows: We're conservatives who believe in things like liberty, free markets, limited government, personal responsibility, constitutionalism, growth and opportunity, the defense of American ideas and institutions at home and abroad, modesty, prudence, aspiration, and inclusion. We are conservatives in the great tradition that stretches back to Burke, Tocqueville, Buckley, and Reagan. But that means that we are not part of what the conservative movement or the GOP has become.

What does it mean to be a contrarian? It does not mean mindless opposition. When the Trump administration or congressional Republicans are right, we should support them; when possible, we'll nudge them to do the right thing. But we will have no problem adopting a spirit of contradiction when they go wrong or lose their way. Contrarians have no obligation to defend the indefensible or reverse their positions based on the leader's whims or tweets. They can step out of the alternative reality silos and look at things as they actually are, rather than relying on what Trump aide Kellyanne Conway called "alternative facts." These independent conservatives can affirm that Trump won the election fairly and freely, but they can also recognize the gravity and implications of Russia's interference in the campaign. They can support tougher border controls and still be appalled by the cruelty and incompetence of his immigration bans. Independent conservatives can applaud Trump's support for Israel and still be thoroughly appalled by his slavish adulation of Vladimir Putin and his flirtations with proto-fascists like France's Marine Le Pen. Most important of all, they will take the long view, recognizing that electoral victories do not change eternal verities or the essential correctness of traditionally conservative insights into human nature and society.

Opposition in the face of power is not a sign of weakness, but rather an indication of the ongoing intellectual vigor of the conservative idea. We should draw inspiration from Frederick Douglass, who observed, "One and God make a majority." Undoubtedly, this will be lonely work and we may lose a lot of friends; but it should also be familiar to conservatives who have a long history of being out of step with the spirit of the age. William F. Buckley Jr. sharpened the definitions of the new conservativism by contrasting it with the "modern" Republicanism of the Eisenhower years. Later, conservative spokesmen were full-throated and active in their opposition to Nixonism. It is not a coincidence that there is no such thing today as a "Nixon conservative."

MODESTY VERSUS BINARY

Although it may sound heretical, conservatives need to step back from the cycle of win-at-all-costs politics in which we are told that each election is the Apocalypse. That cycle contributes to the sense of desperation in our politics today, the conviction that defeat means disaster because our foes are so malign, so vicious, so destructive, that they must be stopped at any price.

This may, in fact, be a teachable moment for conservatives in exile: We simply should not care about politics as much as we do, because it should not be as important as it has become. The question of who serves in political office should not be as consuming as it has become, but is a consequence of the concentration of power and expectations. There is a lesson here for both sides of the political spectrum. Our politics have become too toxic and scary, in large part because our government is too large and consequential.

The English political theorist Michael Oakeshott said that the role of government is "not to inflame passion and give it new objects to feed upon, but to inject into the activities of already too passionate men an ingredient of moderation."[1] But our politics has morphed into a rough beast that inflames passions and crushes voices of moderation. Inevitably, the word "moderation," will be misunderstood as a sort of political squishiness. Rather, it should be understood in the sense that Edmund Burke used it—as a call to modesty in our politics. Peter Wehner notes that political modesty entails a sense of "prudence, the humility to recognize limits (including our own), the willingness to balance competing principles, and an aversion to fanaticism. Moderation accepts the complexity of life in this world and distrusts utopian visions and simple solutions."[2]

A politics of modesty does not, Wehner argues, "see the world in Manichaean terms that divide it into forces of good (or light) and agents of evil (or darkness)." This does not mean quiescence or surrender. Conservatives can believe that "bold and at times even radical steps" may be necessary to "advance moral ends." But a sense of modesty, Wehner wrote, "takes into account what is needed at any given moment; it allows circumstances to determine action in the way that weather patterns dictate which route a ship will follow." By embracing the politics of perpetual outrage and ideological purity, conservatives have lost sight of that tradition and the very real dangers of immodest authoritarianism.

CONSERVATISM IS NOT POPULISM

The rejection of populism runs deep in the conservative tradition, which has long recognized the threat that it poses both to limited government and to individual freedom. Writing nearly two centuries ago, Tocqueville warned that the greatest threat to American democracy was the tyranny of the majority. Long before public opinion polls or social media could define majority opinion or enforce conformity, Tocqueville warned of the potentially suffocating effects of believing *vox populi, vox dei* ("the voice of the people is the voice of God.") "No monarch is so absolute as to combine all the powers of society in his own hands and to conquer all opposition, as a majority is able to do," Tocqueville noted, "which has the right both of making and of executing the laws." He recognized the potential problem of demanding that we all be "in touch" with majority sentiment. "I know of no country in which there is so little independence of mind and real freedom of discussion as in America," Tocqueville wrote.

Tocqueville's skepticism has been shared by modern conservatives, including Barry Goldwater, who had declared that "true Conservatism has been at war equally with autocrats and with 'democratic' Jacobins." In 1960, he wrote in *The Conscience of a Conservative*:

> Was it then a Democracy the framers created? Hardly. The system of restraints, on the face of it, was directed not only against individual tyrants, but also against a tyranny of the masses. The framers were well aware of the danger posed by self-seeking demagogues—that they might persuade a majority of the people to confer on government vast powers in return for deceptive promises of economic gain.
>
> Our tendency to concentrate power in the hands of a few men deeply concerns me. We can be conquered by bombs or by subversion; but we can also be conquered by neglect—by ignoring the Constitution and disregarding the principles of limited government.[3]

Since the sixties, conservatives have recognized the need for that careful balancing of their opposition to both elitist autocracy and populist demagoguery, because both pose a danger to constitutional balance and individual freedom. Even in the nineteenth century, Tocqueville blamed what he called the despotism of the majority in America for the small number of "distinguished men in political life." Nowadays, Tocqueville would be accused of "elitism," but he celebrated the small number of men "who displayed that manly candor and masculine independence of opinion which frequently distinguished the Americans in former times, and which constitutes the leading feature in distinguished characters wherever they may be found."[4]

At the risk of using sexist language, that is precisely what we need now, conservatives with a "manly candor and masculine independence of opinion," or, in other words, contrarians. As isolated as they are now, that small band of brothers and sisters will play a vital role in the looming political confrontations.

CAN CONSERVATIVES SAVE AMERICA?

A Venn diagram of conservatism and modern liberalism would show only a small overlap; but, however limited, a handful of commentators have noticed that common ground does exist and that it is crucial. "Unfortunately, few people properly understand conservatives," Conor Friedersdorf admitted after the election. "In fact, many erroneously conflate them with authoritarians. And that is a very dangerous mistake."[5]

Imagining that all conservatives share a common vision is especially dangerous because it precludes the sort of ad hoc alliance that may be urgently needed in the new political era. As previously noted, political scientist Karen Stenner has stated that, "If properly understood and marshaled," conservatives "can be a liberal democracy's strongest bulwark against the dangers posed by intolerant social movements." Stenner urged critics on the Left to get over their belief "that distaste for change implies distaste for other races, or that commitment to economic freedom somehow suggests an interest in moral regulation and political repression."[6]

Clinging to cartoon images of conservatives has "significant implications," she wrote. "It can drive those who are merely averse to change into unnatural and unnecessary political alliances with the hateful and intolerant, when they could be rallied behind tolerance and respect for difference under the right conditions." Those "right conditions" include a respect for the rule of law and a sense of stability and responsibility. She further noted:

> It is no secret that liberal democracy is most secure when individual freedom and diversity are pursued in a relatively orderly fashion, in a well-established institutional framework, under responsible leadership, within the bounds set by entrenched and consensually accepted "rules of the game."[7]

She draws the key distinction: "[The] prospect of some wholesale overthrow of the system in pursuit of greater unity should be appealing, even exciting, to authoritarians, but appalling to conservatives."[8]

Admittedly, it seems naïve to suggest that there is any meaningful Left-Right common ground left, but it is also worth noting that Trumpism will only succeed if both the Right and the Left fail to understand the tenuous relationship between conservatism and the nativist authoritarianism with which it has become temporarily allied.

What possible common ground could they find? We could start with a renewed appreciation for a reality-based politics, truth, ethics, checks and balances, civil liberties, and the constitutional limits on executive power. However tenuous, there should also be a mutual acknowledgment of the importance of diversity (of ideas as well as identity), tolerance (which needs to go both ways), and a commitment to America as an idea rather than a walled and isolated city.

But this will also require a period of serious introspection for conservatives, especially as they deal with the temptations, compromises, and challenges of the Age of Trump.

A CONSERVATIVE EXORCISM

After the defeat in the 2012 presidential election, GOP leaders commissioned what became known as an "autopsy" of the failed campaign. In victory, however, conservatives will need something very different—an exorcism of the forces that have possessed and, ultimately, distorted, conservativism. Conservatives need to:

1. Address the legitimate grievances that buoyed Trump with the white working class, but find a way to separate them from the toxic elements of Trumpism, including its authoritarianism, racism, misogyny, and isolationism.

2. Return to first principles and revive classical liberalism as an alternative to progressivism on the Left and authoritarian nationalism on the Right.

3. Revitalize a policy agenda that has grown tired and nostalgic. While conservatives need to reclaim the optimism of Reagan, simply repeating the mantras of the Reagan years is no longer enough, and demanding ideological purity is a self-defeating strategy. The alternative may include taking a fresh look at what so-called Reformicons and others have been saying for the last decade.

4. Be willing to tell hard truths, about the importance of limited government (even if it means we don't get everything we want), free markets (and why governments should not pick winners and losers), and the need for American leadership in the world (despite the siren call of the new isolationism).

5. Break free from the toxic thrall of corporate cronyism and K Street lobbyists. Recognize that being pro-business is not the same thing as being pro–free market if it means handing out favors and goodies to special-interest moochers. The 2016 election was a revolt against this kind of rigged, insider-dealing culture, and the GOP had it coming.

6. Realize the demographic bomb that Trump has planted in the GOP. The appeasement of Trump may have alienated Hispanics, Asian Americans, Muslim Americans, African Americans, and women for a generation. Restoring the party's ability to appeal to those groups will require more than a cosmetic

makeover, but failure to do so will consign the party to political oblivion.

7. Drain their own swamp, starting with the Alt Right and its bigoted, anti-Semitic minions. Lines must be drawn, lest the GOP morph into a European-style National Front party.

8. Confront the conservative media that boosted and enabled Trumpism and created a toxic alternative reality bubble that threatens the credibility and sanity of the conservative movement. Conservatives cannot continue to outsource their message to the drunk at the end of the bar or the cynical propagandists on the internet.

SOME MODEST ADVICE FOR FELLOW CONSERVATIVES

Finally, let me offer some free counsel for perplexed conservatives who are struggling to navigate their way through the brave new political age:

*Be worthy of the movement but make sure the movement is worthy of you. The conservative movement is (or ought to be) about ideas. When the movement ceases to be about those things, question your allegiances.

*As the Psalmist reminds us, "Put not your faith in princes." Don't sacrifice your principles on the altar of other people's individual ambitions. Ultimately, our politics cannot simply be about politicians; they come and go, dissemble, flip-flop. There is a fundamental difference between movements based on ideas and cults of personalities. Princes will inevitably let you down. This is not a glitch, it's a feature.

*You should care about what other people think, but only those people whose opinions you respect. The troll who writes in ALL CAPS, not so much. A corollary (one that applies to our lives outside of politics as well): The loudest voice in the room is not always the one you want to listen to; the most extreme opinion is not always the most honest and cogent.

*Opposing bad ideas is absolutely essential, but being opposed to bad ideas is not the same thing as having good ideas. We have to have better ideas than the other side, which is why policy and principles matter, even in campaigns. Conservatives can be anti-elitist without being anti-intellectual or worse, anti-intelligent.

*Develop a well-honed BS meter. To be effective, you need to know what is real, because your credibility is one of your most important and precious assets. But it is also essential in this brave new world where we are inundated with "facts" and information that are often completely bogus. Ask questions: What is the source? How do we know this? Is it credible? Do not suffer crackpots lightly. Do not forward chain emails.

*Be willing to step out of the bubble. Our politics have become increasingly tribal, with each tribe having his own facts and its own reality. But if we are to succeed politically we need to reach beyond those tribal loyalties. The sad truth is that it is easy to get trapped in the alternative reality silos that we have created. If you take your view of reality and your facts from Infowars or Breitbart or the other alternative reality sites, you will eventually find yourself in a corner, isolated from the people you need to persuade. (P.S. If your Facebook feed is your primary source of news/opinion, you need to reexamine your life choices.)

*Fight against political correctness, but recognize what the term actually means. Sometimes boorishness and vulgarity are just boorishness and vulgarity.

*Don't become what we despise. If the other side abandons all pretense of ethics and values, that is not an excuse for us to do the same. Otherwise we become indistinguishable from what we fight against.

*Be willing to be unpopular. You know this because you are conservatives, so you know what it is to be marginalized, despised, and unpopular in the broader culture. But I mean something more: be prepared to lose friends—on our side. Be willing to challenge the conventional wisdom, even among your friends. Stand up for what you believe and decide whether what you believe is worth the price you sometimes have to pay.

*Politics is a team sport, but you are still an individual who can think for yourself. Of all of the areas of American life, politics may be one of the very few where you can get booed for saying that people should follow their conscience. Any movement that tells you to ignore your conscience is a movement that should be met with skepticism.

*Be willing to take the long view. In the end it will be far more important that you preserve your personal integrity, and fight for what you believe, than that you win this or that specific election. Every used car salesman, every fund-raising pitch tries to convince you that you have to make the deal right now; politicians insist that the apocalypse is upon on us. Be willing to step back. As unfashionable as it may be to say these days, there are no permanent victories and no permanent defeats. Which leads to . . .

*Winning is great, but weigh the cost. My father always used to say that sometimes the only fights worth fighting for were the lost causes. I never really understood that, but as I've gotten older and seen more, I've come to appreciate it. There is nothing dishonorable about losing, but there is something shameful about abandoning your principles. After all, what profits it a man to win the whole world, if he loses his soul? But for an election? Any election?

"You can resolve to live your life with integrity," Aleksandr Solzhenitsyn once wrote. "Let your credo be this: Let the lie come into the world, let it even triumph. But not through me."

When you look back on your life and on your career in politics, you will want to know whether you made a difference. You will also want to know whether you stood for what you believe to be right. You will win some elections and you will lose some elections. But what you will find most important is whether you stood firm in the truth.

ACKNOWLEDGMENTS

I am, as always, indebted to others for their insight, encouragement, and inspiration. But I am especially grateful for the handful of courageous voices who served as beacons of sanity. They provided me with both moral and intellectual support and, perhaps most important, reassured me throughout this tumultuous period that we were not the ones who were losing our minds. We are, indeed, a rather small band of brothers and sisters. I am especially grateful to principled conservatives like George Will, Stephen Hayes, Max Boot, Bret Stephens, David Frum, Rich Lowry, Kevin Williamson, Ross Douthat, Peter Wehner, Jonah Goldberg, Noah Rothman, David French, Bill Kristol, Jennifer Rubin, Charles Krauthammer, Charles Murray, Ben Shapiro,

Erick Erickson, Rick Wilson, and John Podhoretz for their often eloquent commentaries and dissents from the new orthodoxies. They reminded me that integrity is in shorter supply than ambition. I'm also indebted to Matthew Continetti for his discussions of the history of the conservative movement and to Conor Friedersdorf for his insightful commentaries on the conservative movement. Historian Nicole Hemmer provided invaluable insights into the development of conservative media. Russell Moore, of the Southern Baptist Convention, helped me understand what happened to evangelical Christian leaders and voters in the last campaign. As readers will notice, I am also indebted to commentators on the left, like E. J. Dionne, who helped me look at the last few years from a different perspective. WNYC radio, MSNBC, and the editors of *Politico* and the *New York Times* also provided me forums in which to work out some of the themes and arguments that appear in this book. As always, I'm grateful for the trust and support of my editor George Witte and the team at St. Martin's Press. Finally, a special thanks to all of the members of my family, especially my wife Janet, who endured the last two years with patience and fortitude. I'll try to make it up to you.

PREFACE TO THE PAPERBACK EDITION

1. Stephen F. Hayes, "Paul Ryan and the End of an Era," *Weekly Standard*, April 13, 2018, www.weeklystandard.com/stephen-f-hayes/hayes-paul-ryan-and-the -end-of-an-era.

2. Philip Bump, "Trump Is the Republican Party, and the Party Is Trump," *Washington Post*, February 7, 2018, www.washingtonpost.com/news/politics/wp /2018/02/07/trump-is-the-republican-party-and-the-party-is-trump/?utm_term= .8873480279c1.

3. "Trump Is No Role Model for Children, U.S. Voters Say 2–1; Quinnipiac University National Poll Finds; He Does Not Provide Moral Leadership, Voters Say," Quinnipiac Poll, January 25, 2018, poll.qu.edu/images/polling/us/us01252018 _uboe26.pdf.

4. Scott Clement and Emily Guskin, "Post-ABC Poll: Majority of Americans Support Mueller's Probe of Russia, Trump Campaign," *Washington Post*, April 13, 2018,

www.washingtonpost.com/politics/post-abc-poll-majority-of-americans-support
-muellers-probe-of-russia-trump-campaign/2018/04/12/fd5326f6-3e87-11e8-8d53
-eba0ed2371cc_story.html?utm_term=.20b024d423c9.

5. Rich Lowry, "But Gorsuch . . . and Other Excellent Judicial Picks . . . and a
Tax Cut . . . and Major Deregulatory Actions . . . and Immigration Enforcement . . .
and the End of the Individual Mandate . . . and a Roll Back of the HHS Mandate . . . ,"
National Review, December 3, 2017, www.nationalreview.com/corner/gorsuch
-trump-administration-accomplishments.

6. Charles J. Sykes, "Absolute Trump Corrupts Absolutely," *Weekly Standard,*
May 2, 2018, www.weeklystandard.com/charles-j-sykes/mike-pence-shoutout-to
-joe-arpaio-was-shameless-and-disgraceful.

7. David M. Drucker, "Congressional Republicans Hesitant to Antagonize
Trump over Russia Probe," *Washington Examiner,* March 21, 2018, www.washington
examiner.com/news/campaigns/congressional-republicans-hesitant-to-antagonize
-trump-over-russia-probe.

8. James Hohmann, "The Daily 202: Loyalty to Trump Emerges as a Top Issue
in Republican Primary Campaign Commercials," *Washington Post,* March 29, 2018,
www.washingtonpost.com/news/powerpost/paloma/daily-202/2018/03/29/daily
-202-loyalty-to-trump-emerges-as-a-top-issue-in-republican-primary-campaign
-commercials/5abc494530fb042a378a2f32/?utm_term=.259a0e19fcdd.

9. Harvard Institute of Politics, "Spring 2018, Youth Opinion Poll," April 11,
2018, iop.harvard.edu/spring-2018-poll.

10. "Breitbart Cuts Ties with Paul Ryan Rival Paul Nehlen over anti-Semitic
Rhetoric," *Haaretz,* December 28, 2017, www.haaretz.com/us-news/breitbart-cuts
-ties-with-paul-nehlen-over-anti-semitic-rhetoric-1.5629837.

11. John Bowden, "Ann Coulter: Trump Is a 'Shallow, Lazy Ignoramus,'" *Hill,*
March 28, 2018, thehill.com/blogs/blog-briefing-room/news/380612-ann-coulter
-trump-is-a-shallow-lazy-ignoramus.

12. Mona Charen, "I'm Glad I Got Booed at CPAC," *New York Times,* February 25, 2018, www.nytimes.com/2018/02/25/opinion/im-glad-i-got-booed-at-cpac
.html.

13. Tweet from Franklin Graham, twitter.com/franklin_graham/status
/931603580125097985.

14. Edward-Isaac Dovere, "Tony Perkins: Trump Gets 'a Mulligan' on Life,
Stormy Daniels," *Politico Magazine,* January 23, 2018, www.politico.com/magazine
/story/2018/01/23/tony-perkins-evangelicals-donald-trump-stormy-daniels-216498.

15. Emily Jashinsky, "Rep. Massie's theory: Voters Who Voted for Libertarians and Then Trump Were Always Just Seeking the 'Craziest Son of a Bitch in the
Race,'" *Washington Examiner,* March 17, 2017, www.washingtonexaminer.com
/rep-massies-theory-voters-who-voted-for-libertarians-and-then-trump-were
-always-just-seeking-the-craziest-son-of-a-bitch-in-the-race.

16. Ted Cruz, "Donald Trump," *Time,* time.com/collection/most-influential
-people-2018/5217621/donald-trump-2.

17. Emily Stewart, "Republican Confidence in the FBI Has Declined in the Age of Trump," Vox, February 3, 2018, www.vox.com/latest-news/2018/2/3/16968372/trump-fbi-republican-poll-confidence.

18. McKay Coppins, "What If the Right-Wing Media Wins?" *Columbia Journalism Review*, Fall 2017, www.cjr.org/special_report/right-wing-media-breitbart-fox-bannon-carlson-hannity-coulter-trump.php.

19. Stephen Battaglio and Matt Pearce, "Backlash Grows over Sinclair Broadcast Group's 'Must-Run' Conservative Content on Local TV Stations," *Los Angeles Times*, April 5, 2018, www.latimes.com/business/hollywood/la-fi-ct-sinclair-promo-20180405-story.html.

20. Hadas Gold and Oliver Darcy, "Salem Executives Pressured Radio Hosts to Cover Trump More Positively, Emails Show," CNN Money, May 9, 2018, money.cnn.com/2018/05/09/media/salem-radio-executives-trump/index.html.

21. Michael M. Grynbaum, "Family of Seth Rich Sues Fox News over Retracted Article," *New York Times*, March 13, 2018, www.nytimes.com/2018/03/13/business/fox-news-seth-rich-lawsuit.html.

22. Paul Farhi, "Fox News Commentator Exits with a Searing Attack on Fox News," *Washington Post*, March 20, 2018, www.washingtonpost.com/lifestyle/style/fox-news-commentator-exits-with-a-searing-attack-on-fox-news/2018/03/20/fc876fc4-2c81-11e8-8ad6-fbc50284fce8_story.html?utm_term=.6acd2aa688db.

23. Rich Lowry, "The Never Trump Delusion," *National Review*, March 30, 2018, www.nationalreview.com/2018/03/never-trump-delusion-trumpism-not-going-to-disappear.

24. Charles P. Pierce, "Donald Trump Was the Inevitable Result of Republicanism," *Esquire*, January 25, 2018, www.esquire.com/news-politics/politics/a15886291/trump-republican-prion-disease.

INTRODUCTION

1. John Hood, "What Bill Bennett Used to Understand, *National Review*, August 23, 2016, www.nationalreview.com/corner/439360/bill-bennett-donald-trump-wrong.

2. Larry O'Connor, "Bennett: #NeverTrump-ers Put Vanity Above Country; 'Terrible Case of Moral Superiority,'" Hotair.com, August 19, 2016, hotair.com/archives/2016/08/19/bennett-nevertrump-ers-put-vanity-above-country-terrible-case-of-moral-superiority.

3. William Bennett, "What a Clinton Supreme Court Would Mean for America," RealClearPolitics.com, August 23, 2016, www.realclearpolitics.com/articles/2016/08/23/what_a_clinton_supreme_court_would_mean_for_america_131586.html.

4. Jonathan Haidt, *The Righteous Mind: Why Good People Are Divided by Politics and Religion* (New York: Vintage Books, 2013), 342.

I. HOW THE RIGHT LOST ITS MIND

1. DID WE CREATE THIS MONSTER?

1. Stephen King, Tweet, March 2, 2016; twitter.com/stephenking/status /705228758840643584?lang=en.

2. Tim Alberta, "The Conservative Movement Is Donald Trump: Trump's Takeover of Conservatism Is Faster and More Decisive Than Anyone Expected," *Politico*, February 26, 2017.

3. Joel Kotkin, "Trump's Choice: Populism or Corporatism," *Orange County Register*, April 17, 2017.

4. Peter Wehner, "The Party of Reagan Is No More," *Time*, March 10, 2016.

5. David Wasserman, "Introducing the 2017 Cook Political Report Partisan Voter Index," *Cook Political Report*, April 7, 2017.

6. Mike Allen, "1 Big Thing: Why Washington Is Broken," *Axios*, April 9, 2017, www.axios.com/axios-am-2352154986.html?utm_source=newsletter&utm _medium=email&utm_campaign=newsletter_axiosam.

7. Bill Bishop, "Caught in a Landslide—County-level Voting Shows Increased Sorting," *Daily Yonder*, November 21, 2016, www.dailyyonder.com/caught-in-a -landslide-county-level-voting-shows-increased-sorting/2016/11/21/16361.

8. Jonathan Haidt, *The Righteous Mind*, 363.

9. Conor Friedersdorf, "How the Conservative Movement Enabled the Rise of Trump," *Atlantic*, February 25, 2016, www.theatlantic.com/politics/archive/2016 /02/how-the-conservative-movement-enabled-donald-trumps-rise/470727.

10. Charles J. Sykes interview with George Will, December 15, 2016, www .rightwisconsin.com/shows/charlie-sykes/charlie-sykes-podcast/george-will -salutes-charlies-radio-career-12-15-2016.

11. For a full discussion, see Kimberley Strassel, *The Intimidation Game: How the Left Is Silencing Free Speech* (New York: Hachette Book Group, 2016), ff.

12. "Video Shows NYC Protesters Chanting for 'Dead Cops,'" NBC New York, December 15, 2014, www.nbcnewyork.com/news/local/Eric-Garner-Manhattan -Dead-Cops-Video-Millions-March-Protest-285805731.html.

13. "Black Lives Matter Protesters Chant: 'Pigs in a Blanket, Fry 'Em Like Bacon,'" *Daily Caller*, August 29, 2015 (Video), dailycaller.com/2015/08/29/black-lives -matter-protesters-chant-pigs-in-a-blanket-fry-em-like-bacon-video.

14. Karen Stenner, *The Authoritarian Dynamic* (Cambridge: Cambridge University Press, 2005).

15. Ibid., p. 178.

16. Conor Friedersdorf, "How Conservatives Can Save America," *Atlantic*, February 2, 2017.

17. Ben Howe, "I Lied to Myself for Years About Who My Allies Were. No More," *RedState*, May 2, 2016, www.redstate.com/aglanon/2016/05/02/i-lied-to-myself-for-years/.

18. Kathleen Hall Jamieson and Joseph N. Capella, *Echo Chamber: Rush Limbaugh and the Conservative Media Establishment* (Oxford: Oxford University Press, 2008).

19. Matthew Sheffield, "Donald Trump, Mainstream Conservative: Those Who Have Long Stoked the Flames of Populism Should Not Be Surprised by the Results," *American Conservative*, June 10, 2016.

20. Philip N. Howard, Gillian Bolsover, Bence Kollanyi, Samantha Bradshaw, Lisa-Maria Neudert. "Junk News and Bots During the U.S. Election: What Were Michigan Voters Sharing Over Twitter?" Data Memo 2017.1. Oxford, UK: Project on Computational Propaganda. www.politicalbots.org.

21. John Markoff, "Automated Pro-Trump Bots Overwhelmed Pro-Clinton Messages, Researchers Say," *New York Times*, November 17, 2016.

22. Danny Westneat, "UW Professor: The Information War Is Real, and We're Losing It," *Seattle Times*, March 29, 2017.

23. James Poniewozik, "In Conservative Prime Time, It's Now Fox and Enemies, *New York Times*, May 3, 2017.

24. Charles J. Sykes, "If Liberals Hate Him, Then Trump Must Be Doing Something Right," *New York Times*, May 12, 2017.

2. CONFESSIONS OF A RECOVERING LIBERAL

1. These quotes are taken from an unpublished manuscript: Jay G. Sykes, "The Levelled Society: The Legacy of Liberalism," 1976.

2. Charlie Sykes, "The Trump Temptation," *Right Wisconsin*, August 15, 2015, www.rightwisconsin.com/opinion/perspectives/the-trump-temptation.

3. Peter Wehner, "Why I Will Never Vote for Donald Trump," *New York Times*, January 14, 2015.

3. THE ATTACK ON THE CONSERVATIVE MIND

1. "GOP Quickly Unifies Around Trump; Clinton Still Has Modest Lead," Public Policy Poll, May 10, 2016, www.publicpolicypolling.com/main/2016/05/gop-quickly-unifies-around-trump-clinton-still-has-modest-lead.html.

2. Ilya Somin, "What No One Talks About During Election Season: Voter Ignorance," Forbes.com, November 3, 2014, www.forbes.com/sites/realspin/2014/11/03/what-no-one-talks-about-during-election-season-voter-ignorance/#2eb1b1dc3a22.

3. Nicholas Kristof, "Lessons from the Media's Failures in Its Year with Trump," *New York Times*, December 31, 2016.

4. Justin Kruger and David Dunning, "Unskilled and Unaware of It: How Difficulties in Recognizing One's Incompetence Lead to Inflated Self-Assessments," *Journal of Personality and Social Psychology*, 77, No. 6 (1999), psych.colorado.edu/~vanboven/teaching/p7536_heurbias/p7536_readings/kruger_dunning.pdf.

5. David Dunning, "The Psychological Quirk That Explains Why You Love Donald Trump: The Popularity of the GOP Front-runner Can Be Explained by the Dunning-Kruger Effect," *Politico Magazine*, May 25, 2016.

6. James Hohmann, "The Daily 202: Trump's Pollster Says He Ran a 'Post-ideological' Campaign," *Washington Post*, December 5, 2016, www.washingtonpost

.com/news/powerpost/paloma/daily-202/2016/12/05/daily-202-trump-s-pollster
-says-he-ran-a-post-ideological-campaign/5844d166e9b69b7e58e45f2a/?tid=a
_inl&utm_term=.16974f4ebdab.

7. Matt K. Lewis, *Too Dumb to Fail: How the GOP Betrayed the Reagan Revolution to Win Elections (and How It Can Reclaim Its Conservative Roots)* (New York: Hachette Books, 2015), 105.

8. Kevin Williamson, "Translating 'Make America Great Again' into English," *National Review,* January 24, 2016.

9. Ibid.

10. Nahema Marchal, "'White Anchor' Tomi Lahren Under Fire for Suggesting the Clintons Murdered DNC Staffer Seth Rich," *Heat Street,* October 24, 2016, heatst.com/politics/white-anchor-tomi-lahren-under-fire-for-suggesting-the-clintons-murdered-dnc-staffer-seth-rich.

11. Jonah Engel Bromwich, "Tomi Lahren: Young, Vocal and the Right's Rising Media Star," *New York Times,* December 4, 2016.

12. Jamie Weinstein, "Tomi Lahren on Conservatism, Her Support for Trump and Her Influences," *Daily Caller,* October 23, 2016, dailycaller.com/2016/10/23/tomi-lahren-on-conservatism-her-support-for-trump-and-her-influences/#ixzz4YzMq8QoR.

13. Marc Fisher, "Donald Trump Doesn't Read Much. Being President Probably Wouldn't Change That," *Washington Post,* July 17, 2016.

14. Kiron K. Skinner, Annelise Anderson, and Martin Anderson, eds., *Reagan in His Own Hand* (New York: Free Press, 2001).

15. Lionel Trilling, *The Liberal Imagination* (New York: New York Review Books, 2008), xv.

16. Clinton Rossiter, *Conservatism in America* (New York: Alfred Knopf, 1955).

4. THE CONSERVATIVE IDEA

1. William F. Buckley Jr., *The Unmaking of a Mayor* (New York: Encounter Books, 2015), xiv.

2. Ibid., xiii.

3. Ibid., 144.

4. Ibid., xvii.

5. "Publisher's Statement," *National Review,* November 19, 1955.

6. Ibid.

7. Lee Edwards, "The Conservative Consensus: Frank Meyer, Barry Goldwater, and the Politics of Fusionism," *Heritage Foundation,* January 22, 2007.

8. Ibid.

9. George Nash, *The Conservative Intellectual Movement in America Since 1945* (New York: Basic Books, 1976). See also: George Nash, "The Conservative Intellectual Movement in America: Then and Now," *National Review,* April 26, 2016.

10. Barry Goldwater, *The Conscience of a Conservative* (New York: Hillman Books, 1960), 7.

11. Ibid., 7.

12. Ibid., 8.

13. E. J. Dionne, *Why the Right Went Wrong* (New York: Simon & Schuster), 462.

14. Barry Goldwater, *The Conscience of a Conservative*, 9.

15. Matthew Continetti, "The Coming Conservative Dark Age," *Commentary*, April 12, 2016.

16. William F. Buckley Jr., *Up from Liberalism* (New York: Hillman 1959), 192.

17. Matthew Continetti, "The Coming Conservative Dark Age."

18. Whittaker Chambers, "Big Sister Is Watching You," *National Review*, December 28, 1957.

19. William F. Buckley Jr., *National Review*, 12 (1962), 88. See also William F. Buckley Jr., "Goldwater, the John Birch Society, and Me," *Commentary*, March 1, 2008.

20. William F. Buckley Jr., "Goldwater, the John Birch Society, and Me."

21. Matthew Continetti, "Crisis of the Conservative Intellectual Column: How Populism Displaced Conservatism in the Republican Party," *Washington Free Beacon*, October 21, 2016, freebeacon.com/columns/crisis-conservative-intellectual.

22. Ibid.

23. Nicole Hemmer, *Messengers of the Right: Conservative Media and the Transformation of American Politics* (Philadelphia: University of Pennsylvania Press, 2016), 241.

24. "Why the South Must Prevail," *National Review*, August 14, 1957.

25. "Foul," *National Review*, April 18, 1956.

26. Quoted in Alvin S. Felzenberg, *A Man and His Presidents: The Political Odyssey of William F. Buckley Jr.* (New Haven: Yale University Press, 2017) 159–60.

27. Continetti, "Crisis of the Intellectual Column."

28. Ibid.

29. Alvin S. Felzberg, *A Man and His Presidents*, 299.

30. Ibid. 274.

31. Nicole Hemmer, *Messengers of the Right*, xvi.

32. Ibid., 253.

33. Ibid., 264.

34. Ibid., 272.

5. STORM WARNINGS

1. Ross Douthat and Reihan Salam, "The Party of Sam's Club: Isn't It Time the Republicans Did Something for Their Voters?," *Weekly Standard*, November 14, 2005.

2. Ibid.

3. David Frum, "Republicans Must Change to Win," *Financial Times*, May 7, 2008.

4. Ross Douthat and Reihan Salam, "The Party of Sam's Club."

5. John Avlon, *Wingnuts: Extremism in the Age of Obama* (New York: Beast Books, 2014), 35.

6. Ibid., 41.

7. Ibid., 146.

8. Ibid., 45.

9. Ibid., 123.

10. Charles J. Sykes, "Fall Reckoning: The Voters Exact Vengeance upon the Disdainful Democrats," *Wisconsin Interest Magazine* 19, no. 3 (November 2010).

11. Michael Murray, "Tea Party Protests: 14-Year-Old Wisconsin Activist Reacts to Hecklers," ABC News, April 21, 2011, abcnews.go.com/US/tea-party-hecklers-14-year-wisconsin-tea-party/story?id=13421116.

12. Patrick McIlheran, "Rep. Gordon Hintz Says He's So (Expletive) Sorry," *Milwaukee Journal-Sentinel*, March 1, 2011.

13. "WTDY Host John 'Sly' Sylvester Insults Wisconsin Lt. Gov. Rebecca Kleefisch." Available at www.youtube.com/watch?v=bp-DFsUvYn0.

14. Scott K. Walker, *Unintimidated: A Governor's Story and a Nation's Challenge* (New York: Sentinel, 2014), 61.

15. Michael Savage, "Savage Predicts 'A Revolution in This Country if This Keeps up Because the White Male . . . Has Nothing to Lose,'" *Savage Nation*, August 21, 2009.

16. John Avlon, *Wingnuts*, 48.

17. David Frum, "When Did the GOP Lose Touch with Reality?," *New York Magazine*, November 20, 2011.

18. Charles J. Sykes, "Time to Confront Crackpots," *Wisconsin Interest Magazine* 22, no. 1 (April 2013). www.buzzfeed.com/craigsilverman/partisan-fb-pages-analysis?utm_term=.thBXrODwx#.laEMdaBNR.

19. Nicole Duran, "Ryan Warns GOP Wisconsin Could Turn Blue Again," *Washington Examiner*, December 19, 2016. See also Bill Glauber, "Paul Ryan Thanks Charlie Sykes for Lifting Conservative Ideas," *Milwaukee Journal Sentinel*, December 19, 2016.

20. Matt K. Lewis, "How Paul Ryan Went from Wingnut to RINO: The Surprising Reasons Why the Onetime Conservative Wunderkind Is Now Considered a Traitor by Many on the Right." *Daily Beast*, October 26, 2015.

21. Josh Feldman, "Palin in 2010: 'I'm Very Impressed with Paul Ryan,' 'He Is Sharp, He Is Smart'," *Mediaite*, May 8, 2016, www.mediaite.com/tv/palin-in-2010-im-very-impressed-with-paul-ryan-he-is-sharp-he-is-smart/.

22. Ibid.

23. Alex Griswold, "Coulter: I Don't Care If Donald Trump Performs Abortions in the White House," *Mediaite*, August 16, 2015, www.mediaite.com/online/coulter-i-dont-care-if-donald-trump-performs-abortions-in-the-white-house.

24. Matt Vespa, "Poll: Paul Ryan's Approval Collapses, More GOP Voters Say Trump Best Represents Their View of the Party," *Townhall*, October 21, 2016.

25. Sahil Kapur, "Poll Shows Republicans Less Committed to Trump in Defeat: Just 24 Percent of Republicans and Those Who Lean That Way Say Trump Should Be the Face of the Party Nationally if Clinton Wins," Bloomberg, October 20, 2016.

6. THE PERPETUAL OUTRAGE MACHINE

1. Paul H. Jossey, "How We Killed the Tea Party," *Politico*, August 14, 2016, www.politico.com/magazine/story/2016/08/tea-party-pacs-ideas-death-214164.

2. Matea Gold, "Tea Party PACs Reap Money for Midterms, But Spend Little on Candidates," *Washington Post,* April 26, 2014.

3. Kenneth P. Vogel, "The Rise of 'Scam PACs': Conservatives Sound Alarms About Self-Dealing Fundraisers," *Politico,* January 26, 2015, www.politico.com/story/2015/01/super-pac-scams-114581.

4. Ibid.

5. Brian Sikma, "Scam PACs Enrich Vendors, Waste Donor Dollars: Little to No Money Goes to Where it Claims It Will," *Right Wisconsin,* August 30, 2016, www.rightwisconsin.com/opinion/daily-takes/scam-pacs-enrich-vendors-waste-donor-dollars.

6. Brim, Sikma, "Faux Tea Party Groups Enrich Vendors, Waste Donor Dollars," Media Trackers, August 29, 2016.

7. Vogel, Kenneth P. "The Rise of 'Scam PACs.' "

8. Ibid.

9. Quoted in Matt K. Lewis, *Too Dumb to Fail,* 131.

10. David French, "Conservative Scams Are Bringing Down the Conservative Movement," *National Review,* August 15, 2016.

11. Charles C. W. Cooke, "Against the Dangerous Myth That the GOP Has 'Given Obama Everything He Wanted,' " *National Review,* May 6, 2016.

12. Ibid.

13. E. J. Dionne, *Why the Right Went Wrong,* 3.

14. Andrew Blasko, "Reagan and Heritage: A Unique Partnership," The Heritage Foundation, June 7, 2004, www.heritage.org/research/commentary/2004/06/reagan-and-heritage-a-unique-partnership.

15. Ibid.

16. Paul Blumenthal, "Jim DeMint, Heritage Foundation Merger Brings Politics to Forefront," *Huffington Post,* December 7, 2012, www.huffingtonpost.com/2012/12/07/jim-demint-heritage-foundation_n_2258631.html.

17. Zeke J. Miller, "Hidden Hand: How Heritage Action Drove DC to Shut Down: Harnessing the Power of the Tea Party, the Political Action Arm of the Once-esteemed Heritage Foundation Has Perfected the Art of Disrupting DC, Whatever the Cost," *Time,* September 30, 2013.

18. Ibid.

19. Kenneth P. Vogel and Mackenzie Weinger, "The Tea Party Radio Network," *Politico,* April 17, 2014.

20. Matt Fuller, "Heritage Action Leaves GOP 'In the Lurch' on Government Shutdown," *Roll Call,* July 31, 2013.

21. Pete Dominick, "Mark Levin–Ron Johnson Fight Explains the Shutdown Perfectly," *Daily Beast,* October 18, 2013.

22. "Limbaugh Bashes GOP 'Establishment': 'Embarrassed' to Be Associated with 'Lunatic' Cruz," *Mediaite,* October 17, 2013.

23. "As Sequester Deadline Looms, Little Support for Cutting Most Programs," Pew Research Center, February 22, 2013, www.people-press.org/2013/02/22/as-sequester-deadline-looms-little-support-for-cutting-most-programs.

24. "In U.S., Support for Tea Party Drops to New Low," Gallup Poll, October 26, 2015, www.gallup.com/poll/186338/support-tea-party-drops-new-low.aspx.

25. Neil King Jr. and Scott Greenberg, "Poll Shows Budget-Cuts Dilemma: Many Deem Big Cuts to Entitlements 'Unacceptable,' but Retirement and Means Testing Draw Support," *Wall Street Journal*, March 3, 2011.

26. Caleb Howe, "Donald Trump Is Talk Radio's Frankencandidate," *RedState*, August 30, 2016, www.redstate.com/absentee/2016/08/30/trump-talk-radios -frankencandidate/.

II. THE POST-TRUTH POLITICS OF THE RIGHT

7. THE ALT REALITY MEDIA

1. David Bauder, "Divided America: Constructing Our Own Intellectual Ghettos," Associated Press, June 16, 2016.

2. Yochai Benkler, Robert Faris, Hal Roberts, and Ethan Zuckerman, "Study: Breitbart-led Right-wing Media Ecosystem Altered Broader Media Agenda," *Columbia Journalism Review*, March 3, 2017.

3. Matea Gold, "The Mercers and Stephen Bannon: How a Populist Power Base Was Funded and Built," *Washington Post*, March 17, 2017.

4. Ibid.

5. Nicole Hemmer, *Messengers of the Right*, xiii.

6. Ibid.

7. Howard Kurtz, "Evangelical Outrage," *Washington Post*, February 6, 1993.

8. Kathleen Hall Jamieson and Joseph N. Capella, *Echo Chamber*, x.

9. "Yes, I'd Lie to You: Dishonesty in Politics Is Nothing New; But the Manner in Which Some Politicians Now Lie, and the Havoc They May Wreak by Doing So, Are Worrying," *Economist*, September 10, 2016.

10. Multiple authors, "Hyperpartisan Facebook Pages Are Publishing False and Misleading Information at an Alarming Rate," BuzzFeed, October 20, 2016, www.buzzfeed.com/craigsilverman/partisan-fb-pages-analysis?utm_term= .tfZLVla9z#.suLnW5Ne1.

11. Olivia Solon, "Facebook's Failure: Did Fake News and Polarized Politics Get Trump Elected?," *Guardian*, November 10, 2016.

8. THE POST-TRUTH POLITICS OF THE RIGHT

1. Caitlyn Dewey, "Facebook Fake-news Writer: 'I Think Donald Trump Is in the White House Because of Me,'" *Washington Post*, November 17, 2016.

2. Cited in "Yes, I'd Lie to You."

3. twitter.com/kasparov63/status/808750564284702720?lang=en.

4. I discussed this in Charles J. Sykes, "Why Nobody Cares the President Is Lying," *New York Times*, February 4, 2017.

5. Jeremy W. Peters, "Wielding Claims of 'Fake News,' Conservatives Take Aim at Mainstream Media," *New York Times,* December 25, 2016.

6. Margaret Sullivan, "It's Time to Retire the Tainted Term 'Fake News,'" *Washington Post,* January 8, 2017.

7. "Facebook's Fake Fix for Fake News: Liberal Fact-checkers Are Not the Way to Ensure a More Informed Public," *Wall Street Journal,* December 18, 2016.

8. Matt Shapiro, "Running the Data on PolitiFact Shows Bias Against Conservatives," *Federalist,* December 16, 2016, thefederalist.com/2016/12/16/running-data -politifact-shows-bias-conservatives.

9. Ibid.

10. Shanika Gunaratna, "Facebook Apologizes for Promoting False Story on Megyn Kelly in #Trending," CBS News, August 29, 2016.

11. Danny Westneat, "UW Professor: The Information War Is Real, and We're Losing It," *Seattle Times,* March 29, 2017.

12. Kate Starbird, "Examining the Alternative Media Ecosystem Through the Production of Alternative Narratives of Mass Shooting Events on Twitter," faculty .washington.edu/kstarbi/Alt_Narratives_ICWSM17-CameraReady.pdf.

13. Ibid.

14. Ibid.

15. Ben Collins, "The Vigilante Faking WikiLeaks Docs to Dupe Trump Trolls: An Expense Report That Shows Hillary Giving Money to the 'Sharia Law Center' Should Be Too Stupid to Believe. But Somehow It Wasn't. Meet the Man Who Made It—and Is Baffled High-Profile People Fell for It," *Daily Beast,* October 12, 2016, www.thedailybeast.com/articles/2016/10/16/the-vigilante-faking-wikileaks-docs-to -dupe-trump-trolls.html.

16. Ibid.

17. John Herman, "Inside Facebook's (Totally Insane, Unintentionally Gigantic, Hyperpartisan) Political-Media Machine: How a Strange New Class of Media Outlet Has Arisen to Take Over Our News Feeds," *New York Times Magazine,* August 24, 2016.

18. "Hyperpartisan Facebook Pages Are Publishing False and Misleading Information at an Alarming Rate," BuzzFeed, October 20, 2016, buzzfeed.com/craigsilverman/partisan-fb-pages-analysis?utm_term=.thBXrODwx#.IaEMdaBNR.

19. Cited in "Yes, I'd Lie to You."

20. Jonathan Haidt, *The Righteous Mind,* 365.

21. Ibid, 100.

22. Ibid, 103.

23. Ibid, 98.

24. Lindsey Ellefson, "Scottie Nell Hughes Straight-Up Said 'There's No Such Things' as Fact," *Mediaite,* December 1, 2016, www.mediaite.com/online /scottie-nell-hughes-straight-up-said-theres-no-such-things-as-facts.

25. Stephen Colbert, interview by Nathan Rabin, The A.V. Club, January 25, 2006.

26. "Ballot Bluffing: A Disingenuous Article Falsely Claimed That 'Tens of Thousands' of Fraudulent Ballots Were Discovered in a Warehouse in Ohio," Snopes.com, October 6, 2016, www.snopes.com/clinton-votes-found-in-warehouse.

27. Charlie Warzel, "The Right Is Building a New Media 'Upside Down' to Tell Trump's Story," BuzzFeed, January 23, 2017.

28. Abby Ohlheiser, "How the War Against Fake News Backfired," *Washington Post*, December 7, 2016.

29. Callum Borchers, "Blog Known for Spreading Hoaxes Says It Will Have a Correspondent in Trump White House," *Washington Post,* January 20, 2017.

30. Eric Hananoki, "22 Times Jim Hoft and the Gateway Pundit Were Absurdly Wrong," Media Matters for America, January 25, 2017.

31. Ibid.

32. Ibid.

33. "North Carolina Hillary Supporter Votes Multiple Times: Claims of Voter Fraud in North Carolina Turned Out to Be Merely a Facebook Joke," Snopes .com, October 29, 2016.

34. "Clinton's Campaign Manager Robby Mook Deleted All of His Tweets Because He Was 'Spooked' by an FBI Investigation," Snopes.com, October 29, 2016.

35. Brian Stelter, "Fake Story About Obamas, Hillary Clinton Ensnares Sean Hannity," CNN, November 1, 2016.

36. Jim Hoft, "WikiLeaks Document Shows John McCain Requested Donations from Russians" (Updated), Gateway Pundit, February 22, 2017, www .thegatewaypundit.com/2017/02/wow-wikileaks-document-shows-john-mccain -requested-donations-russians.

37. Joe Concha, "Hannity Apologizes for Sharing 'Inaccurate' Story About McCain," *Hill*, February 23, 2017.

38. Charlie Warzel, "Here's Where Donald Trump Gets His News," BuzzFeed, December 3, 2016, www.buzzfeed.com/charliewarzel/trumps-infor mation-universe?utm_term=.shqp8AlRw#.gwKz5PAXx.

39. Eric Hananoki, "22 Times Jim Hoft and the Gateway Pundit."

40. Julie Alderman and Brendan Karet, "What *60 Minutes* Didn't Mention About 'Alt-Right' Men's Rights Activist Mike Cernovich," Media Matters for America, March 27, 2017.

41. Matthew Rosenberg, Maggie Haberman, and Eric Schmitt, "Trump Fires Adviser's Son from Transition for Spreading Fake News," *New York Times*, December 6, 2016.

42. Kellyanne Conway, Twitter, April 3, 2017.

43. Donald J. Trump Jr., Twitter, April 4, 2017.

44. Adam Shaw, "Pro-Trump Blogger Cernovich Getting Big Scoops, Mainstream Attention," Fox News, April 14, 2017, www.foxnews.com/politics/2017/04/14 /pro-trump-blogger-cernovich-getting-big-scoops-mainstream-attention.html.

9. DRUDGE AND THE POLITICS OF PARANOIA

1. Sam Reisman, "Drudge Report Ranks #3 for All Media Publishers for Month of June," *Mediaite*, July 12, 2016.

2. John Ziegler, "Gretchen Carlson's Lawsuit Exposes the Left/Right Media Scam," *Mediaite*, July 7, 2016.

3. Eric Hananoki, "A Comprehensive Guide to Alex Jones: Conspiracy Theorist and Trump 'Valuable Asset,'" Media Matters for America, December 1, 2016.

4. Ibid. See also Genesis Communications Network, *The Alex Jones Show*, January 13, 2015.

5. Ibid.

6. Genesis Communications Network, *The Alex Jones Show*, October 10, 2016.

7. Eric Bradner, "Trump Praises 9/11 Truther's 'Amazing' Reputation," CNN, December 2, 2015.

8. Manuel Roig Franza, "How Alex Jones, Conspiracy Theorist Extraordinaire, Got Donald Trump's Ear," *Washington Post*, November 16, 2016.

9. Jonathan Tilove, "In Travis County Custody Case, Jury Will Search for Real Alex Jones," *Austin American-Stateman*, April 16, 2017.

10. Manuel Roig Franza, "How Alex Jones, Conspiracy Theorist Extraordinaire, Got Donald Trump's Ear."

11. Paul Joseph Watson, "Bilderberg-Approved Perry Set to Become Presidential Frontrunner," *Infowars*, June 20, 2011.

12. KEVINAW2, "Why Is Drudge Linking to Alex Jones's 'Info Wars' Site?," *RedState*, June 20, 2011, www.redstate.com/diary/kevinaw2/2011/06/20/why-is-drudge-linking-to-alex-joness-info-wars-site.

13. "A Strange Man Is Following You," *New York*, April 4, 2011, nymag.com/nymag/features/alex-jones-2011-4/index2.html.

14. Ben Dimiero, "How Matt Drudge Serves as Alex Jones' Web Traffic Pipeline; Drudge Report Has Linked to Jones' Infowars Site 244 Times in Two Years," Media Matters for America, April 26, 2013.

15. Ibid.

16. Tweet from *RedState* editor Ben Howe, mediamatters.org/blog/2013/04/26/how-matt-drudge-serves-as-alex-jones-web-traffic/193780.

17. Adan Salazar, "Drudge: 'Why Aren't We Seeing Hillary's Lovers?': Media Mogul Questions Lack of Investigative Reporting into Leading Democrat Presidential Candidate," Infowars.com, October 7, 2015.

18. CNN.com, October 6, 2015.

19. Adan Salazar, "Drudge: 'Why Aren't We Seeing Hillary's Lovers?'"

20. Richard Hofstadter, "The Paranoid Style in American Politics," *Harper's*, November 1964.

21. Ibid.

22. Ibid.

23. Laura Miller, "The Paranoid Style in American Punditry: Richard Hofstadter's Seminal Take on Right-Wing Crackpots Sheds Light on the Current Anti-Muslim Panic," Salon.com, September 15, 2010, www.salon.com/2010/09/15/hofstadter.

24. Jonathan Merritt, "Pat Robertson, Christianity's Crazy Uncle," *Week*, October 17, 2016.

25. "ADL Outraged at Pat Robertson's Remarks Blaming Sharon's Stroke on the Wrath of God," Anti-Defamation League, January 5, 2006, archive.adl.org/presrele/islme_62/4847_62.html.

26. "Press release: Pat Robertson's Statement Regarding Terrorist Attack on America," accessed January 16, 2017, www.patrobertson.com/PressReleases/TerroristAttack.asp.

27. Marc Ambinder, "Falwell Suggests Gays to Blame for Attacks," ABC News, September 14, 2001.

28. Pat Robertson, *The New World Order* (Dallas: Word Publishing, 1991), 96.

29. Richard C. Longworth, "Nobody Loves a Conspiracy Theory More Than Donald Trump," *Chicago Tribune,* October 21, 2016.

30. Daniel Pipes, *Conspiracy: How the Paranoid Style Flourishes and Where It Comes From* (New York: Touchstone, 1999).

31. Michael Lind, "Rev. Robertson's Grand International Conspiracy Theory," *New York Review of Books,* February 3, 1995. See also Ephraim Radner, "New World Order, Old World Anti-Semitism," *Christian Century* 112, no. 26 (September 13, 1995).

32. Jacob Heilbrunn, "His Anti-Semitic Sources," *New York Review of Books,* April 20, 1995.

33. Michael Lind, "Rev. Robertson's Grand International Conspiracy Theory."

34. Steve Benen, "The Birthers," *Washington Monthly,* March 2, 2009. See also Gregory Krieg, "14 of Trump's Most Outrageous 'Birther' Claims—Half from After 2011," CNN.com, September 9, 2016.

35. Ibid.

36. "Romney and the Birthers," Public policy polling, February 15, 2011, publicpolicypolling.blogspot.com/2011/02/romney-and-birthers.html.

37. Steve Benen, "The Birthers."

38. E. J. Dionne, *Why the Right Went Wrong,* 436.

39. Josh Voorhees, "All of Donald Trump's Birther Tweets," Slate.com, September 16, 2016, www.slate.com/blogs/the_slatest/2016/09/16/donald_trump_s_birther_tweets_in_order.html.

40. Michael Barbaro, "Trump Clung to Birther Lie for Years, and Still Isn't Apologetic," *New York Times,* September 16, 2016.

41. Eric Levitz, "Trump Says His Accusers Are Pawns in a Globalist Conspiracy to End U.S. Sovereignty," *New York Magazine,* October 13, 2016, nymag.com/daily/intelligencer/2016/10/trump-my-accusers-are-part-of-a-global-plot-to-end-the-u-s.html.

42. Zeke J. Miller, "Donald Trump Has a Grand Unified Campaign Conspiracy Theory," *Time,* October 13, 2016, time.com/4530568/donald-trump-hillary-clinton-conspiracy.

43. Ron Kampeas, "Donald Trump's 'International Bankers' Speech Leaves Some Uneasy," *Jewish Telegraph Agency,* October 14, 2016, www.jta.org/2016/10/14/news-opinion/politics/donald-trumps-conspiracy-theories-stir-uneasy-echoes.

III. THE TRUMPIAN TAKEOVER

10. THE FOX NEWS PRIMARY

1. Yochai Benkler, Robert Faris, Hal Roberts, and Ethan Zuckerman, *Columbia Journalism Review*, March 3, 2017, "Study: Breitbart-led Right-wing Media Ecosystem Altered Broader Media Agenda."

2. Scott Eric Kaufman, "Conservative Radio Host Mark Levin: Fox News Is 'Trump Super PAC' That Will Be 'Rubbing Their Faces in Their Own Feces' Come November: He Isn't Happy About the State of the GOP or Its Unofficial Fair-and-Balanced Organ," Salon.com, May 4, 2016, www.salon.com/2016/05/04/conservative_radio_host_mark_levin_fox_news_is_trump_super_pac_that_will_be_rubbing_their_faces_in_their_own_feces_come_november/.

3. Amy Mitchell, Jeffrey Gottfried, Jocelyn Kily, and Katerina Eva Matsa, "Political Polarization & Media Habits," Pew Research Center, October 21, 2014.

4. Gabriel Sherman, *The Loudest Voice in the Room; How the Brilliant, Bombastic Roger Ailes Built Fox News—and Divided a Country* (New York: Random House, 2014), 33.

5. Ibid., 254.

6. Ibid., 344.

7. Ibid., 372.

8. Ibid., 373.

9. Eliana Johnson," How Trump Blew Up the Conservative Media: The Right-wing Media Won the Presidency—but Lost Control of Their Audience. Inside the New Power Dynamics Roiling Fox, Breitbart and the *Wall Street Journal*," *Politico Magazine*, May/June 2017.

10. Rob Savillo, "STUDY: Trump Won the Fox Primary, Doubling Any Other Candidate in Interview Airtime," Media Matters for America, May 5, 2016, mediamatters.org/blog/2016/05/05/study-trump-won-fox-primary-doubling-any-other-candidate-interview-airtime/210249.

11. "'Ted Cruz: Rupert Murdoch and Roger Ailes 'Have Turned Fox News into the Donald Trump Network,'" Media Matters for America, May 3, 2016, mediamatters.org/video/2016/05/03/ted-cruz-rupert-murdoch-and-roger-ailes-have-turned-fox-news-donald-trump-network/210192.

12. Jennifer Senior, "Review: Megyn Kelly Tells Tales Out of Fox News in Her Memoir, 'Settle for More,'" *New York Times*, November 10, 2016.

13. Dylan Byers and Dana Bash, "How Roger Ailes Is Shaping Donald Trump's Debate Prep," CNNMoney.com, September 7, 2016, money.cnn.com/2016/09/07/media/roger-ailes-donald-trump-presidential-debate-preparation.

14. Ibid.

15. "New York's Gabriel Sherman: Sexual Harassment 'Was Encouraged and Protected' at Fox News Under Roger Ailes," Media Matters for America, July 26, 2016.

16. Gabriel Sherman, "Rupert Murdoch Is Turning Fox News into Trump TV," *New York Magazine*, January 5, 2017.

17. Eliana Johnson, "How Trump Blew Up the Conservative Media."

11. LIMBAUGH'S FLOP

1. Rush Limbaugh, "If Donald Trump Didn't Exist, the GOP Would Have to Invent Him to Win," Media Matters for America, December 17, 2015.

2. Nicole Hemmer, *Messengers of the Right*, 263.

3. Ibid., 271.

4. John Ziegler, "How and Why the Conservative Media Sold Its Soul to Facilitate Trump's Nomination," *Mediaite*, March 15, 2016.

5. Ethan Epstein, "Is Rush Limbaugh in Trouble? The Talk Radio Host Is as Influential as Ever, but His Business Model Is on Shaky Ground," *Politico*, May 24, 2016, www.politico.com/magazine/story/2016/05/is-rush-limbaugh-in-trouble-talk-radio-213914.

6. "Butt Sisters are Safe from Newt and Rick," *Rush Limbaugh Show*, Transcript, February 29, 2012.

7. "Updated: Limbaugh's Misogynistic Attack on Georgetown Law Student Continues with Increased Vitriol," Media Matters for America, retrieved on March 5, 2012.

8. Ibid.

9. David Jackson, "Limbaugh Apologizes to Sandra Fluke," *USA Today*, March 3, 2012.

10. "Sandra Fluke Says Rush Limbaugh's Apology Doesn't Change Anything," ABC News, retrieved on March 6, 2012.

11. Ethan Epstein, "Is Rush Limbaugh in Trouble?"

12. "Are We Being Fair to Rush Limbaugh?," CNN.com, March 5, 2012.

13. "George Will: Republican Leaders Are Afraid of Rush Limbaugh," ABC News, March 4, 2012.

14. Eric Boehlert, "Why Reports About Rush Limbaugh's Contract Renewal Don't Mention the Price," Media Matters for America, August 2, 2016.

15. Eric Boehlert, "Rush Limbaugh Demoted to Another Irrelevant, Ratings-Challenged Station in a Major Market," Media Matters for America, June 17, 2015.

16. Darryl Parks, "How's Limbaugh's Station in Pittsburgh Doing?," blog post, July 26, 2016, darrylparks.com/2016/07/26/hows-limbaughs-station-in-pittsburgh-doing.

17. Caleb Howe, "Limbaugh: I Never Took Trump Seriously on Immigration Anyway," *RedState*, August 29, 2016.

18. Tim Mak, "Talk Radio Gets Angrier as Its Revenues Drop," *FrumForum*, August 6, 2009.

19. John Avlon, *Wingnuts*, 112.

20. Jon Favreau, "Longtime Listener, First-Time Candidate," *Ringer*, September 6, 2016, theringer.com/how-the-far-right-media-controls-donald-trump-3d077ca46a21#.igawfzvkp.

21. Maggie Haberman, "Rush Limbaugh Rallies Listeners to Donald Trump's Defense," *New York Times*, July 20, 2015.

22. Premiere Radio Networks, *Rush Limbaugh Show*, November 11, 2015.

23. "Limbaugh: I Never Took Trump Seriously," Daily Rushbo, August 29, 2016, dailyrushbo.com/limbaugh-i-never-took-trump-seriously.

24. Allahpundit, "Rush on Trump's Maternity Leave Plan: Do You Really Think People Still Care About Small Government?," Hotair.com, September 14, 2016, hotair .com/archives/2016/09/14/rush-trumps-maternity-leave-plan-really-think-people -still-care-small-government. See also Allahpundit, "Rush: If Done Right, a Gigantic Infrastructure Stimulus Could Be Popular and an Economic Boon," Hotair.com, December 5, 2016.

25. Ibid.

26. Michael Gerson, "Rush Limbaugh's Blessing of Trump Is Killing Conservatism," *Washington Post,* March 28, 2016.

27. Charlie Sykes, "Yes, Talk Radio Is Different in Wisconsin," *Right Wisconsin,* March 28, 2016, www.rightwisconsin.com/opinion/perspectives/yes-talk -radio-is-different-in-wisconsin. See also Nolan D. McCaskill, "Trump Walks Into #Nevertrump Radio Buzzsaw," *Politico,* March 28, 2016.

28. David Weigel, "'Stop Trump' Forces See an Opportunity in Scott Walker's Wisconsin," *Washington Post,* March 23, 2016.

29. Rush Limbaugh, May 3, 2017, dailyrushbo.com/Limbaugh-media-are -jealous-as-they-can-be-that-trump-responded-to-criticism-from-me/.

12. THE BIGOTS AMONG US

1. John Hayward, "Paul Nehlen: Paul Ryan Is a 'Soulless, Globalist Snake, and We Smoked Him Out of the Snake Hole,'" Breitbart.com, August 9, 2016.

2. Julia Hahn, "Paul Ryan Plummets to 43 Percent in New Primary Poll," Breitbart.com, July 9, 2016.

3. James Wigderson, "Stunning: Paul Nehlen Suggests Deporting All Muslims," *Right Wisconsin,* August 4, 2016, video available at youtube/PI88ehLJtEM.

4. Erick Trickey, "Charlie Sykes' Air War: How One of the Most Influential #Nevertrumpers Is Battling His Party's Nominee and Questioning Some Long-Held Beliefs," *Politico,* August 21, 2016.

5. Ibid.

6. Robert Draper, "How Donald Trump Set Off a Civil War Within the Right-Wing Media," *New York Times Magazine,* September 29, 2016.

7. Carl M. Cannon, "Who's to Blame for Trump?," RealClearPolitics, October 30, 2016, www.realclearpolitics.com/articles/2016/10/30/who_is_to_blame_for_trump _132199.html.

8. Jonah Goldberg, "How the Media's History of Smearing Republicans Now Helps Trump," *National Review,* July 27, 2016.

9. Frank Bruni, "Crying Wolf, Then Confronting Trump," *New York Times,* September 1, 2016.

13. THE RISE OF THE ALT RIGHT

1. Sarah Posner, "How Donald Trump's New Campaign Chief Created an Online Haven for White Nationalists," *Mother Jones,* August 22, 2016.

2. Benjamin Welton, "What, Exactly, Is the 'Alternative Right?' A Taxonomy," *Weekly Standard*, December 21, 2015.

3. Michael Knowles, "An Actual Conservative's Guide to the Alt-Right: 8 Things You Need to Know," *Daily Wire*, September 26, 2016, www.dailywire.com /news/9441/actual-conservatives-guide-alt-right-8-things-you-michael-knowles.

4. Ibid.

5. Benjamin Welton, "What, Exactly, Is the 'Alternative Right?'"

6. "'Cuckservative' Is a Racist Slur, Part 2" *Ace of Spades HQ* blog, July 29, 2015, ace.mu.nu/archives/358148.php.

7. Erick Erickson, "'Cuckservative' Is a Racist Slur and an Attack on Evangelical Christians," *RedState*, July 29, 2015.

8. David French, "'Cuckservative' Has Got to Go," *National Review*, September 18, 2015.

9. Matt K. Lewis, "What's Behind the 'Cuckservative' Slur? (NSFW)," *Daily Caller*, July 23, 2015, dailycaller.com/2015/07/23/whats-behind-the-cuckservative -slur-nsfw/#ixzz4W9A2rNHh.

10. Milo Yiannopoulos, "'Cuckservative' Is a Gloriously Effective Insult That Should Not Be Slurred, Demonised, or Ridiculed," Breitbart.com, July 28, 2015, www.breitbart.com/big-government/2015/07/28/cuckservative-is-a-gloriously -effective-insult-that-should-not-be-slurred-demonised-or-ridiculed.

11. David Weigel, "'Cuckservative'—the Conservative Insult of the Month, Explained," *Washington Post*, July 29, 2015.

12. Michael Knowles, "An Actual Conservative's Guide to the Alt-Right."

13. Betsy Woodruff, "Rush Limbaugh's Favorite New White-Power Group: The Talk Radio Host May Not Know What the 'Alternative Right' Is—but He Gave It a Huge Endorsement Last Week," *Daily Beast*, December 3, 2015, www.thedailybeast .com/articles/2015/12/03/rush-limbaugh-s-favorite-new-white-power-group.html.

14. "'Nationalism Trumps Conservatism,'" Says Limbaugh: Rush Explains How Movement Is Remaking the American Right," *World Net Daily*, January 20, 2016, www.wnd.com/2016/01/nationalism-trumps-conservatism-says-limbaugh.

15. "Conservative Pundits Use White Nationalist Sam Francis to Explain Trump's Popularity," Southern Poverty Law Center, January 29, 2016, www .splcenter.org/hatewatch/2016/01/29/conservative-pundits-use-white-nationalist -sam-francis-explain-trumps-popularity.

16. Ibid.

17. Ibid.

18. Robert Farley, "Trump Retweets Bogus Crime Graphic," FactCheck .org, November 24, 2015, www.factcheck.org/2015/11/trump-retweets-bogus -crime-graphic. See also Margaret Hartmann, "Donald Trump Makes Racist Point with Wildly Incorrect Tweet," *New York Magazine*, November 22, 2015, nymag .com/daily/intelligencer/2015/11/trump-makes-racist-point-with-incorrect-tweet. html#; Philip Bump, "Donald Trump Retweeted a Very Wrong Set of Numbers on Race and Murder," *Washington Post*, November 22, 2015, www.washingtonpost

.com/news/the-fix/wp/2015/11/22/trump-retweeted-a-very-wrong-set-of
-numbers-on-race-and-murder/?tid=sm_tw&utm_term=.79fb6c7346bc.

19. Tal Kopan, "Donald Trump Retweets 'White Genocide' Twitter User,"
CNN, January 22, 2016, www.cnn.com/2016/01/22/politics/donald-trump
-retweet-white-genocide.

20. Eric Hananoki, "Donald Trump's Campaign Gave Press Credentials to a
White Nationalist Radio Program," Media Matters for America, March 1, 2016.

21. Tommy Christopher, "Donald Trump Jr. Explains That White Supremacist Radio Interview Was an Accident," *Mediaite*, March 3, 2016.

22. Abby Ohlheiser and Caitlin Dewey, "Hillary Clinton's Alt-Right Speech,
Annotated," *Washington Post*, August 25, 2016, www.washingtonpost.com/news
/the-fix/wp/2016/08/25/hillary-clintons-alt-right-speech-annotated/?utm_term
=.e3413bdf2ca3.

23. Mytheos Holt, "The Intellectual Case for Trump I: Why the White Nationalist Support?," *Federalist*, March 30, 2016, thefederalist.com/2016/03/30/the
-intellectual-case-for-trump-i-why-the-white-nationalist-support.

24. Ibid.

25. Allum Bokhari and Milo Yiannopoulos, "An Establishment Conservative's Guide to the Alt-Right," Breitbart.com, March 29, 2016, www.breitbart.com
/tech/2016/03/29/an-establishment-conservatives-guide-to-the-alt-right.

26. Ibid.

27. Ben Shapiro, "Leftist Web Site Releases 'Punch a Nazi' Game: Punch
Spencer, Yiannopoulos, Hitler," *Daily Wire*, February 3, 2017.

28. Daniel J. Solomon, "Milo Yiannopoulos Slams 'Thick as Pig-S**t Media
Jews,'" *Forward*, January 3, 2017.

29. Charlie Warzel, "Twitter Permanently Suspends Conservative Writer Milo
Yiannopoulos," BuzzFeed, July 20, 2016, www.buzzfeed.com/charliewarzel/twitter
-just-permanently-suspended-conservative-writer-milo?utm_term=.tfZLVla9z#
.wnVvw/jyZ.

30. Allum Bokhari and Milo Yiannopoulos, "An Establishment Conservative's Guide to the Alt-Right."

31. Ibid.

32. Ibid.

33. Bethany Mandel, "My Trump Tweets Earned Me So Many Anti-Semitic
Haters That I Bought a Gun," *Forward*, March 21, 2016, forward.com/opinion
/336159/my-trump-tweets-earned-me-so-many-anti-semitic-haters-that-i-bought
-a-gun.

34. ADL Task Force Issues Report Detailing Widespread Anti-Semitic Harassment of Journalists on Twitter During 2016 Campaign, October 19, 2016, www.adl
.org/press-center/press-releases/anti-semitism-usa/task-force-report-anti-semitic
-harassment-journalists-twitter-2016-campaign.html?referrer www.google.com
/#.WGUay_krKUk.

35. Ibid.

36. "The Daily Stormer," Wikipedia, accessed April 24, 2017, en.wikipedia .org/wiki/The_Daily_Stormer.

37. Andrew Anglin, "A Normie's Guide to the Alt-Right," Daily Stormer, August 31, 2016, www.dailystormer.com/a-normies-guide-to-the-alt-right/.

38. Melania Trump, Facebook post, April 27, 2016, www.facebook.com /MelaniaTrump/posts/10154069359512808.

39. Ibid.

40. Lauren Gambino, "Melania Trump Hit with Barrage of Antisemitic Abuse," Guardian, April 28, 2016.

41. Eric Hananoki, "Here's What Happens When Trump Refuses to Denounce His Racist Neo-Nazi Supporters: Neo-Nazi Website: Trump's Refusal to Denounce Anti-Semitic Threats Amounts to 'Hail Victory, Comrades!'" Media Matters for America, May 6, 2016, mediamatters.org/blog/2016/05/06/heres-what-happens -when-trump-refuses-denounce-his-racist-neo-nazi-supporters/210275.

42. Andrew Anglin, "Glorious Leader Donald Trump Refuses to Denounce Stormer Troll Army," Daily Stormer, May 6, 2016, www.dailystormer.com /glorious-leader-donald-trump-refuses-to-denounce-stormer-troll-army.

43. Isaac Chotiner, "Melania Trump Says Reporter Who Was Target of Anti-Semitic Attacks 'Provoked Them,'" Slate.com, May 17, 2016, www.slate .com/blogs/the_slatest/2016/05/17/melania_trump_blames_julia_ioffe_for _attacks_against_julia_ioffe.html.

44. David Weigel, "Four Lessons from the Alt-Right's D.C. Coming-out Party," Washington Post, September 10, 2016.

45. Ronald Reagan, Farewell Address to the Nation, January 11, 1989.

46. Hugh Hewitt, "Jonah Goldberg and I on the '#AltRight,'" August 31, 2016, www.hughhewitt.com/jonah-goldberg-altright.

47. Matthew Continetti, "The Coming Conservative Dark Age."

48. Nicole Hemmer, "CPAC's Identity Crisis: Inviting Milo Was a Symptom of What Ails Conservatism. And Disinviting Him Is No Cure," Politico, February 20, 2017.

14. THE BINARY CHOICE

1. "Must Hear!!! Rush Blows the Lights Out in the Final Hour! What This Election Is Really About and What's Really at Stake," Rushlimbaugh.com, February 23, 2016, www.rushlimbaugh.com/daily/2016/02/23/must_hear_rush_blows _the_lights_out_in_the_final_hour_what_this_election_is_really_about_and _what_s_really_at_stake.

2. Ben Howe, "No This Is NOT the 'Flight 93 Election,' Rush," RedState, September 8, 2016, www.redstate.com/aglanon/2016/09/08/flight-93-election -rush.

3. Tré Goins-Phillips, "Michele Bachmann: This Will Be the 'Last Election' if Hillary Clinton Wins the Presidency," Blaze, September 2, 2016, www.theblaze .com/news/2016/09/02/michele-bachmann-this-will-be-the-last-election-if -hillary-clinton-wins-the-presidency.

4. Brian Tashman, "Trump: 'This Will Be the Last Election If I Don't Win,'" *Right Wing Watch*, September 9, 2016, www.rightwingwatch.org/post/trump-this-will-be-the-last-election-if-i-dont-win.

5. Dennis Prager, "Trump, Conservatives, and the 'Principles' Question," *National Review*, September 6, 2016, www.nationalreview.com/article/439712/never-trump-supporters-dont-realize-hillary-clinton-worse-option-donald-trump?utm_source=NR&utm_medium=twitter&utm_campaign=September6prager.

6. Larry O'Connor, "Bennett: #NeverTrump-ers Put Vanity Above Country; 'Terrible Case of Moral Superiority,'" Hotair.com, August 19, 2016, hotair.com/archives/2016/08/19/bennett-nevertrump-ers-put-vanity-above-country-terrible-case-of-moral-superiority.

7. Victor Davis Hanson, "The Case for Trump," *National Review*, October 17, 2016.

8. Publius Decius Mus (Michael Anton), "The Flight 93 Election" *Claremont Review of Books*, Claremont Institute, September 5, 2016, www.claremont.org/crb/basicpage/the-flight-93-election.

9. Conor Friedersdorf, "An Attack on Founding Principles at the Claremont Institute," *Atlantic*, September 9, 2016, www.theatlantic.com/politics/archive/2016/09/an-attack-on-founding-principles-at-the-claremont-institute/499094.

10. Publius Decius Mus (Michael Anton), "The Flight 93 Election."

11. Greg Weiner, "The Flight of Fancy Election," *Library of Law and Liberty*, September 8, 2016, www.libertylawsite.org/2016/09/08/the-flight-of-fancy-election.

12. Ibid.

13. Conor Friedersdorf, "An Attack."

14. Ben Shapiro, "The Widely-Praised 'Flight 93 Election' Essay Is Dishonest and Stupid," *Daily Wire*, September 8, 2016, www.dailywire.com/news/8985/widely-praised-flight-93-election-essay-dishonest-ben-shapiro.

15. Abraham Lincoln, "The Perpetuation of Our Political Institutions: Address Before the Young Men's Lyceum of Springfield, Illinois, January 27, 1838, www.abrahamlincolnonline.org/lincoln/speeches/lyceum.htm.

16. Friedrich Hayek, *The Road to Serfdom* (Chicago: University of Chicago Press, 1944), 10 ff.

17. Ibid.

15. WHAT HAPPENED TO THE CHRISTIANS?

1. Russell Moore, "Can the Religious Right Be Saved?," The 2016 Erasmus Lecture, *First Things*, January 2017, www.firstthings.com/article/2017/01/can-the-religious-right-be-saved.

2. Matthew Sheffield, "Religious Right Suddenly Decide Morality's Not Important in Politics: How in the World Did That Happen?," Salon.com, October 19, 2016.

3. Julie Zauzmer, "Who's in the Photo Behind Trump and the Falwells? A Playboy Model Now in Prison," *Washington Post*, June 22, 2016.

4. "Embarrassing: Porno Mag Photobombs Jerry Falwell Jr., His Wife and Trump," *Right Scoop*, June 21, 2016, therightscoop.com/embarrassing-p0rno-mag-photobombs-jerry-falwell-jr-his-wife-and-trump/.

5. Julie Zauzmer, "Who's in the Photo."

6. Erick Erickson, "I Don't Know Which Jesus Jerry Falwell, Jr. is Worshipping," Resurgent, January 18, 2016, theresurgent.com/i-dont-know-which-jesus-jerry-falwell-jr-is-worshipping.

7. Eugene Scott, "Trump Believes in God, but Hasn't Sought Forgiveness," CNN, July 18, 2015, www.cnn.com/2015/07/18/politics/trump-has-never-sought-forgiveness/.

8. Cal Thomas, "Trump Interview—The Transcript," Tribune Content Agency, LLC, calthomas.com/node/985.

9. Sarah Pulliam Bailey, "Standing by Donald Trump, Pat Robertson Calls Lewd Video 'Macho Talk,'" *Washington Post*, October 10, 2016.

10. Sarah Rodriguez, "Falwell Speaks," *Liberty Champion*, March 8, 2016, www.liberty.edu/champion/2016/03/falwell-speaks/.

11. Erick Erickson, "Jerry Falwell, Jr. Has Taken to Mocking God to Support Donald Trump," Resurgent, March 15, 2016, theresurgent.com/jerry-falwell-jr-has-taken-to-mocking-god-to-support-donald-trump.

12. Bob Eschliman, "After Donald Trump's Salvation, Dr. James Dobson Reminds How to Deal with 'Baby Christians,'" *Charisma News*, June 27, 2016, www.charismanews.com/politics/elections/58066-after-donald-trump-s-salvation-dr-james-dobson-reminds-how-to-deal-with-baby-christians.

13. Katie Glueck, "Trump's God Whisperer: The Woman Who Led the Candidate to Christ Has Many of the Same Problems Connecting with Evangelicals as He Has," *Politico*, July 11, 2016, www.politico.com/story/2016/07/donald-trump-pastor-paula-white-225315.

14. Jonathan Van Maren, "The Uncomfortable Truth About Christian Support for Trump," Lifesitenews.com, September 28, 2016, www.lifesitenews.com/blogs/the-uncomfortable-truth-about-christian-support-for-trump.

15. Anna Giaritelli, "Franklin Graham: Trump Won Because 'God Showed Up,'" *Washington Examiner*, December 17, 2016, www.washingtonexaminer.com/franklin-graham-trump-won-because-god-showed-up/article/2609931.

16. Sarah Pulliam Bailey, "White Evangelicals Voted Overwhelmingly for Donald Trump, Exit Polls Show," *Washington Post*, November 9, 2016.

17. Andy Crouch, "Speak Truth to Trump: Evangelicals, of All People, Should Not Be Silent About Donald Trump's Blatant Immorality," *Christianity Today*, October 10, 2016, www.christianitytoday.com/ct/2016/october-web-only/speak-truth-to-trump.html?start=.

18. Paul A. Djupe, Anand Edward Sokhey, Amanda Friesen, and Andrew R. Lewis, "When Evangelical Clergy Oppose Trump, Their Flocks Listen. But They're Not Speaking Up," *Washington Post*, November 4, 2016.

19. Samuel Smith, "Donald Trump: 'Russell Moore Is Truly a Terrible Representative of Evangelicals,'" *Christian Post*, May 9, 2016, www.christianpost.com/news/donald-trump-russell-moore-is-truly-a-terrible-representative-of-evangelicals-163596/#oQ3XDPVyZsDzgc31.99.

20. Russell Moore, "Why This Election Makes Me Hate the Word 'Evangelical,'" *Washington Post,* February 29, 2016.

21. Russell Moore, "Can the Religious Right Be Saved?"

22. Rod Dreher, "The Religious Right: A Eulogy," *American Conservative,* October 24, 2016, www.theamericanconservative.com/dreher/the-religious-right-a-eulogy/.

23. Russell Moore, "Can the Religious Right Be Saved?"

24. Ibid.

25. Ibid.

26. Ibid.

IV. RESTORING THE CONSERVATIVE MIND

16. TROLLS AND FLYING MONKEYS: THE RIGHT'S NEW CULTURE OF INTIMIDATION

1. Eliana Johnson, "How Trump Blew Up the Conservative Media."

2. Bret Stephens, "Don't Dismiss President Trump's Attacks on the Media as Mere Stupidity," Full Text of Remarks at Daniel Pearl Memorial Lecture, February 16, 2017, published at time.com/4675860/donald-trump-fake-news-attacks/.

3. Ibid.

4. Ibid.

5. Ibid.

6. Eliana Johnson, "How Trump Blew Up the Conservative Media."

7. Jazz Shaw, "Some of Our #Nevertrump Friends Need a Thanksgiving Intervention," Hotair.com, November 15, 2016, hotair.com/archives/2016/11/15/some-of-our-nevertrump-friends-need-a-thanksgiving-intervention.

8. Email from Robert Dohnal to multiple recipients, November 16, 2016, 11:22:11 a.m.

9. Daniel Bice, "Mark Belling Endorses Donald Trump—Reluctantly," *Milwaukee Journal Sentinel,* July 13, 2016.

10. Mark Belling, "Trump Can Learn from Wisconsin," *Waukesha Freeman,* January 4, 2017.

11. Rachel Bade, "Trump Posse Browbeats Hill Republicans: Lawmakers Are Loath to Say Anything Remotely Critical, Fearful They Might Set Off the President-Elect or His Horde of Enforcers," *Politico,* December 21, 2016, www.politico.com/story/2016/12/donald-trump-congress-republicans-232800.

12. truthfeed.com/breaking-rep-bill-flores-has-crafted-a-plan-to-block-trumps-immigration-reform/40170.

13. Robert Tracinski, "Everything Awful About Donald Trump's Campaign in One Tweet," *Federalist,* April 8, 2016, thefederalist.com/2016/04/08/everything-awful-about-donald-trumps-campaign-in-one-tweet/.

14. Lloyd Grove, "How Breitbart Unleashes Hate Mobs to Threaten, Dox, and Troll Trump Critics: Seventeen Million Readers Revel in the Website's Angry

Pro-Trump Populism and Anti-Immigration, Anti-Muslim Message. Is It Stoking Up Dangerous Hatred?," *Daily Beast*, February 29, 2016, www.thedailybeast.com/articles/2016/03/01/how-breitbart-unleashes-hate-mobs-to-threaten-dox-and-troll-trump-critics.html.

15. Tim Mak and Brandy Zadrozny, "Ex-Wife: Donald Trump Made Me Feel 'Violated' During Sex. Ivana Trump Once Accused the Real-Estate Tycoon of 'Rape,' Although She Later Clarified: Not in the 'Criminal Sense,'" *Daily Beast*, July 27, 2015, www.thedailybeast.com/articles/2015/07/27/ex-wife-donald-trump-made-feel-violated-during-sex.html.

16. "Conservative Radio Host: You Embrace Trump, You Embrace Every Slur, Every Insult, Every Outrage, Every Falsehood," Media Matters for America, May 9, 2016, mediamatters.org/video/2016/05/09/conservative-radio-host-you-embrace-trump-you-embrace-every-slur-every-insult-every-outrage-every/210319.

17. Ibid.

18. Erick Erickson, "A Year after Launch: Writers Welcome," Resurgent, January 9, 2017.

19. Ben Schreckinger, "Anti-Trump Operatives Targeted in Online 'Catfishing' Scheme," *Politico*, August 23, 2016, www.politico.com/story/2016/08/anti-trump-operatives-targeted-in-online-catfishing-scheme-227288.

20. Hanna Trudo, "Mark Levin: I Won't Back Trump in the General," *Politico*, April 8, 2016, www.politico.com/story/2016/04/mark-levin-i-wont-back-trump-in-the-general-221754.

21. Andrew Anglin, "Roger Stone: Jew Levin, Others Paid by GOP to Attack Glorious Leader," Daily Stormer, April 9, 2016.

22. Hanna Trudo, "Mark Levin: I Won't Back Trump." See also Charlie Sykes, "Welcome to #NeverTrump, Mr. Levin: Mark Levin Is Late to the Party." April 10, 2016, www.rightwisconsin.com/opinion/perspectives/welcome-to-nevertrump-mr-levin.

17. THE CONTRARIAN CONSERVATIVE

1. Peter Wehner, "One Way Not to Be Like Trump," *New York Times*, December 17, 2016.

2. Ibid.

3. Barry Goldwater, *The Conscience of a Conservative*, 11.

4. Alexis de Tocqueville, *Democracy in America* (Garden City, NY: Doubleday, 1969), 258 ff.

5. Conor Friedersdorf, "How Conservatives Can Save America," *Atlantic*, February 2, 2017.

6. Ibid.

7. Ibid.

8. Karen Stenner, *The Authoritarian Dynamic*.

INDEX